# DIRECTING POSTMODERN THEATER

# Directing Postmodern Theater

## Shaping Signification in Performance

JON WHITMORE

*Ann Arbor*

THE UNIVERSITY OF MICHIGAN PRESS

Copyright © Jon Whitmore 1994
All rights reserved
Published in the United States of America by
The University of Michigan Press
Manufactured in the United States of America
⊗ Printed on acid-free paper

2001   2000            7   6   5

A CIP catalogue record for this book is available from the British Library.

Library of Congress Cataloging-in-Publication Data

Whitmore, Jon.
    Directing postmodern theater : shaping signification in
performance / Jon Whitmore.
        p.     cm. — (Theater—theory/text/performance)
    Includes bibliographical references and index.
    ISBN 0-472-09557-9 (alk. paper). — ISBN 0-472-06557-2 (pbk. :
alk. paper)
        1. Theater—Semiotics. 2. Theater—Production and direction.
I. Title.   II. Series.
PN2041.S45W54    1994
792'.014—dc20                                        94-1272
                                                       CIP

Grateful acknowledgment is made to the following authors, publishers, and institutions for permission to reprint previously published and copyrighted materials.

St. Martin's Press, Incorporated for excerpts from *Director's Theatre* by David Bradby and David Williams. Copyright © 1988 by David Bradby and David Williams. Theatre Communications Group for excerpts from *The Director's Voice* by Arthur Bartow. Copyright © 1988 by Arthur Bartow. Reprinted with permission of Theatre Communications Group. Doubleday for excerpts from *The Hidden Dimension* by Edward T. Hall. Copyright © 1966, 1982 by Edward T. Hall. Reprinted with permission of Doubleday, a division of Bantam Doubleday Dell Publishing Group, Inc. Performing Arts Journal Publications for excerpts from *Languages of the Stage* by Patrice Pavis. Copyright © 1982 by Performing Arts Journal Publications. Reprinted with permission of Performing Arts Journal Publications. Hill and Wang for excerpts from *Reimagining American Theatre* by Robert Brustein. Copyright © 1991 by Robert Brustein. Reprinted with permission of Hill and Wang, a division of Farrar, Straus & Giroux, Inc. Theatre Communications Group for excerpts from *Robert Wilson and His Collaborators* by Laurence Shyer. Copyright © 1989 by Laurence Shyer. Reprinted with permission of Theatre Communications Group. MIT Press for excerpts from "Theatre of Magic and Sacrilege" by Eugenio Barba and Ludwik Flaszen, *Tulane Drama Review 9*, Spring 1965, with permission of the MIT Press. Copyright © 1965, *Tulane Drama Review*. Scarecrow Press for excerpts from *The Essential Delsarte* by John W. Zorn, ed. Copyright © 1968 by John W. Zorn. Reprinted with permission of Scarecrow Press, a division of Grolier Educational Corp. Ken Westerman for excerpts from "The Semiotics of Music: Material and Production" by Ken Westerman (1991). Reprinted with permission of Ken Westerman. The University of Kentucky Press for excerpts from *Practicing Theory and Reading Literature* by Raman Selden. Copyright © 1989 by Raman Selden. Reprinted with permission of The University of Kentucky Press. Routledge for excerpts from *A Dictionary of Theatre Anthropology: The Secret Art of the Performer* by Eugenio Barba and Nicola Saverse, translated by Richard Fowler. Copyright © 1991 by Eugenio Barba and Nicola Saverse. Reprinted with permission of Routledge, a division of Routledge, Chapman & Hall. Routledge for excerpts from *Theatre Audiences* by Susan Bennett. Copyright © 1990 by Susan Bennett. Reprinted with permission of Routledge, a division of Routledge, Chapman & Hall. Theatre Crafts Associates for excerpts from "The Mystery is in the surface" by Rob Baker, *Theatre Crafts 19*, October 1985. Copyright © 1985 by Theatre Crafts Associates. UMI Research Press for excerpts from *Richard Foreman and the Ontological-Hysteric Theatre* by Kate Davy. Copyright © 1981 by Kate Davy. Pantheon Books for excerpts from *Unbalancing Acts* by Richard Foreman. Copyright © 1992 by Pantheon Books, a division of Random House. Methuen Press for "The Field of Drama" by Martin Esslin, published in *The Semiotics of Theatre and Drama*, edited by Keir Elam. Copyright © 1980 by Methuen.

Every effort has been made to trace the ownership of all copyrighted material in this book and to obtain permission for its use.

*To Eurma, Walter, Amy, Ian, and Jennifer*

# Preface

I have always been fascinated with theories of all kinds. What I am most interested in is not the study of theory for theory's sake but, rather, how theories can be applied to solve a problem or how theories can be used to improve the actual practice of a profession.

In this book I posit the question: How might semiotics be useful to the creator of theater performances? That is, how might stage directors come to understand how theater performances communicate, and how might this understanding assist in the day-to-day work of conceptualizing, planning, rehearsing, and constructing a performance in the postmodern theater world? In short, the goal of *Directing Postmodern Theater* is to wed theory to practice.

The second dimension to this inquiry is how directing postmodern productions differs from directing more traditional realistic theater. What is it that postmodernists do that traditionalists do not do (and vice versa)? How are sign systems and signifiers used in performance differently by directors who operate at opposite ends of the postmodern-traditional continuum?

Chapter 1 outlines how theater performances communicate with spectators and how semiotics and reader-response theories can aid the director in transforming a playscript or concept into a performance. Five systems of communication are reviewed: linguistic, visual, aural, olfactoral, and tactile. Twenty sign systems are identified: spectator, audience, framing devices (environment, publicity); the performer's personality, voice, facial expression, gesture, movement, makeup and hairstyle; visual systems of space, setting, costume, properties, lighting, and color; aural systems of music and sound; and smell and touch. Chapters 2 through 7 examine how each sign system contributes to a spectator's construction of the meanings of a performance and how directors can manipulate these sign systems to create complex and distinctive works of art. The final chapter examines the complexity of sign usage during performance and discusses options for foregrounding and backgrounding signifiers and sign systems in order to create unique yet unified performances. The director's rehearsal process and her role as final arbiter, choice maker, and unifier is evaluated.

Throughout the book examples from contemporary and postmodern productions are used to compare how directors employ sign systems differently to communicate with audiences. Emphasis is placed on how post-modernists manipulate signifiers and sign systems to create new paradigms of theatrical communication, downplaying the use of spoken words and highlighting their experiments with visual and aural communication.

I am enormously grateful to many people for their advice and assistance in writing this book. I started the research and writing while at the State University of New York at Buffalo. There I am indebted to John Dings and David Willbern who endured my constant questions with grace and (more important) brilliant answers. Diane Marlinski applied her considerable editorial skills to prepare an early draft manuscript for use by my directing students. Thanks Diane.

At the University of Texas at Austin, where the book was completed, I owe a debt of thanks to Pat Gay, who typed preparatory material for my graduate directing class. Merrilee Burdenski helped with early research. Nina LeNoir and Ken Westerman expertly gathered data and acted as readers of and sounding boards for many of my ideas. Their assistance is acknowledged here, with particular thanks to Nina for overseeing the research and to Ken for teaching me about the semiotics of music and stage technology. Letitia Blalock deserves recognition for her skilled editing of several drafts of the manuscript. The quality of writing, flow of ideas, and final structure were greatly improved by her suggestions. I am pleased to acknowledge Kevin Goodbar, who gave his time to produce the superb graphic elements. Thanks go to Beverly Isackes for the index. LeAnn Fields and the copy editors at the University of Michigan Press deserve praise and thanks both for taking on this book and for thoughtfully editing it. Directing students too numerous to name contributed to this book through their constant questions about semiotics and its use by directors and by their contributions to creative projects, one of which is outlined in the final chapter.

Jennifer, Ian, and Amy get my deepest gratitude for giving up their time with me so that I might complete this project. They are remarkable people.

# Contents

1. The Director Uses Semiotics    1

2. Framing Systems    31

3. Audience Systems    51

4. Performer Systems    65

5. Visual Systems    113

6. Aural Systems    173

7. Olfactoral and Tactile Systems    191

8. Simultaneity in Performance    203

Works Cited    229

Index    235

# Chapter 1

# The Director
# Uses Semiotics

The reason for creating and presenting theater is to communicate meanings. These meanings can result in experiences for spectators ranging from sheer joy to profound emotional stimulation to spiritual awakening to intellectual discovery. Understanding how meanings are communicated to and assembled by spectators can be of enormous help to the director as he works to translate his individual vision of a theater production into a living, three-dimensional work of art. Theater is here defined in its broadest context as encompassing circus, street theater, improvised performance, and the production of a playscript.

Twentieth-century theater and its critical analysis have most notably focused on the performance of playscripts. Many directors, designers, and performers (some past, many current), however, are challenging the centrality and sacredness of playscripts (or at least the dialogue therein contained). These theater artists have concluded that the spoken word does not always need to be the central force of a performance. They may use playscripts, new and old, as a place to begin a production, but they do not feel compelled to treat the playscript as a sacred altar to be devoutly worshiped. Instead, these artists are deconstructing playscripts in order to speak more directly to the contemporary audience; or they are finding highly innovative ways of presenting unaltered scripts in altered environments, styles, and aesthetic contexts; or they are working with playwrights or performers to develop scripts through the rehearsal process, rather than the other way around. Some theater artists are ignoring playscripts altogether; they are developing performances through experimentation with objects, visual images, soundscapes, improvisation, or bits and pieces of disjointed language or information.

The language of the theatre has to be reinvented, as the people of
the Wooster Group are doing. The Wooster Group is speaking the
language that the theatre will speak fifteen to twenty years from
now. I'm talking about the vocabulary of stage language, of what
a set looks like, how lighting behaves, how sound works, how
video works, how all of those things go into creating a total work
of art. The notion that a piece is made of all those various elements
is very important, and in the Group's work is the first time that I've
seen all of those elements combined in a really sophisticated way
to create this *Gesamtkunstwerk*, where the text is as important as the
video image is as important as the sound, and nothing has domi-
nance although the words are very powerful. They are inventing
the only vocabulary that can deal with the material of the last
twenty years once we understand its strangeness. (Peter Sellars
interview, in Bartow 1988a, 283–84)

Some theater productions are becoming richer and more dense as
a result of the revolutionary development of theater technology (computers, lasers, digital sound, video walls) and the accelerated evolution of theater directors who now more fully understand that performances communicate on multiple levels simultaneously. The new
directing approach in which visual and aural elements often take center stage (while linguistic elements are either nonexistent or diminished in importance) creates a vibrant and sonorous environment in
which more complex meanings are communicated.

The process [of directing] is a journey into another "studio," where
you have text *and* you have visual elements—designers, musicians
and maybe fifteen or sixteen actors—where the text does not have
to dominate the event all the time and it allows the lighting designer or the set designer or the composer to "play" loud. Moving
from what I've done in the past to what I'm doing now is analogous
to moving from a four-track studio to a sixteen-track studio. And if
you're doing a mix, everybody has a track, each designer, each
actor has his own score. So we lay out sixteen scores, and the mix
comes when we're in the theatre doing a technical rehearsal or
previews and seeing all the elements at once. Everybody may be
playing all the time, and you have to make some adjustment to one
or more of the scores. The work becomes more assaultive because
it's denser, but it's not *only* the density of language. Not everybody
has to play behind the text, support one melody. Each one can play
his own melody, and there doesn't have to be agreement. There's

a tonality that you look for, but it doesn't have to be harmonic. That creates an unsettling edge that contributes to live performance. (Robert Woodruff interview, in Bartow 1988a, 313)

If the theater as an artistic discipline wants to produce directors who are capable of working in both a theater that embraces performances in which words may be of minimal significance and a more traditional word-oriented theater, an analysis of how performance texts (not playscripts) communicate with spectators is a useful study— hence this book.

## Postmodernists/Postmodernism

Richard Foreman, Peter Brook, Jerzy Grotowski, JoAnne Akalaitis, Robert Wilson, Elizabeth LeCompte, Peter Sellars, Josef Svoboda, Andrei Serban, Ariane Mnouchkine, and Martha Clarke are examples of Western directors who are experimenting with theater and its various communication systems. Examples from the productions of these directors (and others) are used throughout this book to highlight and explain the methods and practices utilized in the postmodern theater world. Not all of the directors listed here or examined later are postmodernists, but their labors have either contributed to the development of the postmodern theater or currently parallel much of the work of hard-core postmodernists.

Since I will be using many examples of productions from postmodern theater in this book, a definition of this complex phenomenon may be useful. Postmodernism is difficult to define precisely, however, because it is usually contrasted with either modernism or the avant-garde. "Thus some critics mean by postmodernism what others call avant-gardism, while others still would call the same phenomenon simply modernism" (Hassan 1980, 120). Postmodernism can be defined as differing from modernism because it carries modernist principles beyond anticipated boundaries or because it rejects modernist principles altogether (Gaggi 1989, 19). For postmodernists, extended modernist principles include widespread experimentation of collage, atonality, nonlinearity, decenteredness, imbalance, skepticism, abstractness, ambiguity, serialization, stream-of-consciousness, and the like. Postmodernist principles that reject modernism include the highlighting of self-referentiality, deconstruction, and popular culture (rejecting the notion that high art is the only art worth investigating).

> Postmodernism veers towards open, playful, optative, disjunctive, displaced, or indeterminate forms, a discourse of fragments, an ideology of fracture, a will to unmaking, an invocation of silence—veers toward all these and yet implies their very opposites, their antithetical realities. (Hassan 1980, 125)

For purposes of this study, *postmodernism* is defined broadly and loosely to encompass performances that are primarily nonlinear, non-literary, nonrealistic, nondiscursive, and nonclosure oriented. Some productions that are used as examples in this book ambiguously reflect or combine elements of modernism, postmodernism, and the avant-garde—so be it. *Postmodernism* is, however, the term used in this study to bring simplicity and consistency to an admittedly bewildering discussion.

## Theater's Communication Systems

In the theater there are five communication systems at work. The primary systems are linguistic (language), visual, and aural; the secondary systems are olfactoral and tactile. Directors can manipulate these systems in order to activate a full range of communicative mechanisms during a performance.

> All the elements of a dramatic performance—the language of the dialogue, the setting, the gestures, costumes, make-up and voice-inflections of the actors, as well as a multitude of other signs—each in their own way contribute to the creation of the "meaning" of the performance. A dramatic performance must, at the most basic level, be regarded as essentially a process by which information about the actions that are to be mimetically reproduced is conveyed to the audience. Each element of the performance can be regarded as a sign that stands for an ingredient of the over-all meaning of a scene, an incident, a moment of the action. (Esslin 1987, 16)

In the theater meanings are generated through the work of many artists and technicians from multiple communication systems. Absolute control of the communication process by a single individual is not possible. Also, the meanings of a performance change with each new enactment and are constructed differently by individual spectators because of each viewer's discrete physical, psychological, intellectual, and emotional constitution. Indeed, the spectators themselves are contributors to the performance's meanings. This, of course, is what makes the theater such an exciting art form. The requirement of immediacy—of direct stimulation and confrontation between the event (with all its diverse elements) and the audience—gives the performance its edge. The theater experience shifts the perceptive capabilities of the spectator into high gear. A performance can thrill its spectators: it can challenge their emotional, spiritual, and intellectual capacities to their fullest—simultaneously. Every sensory perceptor of the spectator is engaged during a performance. Multiple meanings are tendered, and the brightest and most perceptive audience members become immersed in an entertaining, enlightening, disorienting, energizing, or thought-evoking experience. This is the special capability of the theater, and, as the chief architect of the performance, the director has an enormous responsibility and an exhilarating opportunity to engage in meaningful (and meaning-producing) work.

## Semiotics Defined

A useful way to look at a director's task is to imagine all the devices or methods of communication that are at her disposal. What elements actually produce the linguistic, visual, aural, olfactoral, and tactile communication? Once a list is compiled it is possible to understand the array of choices a director contemplates while directing a production.

Here we are aided by semioticians who have done much of the groundwork. Semiotics is a system of knowledge that studies signs and offers explanations about how signs are used to communicate meanings.

> Semiotics can best be defined as a science dedicated to the study of the production of meaning in society. As such it is equally concerned with processes of signification and with those of communication, i.e., the means whereby meanings are both generated and exchanged. Its objects are thus at once the different sign-systems and codes at work in society and the actual messages and texts produced thereby. (Elam 1980, 1)

The value of semiotics for directors is that it can provide a framework for structuring experimentation during the gestation, preparation, and rehearsal stages of creating a production. A knowledge of semiotics compels the director to explore more fully than instinct alone will allow the thousands of different, overlapping choices that might be made to produce a rich, complex, multilayered performance or, for that matter, one that is minimalistic, stripped bare of all but the most essential elements of communication. The discipline imposed by semiotics ironically frees the director to see, hear, feel, taste, and imagine more possibilities for communication than instinct or chance alone are likely to produce.

It might be useful to define some of semiotics' relevant elements more specifically, especially as they relate to this study. There is no single semiotic system; theoreticians have different viewpoints on what constitutes a semiotics of the theater. What follows is a semiotic "possibility" taken from my understanding of the work of Esslin, Elam, Pavis, Eco, Barthes, and many others. Signs and their communicative relationship to the theater audience are immensely complicated and any attempt to simplify semiotic theory leads to a certain amount of superficiality. Nonetheless, some concepts are relevant to the work of the director. Investing the time to understand semiotics can lead a director to enriched communication in performance.

## Signs

Semioticians, led by Ferdinand de Saussure, define a sign as a two-part entity consisting of a signifier (also called a sign-vehicle) and a signified (also called a mental image). "A sign consists of two inseparable aspects—like two sides of a sheet of paper: an acoustic or graphic substance (meaningful sounds or marks), called the 'signifier,' and a concept (what we 'think' when we produce or receive a signifier), called the 'signified'" (R. Selden 1989, 75).

In the theater some examples of signifiers and signifieds are:

| Signifier | Signified |
|---|---|
| Red light | Danger, prostitution, or fire |
| Western hat | Ranch hand |
| Person running | Danger, excitement, or aerobics |
| Briefcase | Executive |
| Nude person | Exhibitionism, poverty, or sexiness |

A single signifier often contains many different possible signifieds. That is, each spectator may read a signifier differently. Furthermore, a single signifier may have a primary denotative meaning for all (or most) of the spectators but secondary connotative meanings for each spectator. For example, *red light* may signify "stop" and "danger" to all members of an audience, while in addition it connotes "fire" to one spectator who recently had a fire in her home and "prostitute" to another spectator who recently returned from Amsterdam, where he toured the red-light district.

C. S. Peirce and many of his followers divide signs into three types: icon, index, and symbol. While it is arguable that the identification of signs by these three categories is of little immediate benefit to the director, it is useful to discuss them briefly here as a way of clarifying the range and complexity of signs in performance.

Some signs are icons; that is, they are an exact visual or aural representation of a specific object. "The entire art forms of representational painting, sculpture and photography can be regarded as systems of iconic signs. But not all icons are visual. The sound of a car horn in a play is an icon of the sound of a car horn" (Esslin 1987, 43).

Signs can serve as indexes. These signs are used as indicators or pointers to actual objects. If a character says, "Here comes Joe," and points in the direction of a character who then enters the stage, the words and gesture are index signs. "These signs derive their meaning from a relationship of continuity to the object they depict" (Esslin 1987, 44).

Signs can be symbols, which have "no immediately recognizable organic relationship to their 'signifieds'" (Esslin 1987, 44). The understanding of symbols comes through a knowledge of specific codes. For example, religious symbolism—the Cross or wine and wafers at communion—requires a learned connection between the sign and the religiously significant meaning (Christ's sacrifice and His blood and flesh).

It is useful for the director to realize that these three categories of signs are understood through different levels of knowledge and understanding. Iconic and indexical signs are typically understood through observation, while symbols have meaning only for those who have learned the code that connects the signifier to the various possible signifieds.

Patrice Pavis (1982) has concluded that, although signs can be subdivided into three categories, it is not necessary to do so in order to understand how signs work or how communication takes place during a performance.

A typology of signs (whether derived from Peirce or from elsewhere) is not a prerequisite for the description of performance. Not only because the degree of iconicity or symbolism is of no relevance when taking into account the syntax and semantics of signs, but also because typology is often too general to take into account the complexities of performance. Rather than types of sign (such as icon, index, symbol, signal), it is now more common to follow Umberto Eco and talk about the *signifying function*, where the sign is conceived of as the result of a semiosis, that is of a correlation and a reciprocal presupposition between the level of expression (the Saussurian signifier) and the level of content (the Saussurian signified). This correlation is not a given fact from the start, it emerges from the "readerly" production reading of the director and the "productive" reading of the spectator. (Pavis 1982, 15–16)

The meanings that emerge from a theatrical performance come from the unique juxtaposition of signifiers in a particular mix that gives a context for reading each signifier not in isolation but, instead, in complex clusters or grids. A single signifier perceived in isolation may emanate a different meaning(s) than the same signifier when placed in a cluster of other signs. For example, a large wooden cross seen as a single sign on stage in nondescript white light may produce a general signification of "religion." The same cross when tipped to the side, bathed in red light, and surrounded by smoke and a dancing performer in a red devil's costume will likely signify a much different signified—perhaps "hell," "terror," or the like.

It is possible to view the performance as a whole as an umbrellalike signifier that produces a multifaceted mental image or signified (meaning) for each spectator. This umbrellalike signifier can be broken down into sign systems, which are clusters of signs that emanate from a single source, such as spoken words, physical gestures, or music. Collectively, these multiple sign systems constitute the sum total of the aesthetic performance experience. Directors are able to conceive of individual productions as emphasizing or deemphasizing different sign systems, which have the potential of producing very different sensory and meaning-producing experiences for spectators.

## Codes

In order to find meaning in the signifier/signified components of a sign system, a spectator must understand the codes at work in the society in which a given performance takes place as well as codes for current theatrical norms and codes unique to the performance. Codes are culturally derived signs that have been assigned meanings that are understood by the inhabitants of a given society. The level of under-standing of codes comes through the spectator's background (educa-tional, environmental, ethnic, political, socioeconomic), theatergoing experience, knowledge of a particular playwright or playscript, and the like.

There are several overarching sets of codes at work during each performance: the three most immediate are cultural, theatrical, and individual performance codes.

Cultural codes are rules or guidelines that govern the operation of a society and its culture. Language, dress, manners, the arts, social strata, and level of education are examples. A spectator who does not understand French will not fully understand a performance in French. Language code knowledge is missing; the potential for complete lin-guistic communication is lost. A spectator who watches a performance of Kathakali dance, in which every gesture has a culturally defined, precise meaning, and who does not know the code will not fully understand or appreciate the dance. In a contemporary performance about racial issues in which the only scenery is a large picture of Abraham Lincoln, a spectator who knows who Lincoln was and what his actions did to affect race relations in the United States will con-struct a significant symbolic meaning from viewing the picture. A spectator who does not know who Lincoln was or what he did will likely not construct a meaning and might well be distracted and con-fused by the pictorial signifier.

Theatrical codes are accepted and understood norms of operation that allow the theater to function as a special aesthetic place. Specta-tors who are familiar with theatrical codes, either through observation or education, have a sophisticated understanding of theatrical conven-tions. Examples of theatrical codes are the suspension of belief that what is actually happening on stage is real, the understanding that if a character speaks an aside to the audience the other characters on-stage do not hear the remark, and the understanding that (at least for most traditional realistic productions) the characters do not know that the audience is out there listening to and watching them. Other theat-rical codes include use of a curtain, stylized movement, amplified speech, and the like (Elam 1980, 53).

Individual performance codes are unique rules guiding the under-standing of an individual performance. For example, in Peter Shaffer's *Black Comedy* the normal light code is reversed. That is, when the stage is in complete darkness, the performers (whom the audience can only hear) move about the stage speaking and acting as if they are in full light. Later, when the lights come on onstage, the performers (who can now be seen by the audience) act as though they are in a completely dark environment. Once the audience understands this special performance code, they join in the topsy-turvy world. Another example is when a director chooses color-blind casting, as when both of Romeo's parents are black and he is white. Cultural codes tell the audience that this is a genetic impossibility, yet the director asks the audience to accept a theatrical code for which genetic code knowledge is to be suspended.

The more fully an individual spectator comprehends a culture and its language, aesthetics, theater, playwrights, and so forth, the more meanings she is going to construct from a performance. The depth of meanings that a spectator assembles is directly dependent upon the depth of code knowledge present at the moment of contact between the event and the person.

Performances are different from real life (even in extreme cases of naturalism), and consequently the codes of the theater, and the codes of a specific performance often conflict with the codes of everyday life. Theatrical and performance codes can contradict cultural codes and in the case of postmodern theater can stand them on their heads and shake them vigorously. Houses that float into the fly tower, amplified words that are distorted beyond recognition, men playing women's roles, and Abraham Lincoln on stilts are images and sounds that defy customary decoding. Because they happen, however, within the context of the theatrical code system, they are perfectly acceptable and perhaps even understandable.

Each sign system has a unique code system. Some code systems, such as language, have tightly controlled signifieds, while others, like music, are much more open to wide-ranging interpretations. When a particular set of specific codes is not understood by a spectator, the signifiers from a production may confuse rather than aid in the construction of meanings. On the other hand, less proscriptive personal codes exist for signifiers such as specific color, sound, and movement; here interpretation relies more on individual taste and experience and less on arbitrarily assigned meanings.

It is precisely at this point that some theoreticians argue that the value of semiotics as a tool for reading performances breaks down. They contend that if a scientifically predictable signified is not identifiable we are no longer dealing with a semiotic analysis. Even if this is true—and most contemporary semioticians argue that it is not—the value of applying semiotic analysis to the work of the director remains a useful tool for structuring his work.

The study of semiotics activates the potential use of a wide range of sign systems and signifiers in the imagination of the director. An awareness of semiotics stretches the director's horizon, gives her a grid upon which to contemplate the choices of thousands of signifiers and how they might be layered, and aids her in understanding how meanings are influenced by the mix of signifiers that are ultimately present in a performance.

> Semiotics does not make anyone more talented, but it can impart that consciousness of the knowledge that more clearly distinguishes between the subjective and objective content of the theatre, eliminating sterile arguments (such as the primordiality of the text, the role of the director, the application of Stanislavsky or Brecht, etc.). . . . In the final analysis, theatre is not made for semiotics, but semiotics can be developed and applied in order to understand theatre better. (Nadin 1979, 120)

Perhaps the chief value of a semiotic approach to directing has to do with realigning a director's perception from a strictly horizontal/ linear method of thinking about and rehearsing a production to one that puts increased focus on a vertical moment-by-moment examination of the performance possibilities. Through this method of conceptualization and rehearsal practice comes a more complex and resonant meaning-producing performance. Further, semiotics provides a concrete method to analyze the choices made in the production process by tying them specifically to the reader/spectator. The concept of the performance as a code to be "read" by an audience is far more complex than simply "telling the story," which is the typical framework in which a director works (LeNoir 1993).

## Theater Sign Systems

Several semioticians (Kowzan 1968, Eco 1976, Elam 1980, Esslin 1987, Alter 1990) have identified systems of signs that are used during a theatrical performance to communicate with an audience. Most, however, do not identify the audience as a sign system within the performance itself. This is puzzling, because theater cannot take place without communication between the event and an audience, and most theorists agree that spectators provide feedback to the performers and to one another. In addition, these same theorists do not include odors or physical touching/sensing as part of the performance sign system scheme, nor do their theories spell out what communication systems each of the sign systems function within. In this book I view the audience as a sign system. I also include the olfactoral and tactile senses as communication systems, since they exist as options, even though they are not commonly utilized by directors. I have made these additions because they are essential for a complete understanding of the performance semiotic/perception/communication process. Figure 1 provides a list of the major sign systems considered in this book, together with the communication systems that are engaged by each of the sign systems.

The sign systems in figure 1 will serve as a reference for further analysis of semiotics and how it may help directors carry out their work. Each of these sign systems communicates to the spectators through the communication systems indicated to the right. These communication systems are engaged simultaneously during a performance.

## Communication Systems

*Linguistics* is defined by Webster as "the study of human speech including the units, nature, structure, and modification of language." Except for mime, most theater performances include spoken words, which produce meanings for all spectators who understand the language of the performance. The same holds true for the reader of a playscript; that is, the reader constructs meanings from a script because of a knowledge of words, the way the words are put together to form phrases, clauses, or sentences, and how they are punctuated. The difference in perception between reading and listening to words, however, is significant: during a performance words exist only at the moment in time when they are spoken—they cannot be read or listened to again. A performance marches on; more words come forth at each new moment. Because the theater experience exists in real time, communication by means of the spoken word is quite different from, and often more difficult than, reading a novel or playscript.

Visual communication results from the observation of color, movement, shape, the actor's body and makeup, printed words, costumes, furniture, doors, windows, and the like. As spectators view (as opposed to hear) a performance, they are bombarded with visual stimuli that give meaning to the experience. If we review the twenty sign systems listed in figure 1, we see that three-fourths use visual communication and that almost half convey meaning solely through visual communication. Modern technology is aiding and encouraging to-

| Sign System | Communication System |
|---|---|
| **Audience** | |
| Spectator (Individual) | Linguistic, visual, aural, olfactoral, tactile |
| Audience (Group) | Linguistic, visual, aural, olfactoral, tactile |
| **Frames** | |
| Environment | Visual, aural, olfactoral, tactile |
| Publicity | Linguistic, visual, aural |
| **Performer** | |
| Personality | Visual, aural |
| Voice (Spoken Word) | Linguistic, aural |
| Facial Expression | Visual |
| Gesture | Visual |
| Movement | Visual |
| Makeup and Hairstyle | Visual |
| **Mise-en-Scène** | |
| Space | Visual |
| Setting | Visual, linguistic |
| Costume | Visual |
| Properties | Visual |
| Lighting | Visual |
| Color | Visual |
| **Aural** | |
| Music | Aural |
| Sound | Aural |
| **Olfactoral** | |
| Smell | Olfactoral |
| **Tactile** | |
| Touch | Tactile |

Fig. 1. Theater sign systems

day's directors and designers to explore how the visual aspects of production can participate more fully in theatrical signification.

Aural communication includes spoken words and paralexical sounds (groans, screams, whimpers); sound effects (wind, a car starting up and driving away); and music, which is either integrated into the action of the play (dance music, a radio playing) or incidental to it (mood music at the beginning and end of scenes, background music during a scene).

Tactile communication takes place through the spectator's skin and body. Being touched by a performer, or feeling a gust of wind and rain at an outdoor performance, becomes a part of the experience of witnessing a performance. While tactile communication may not be a primary sign system in most performances, there exists the potential to transfer significant meanings through the sense of touch.

Olfactoral communication occurs when odors are perceived by the spectator. Odors range from being highly pleasant to pungently acrid and can have a significant effect on the quality and impact of a spectator's experience. While it is rare that a director will use smell as a primary means of communication, it is an available tool.

## Mise-en-Scène

Two of the more interesting discussions that theorists have about the theater focus on whether the director or the playwright is the dominant author of a performance and what exactly a spectator reads when she experiences a performance. There is, of course, no question that the playwright holds claim to ownership of the playscript. But who holds claim to the performance? If the director uses no playscript and creates a performance through the rehearsal process, the director and perhaps the performers are the authors. But, if a playscript is used, what role does the playwright play relative to the director and other creative artists who actively overcode the final product, the living work of art?

Rather than proceeding through a history of the evolution of the thinking in this regard, let me simply agree with Jonathan Miller, Patrice Pavis, and many others who have come to understand that "we, as spectators, perceive in a *mise en scène* the director's reading of the author's text; thus through the performance, we do not have direct access to the text [playscript] which is being staged" (Pavis 1982, 150). Playwrights can only use words as signifiers. They cannot demonstrate movements, provide an actual sound effect, or identify an exact shade of blue (although they might try to describe these signifiers through words).

> The text of a play is surprisingly short on the instructions required to bring a performance into existence. Playwrights do not include— and cannot, because of a shortage of notation—all those details of prosody, inflexion, stress, tempo and rhythm. A script tells us nothing about the gestures, the stance, the facial expressions, the dress, the weight, or the grouping or the movement. So although the text is a necessary condition for the performance it is by no means a sufficient one. It is short of all these accessories which are, in a sense, the *essence* of performance. The literal act of reading the words of a script does not constitute a performance. (Miller 1986, 34)

When we consider that the director, after reading a playscript, is free to make decisions about how he will structure space, choose a cast, develop a design and color scheme, situate the performers, and cut or adapt the written words and that he does so in conjunction with designers and technicians, then we are mightily tempted to conclude that it is the director, designers, technicians, and performers who are the true creators of a performance's meanings and, therefore, the principle authors of the performance. This conclusion is incorrect, however, because it leaves out the spectator. The final meanings of a performance are concocted not by the playwright, not by the director or performers, but by each spectator, uniquely. It is the interaction and negotiation that go on between the signifiers produced by the playwright, director, designers, performers, and the spectators, which are ultimately read by the spectators alone, that constitute the essence of the performance experience. And it is even more complicated than this. The audience responds to itself as part of the content of the performance: spectators are not outside of the performance. Spectators play a creative role in signifying the very meanings that they construct for themselves.

The link between playscript, director, performance, and audience is immensely complicated; it constitutes the heart and mystery of the theater experience. Each playscript can be interpreted by a director in an infinite number of ways. Using the playscript as a touchstone, the director creates a hypothetical production in her mind that is made concrete by the work of the theater artists through the mise-en-scène, which Pavis (1982) elegantly defines as "the establishment of a dialectical opposition between T/P [Text (playscript)/Performance] which takes the form of a *stage enunciation* (of a global discourse belonging to *mise en scène*) according to a *metatext* 'written' by the director and his team and more or less integrated, that is established in the enunciation, in the concrete work of the stage production and the spectator's reception" (146). This definition of mise-en-scène is superior to the traditional one because it is much more dynamic (interactive); it brings the audience into the live experience of constructing meanings through reading a performance that includes itself as signifier. The standard definition of mise-en-scène as the physical elements within a performance, what the spectator sees and hears, leaves out the active involvement of the spectator as both a signifier of meanings and an active participant in the interchange and negotiation present in a performance.

## Reading a Performance

A theatrical performance is pluridimensional. A spectator simultaneously hears spoken words; sees space, color, and movement; hears music and sound effects; and smells odors—all of which are signs that require synthesis, interpretation, and understanding (decoding, in the language of the semioticians). Spectators, however, see and hear different things, depending on where their gaze rests or shifts to from instant to instant, where they are located in the theater, and how much they are concentrating at each moment.

> The audience's freedom to select quite different processes of reading, or even to ignore the play entirely, must not be discounted. Similarly, members of an audience may resist focal points. Instead of accepting the sign-cluster which represents the centre of the action, concentration may be diverted to signs other than those foregrounded by the performance or may even move to read unintentional signs against them. With these caveats, it is nevertheless recognized that a *mise en scène* is inevitably structured so as to give emphasis to a sign or sign-cluster intended to locate audience focalization on that aspect of the drama. (S. Bennett 1990, 160)

Educational level, cultural heritage, social experience, mood, physical impairment, ability to concentrate, and the like all play a part in the spectator's ability to construct meanings from the performance through a reading or decoding of signs. Furthermore, each spectator possesses a different skill level for interpreting the multiple signifiers that the performance offers.

Contemporary criticism has given us "reader-response" and "reception" theories as ways of analyzing the dynamic relationship between a spectator (reader) and the text—a book, concert, or theatrical performance, for example. Reader-response or reception theories in their simplest forms ask the question: What does the reader bring to the act of interpreting, and therefore what does she see, hear, feel, and experience that is unique to her because of her cultural background, education, mood, physical and mental abilities, and other forms of preprogramming? How does a spectator/reader respond to the signifiers, sign systems, and clusters of signs that she experiences when reading the words on a page or when seeing, hearing, feeling, smelling, and touching a performance? These are difficult questions that reader-response theorists have struggled with in order to understand how each reader/spectator consciously and unconsciously interacts with a text. Each reader fashions meanings differently through a dialectical exchange with the text.

Theorists have developed different reader-response theories to help explain how readers read literature and, by extension, they have provided clues about how spectators read productions through the various sign systems. Norman Holland (1975) claims that a reader is predisposed to read a work of literature through the core values and psychological disposition he possesses. "A reader responds to a literary work by assimilating it to his own psychological processes, that is, to his search for successful solutions within his identity theme to the multiple demands, both inner and outer, on his ego" (128). For example, one reader who is highly religious may look for certain themes, symbols, or images in a performance, while another reader, guided by her interest in feminism, seeks out themes, symbols, or images in the same performance that resonate with her specific values.

To analyze the text in formal isolation as so many "words-on-a-page" (in the old formula of the New Criticism) is a highly artificial procedure. A literary text, after all, in an objective sense consists only of a certain configuration of specks of carbon black on dried wood pulp. When these marks become words, when those words become images or metaphors or characters or events, they do so because the reader plays the part of a prince to the sleeping beauty. He gives them life out of his own desires. When he does so, he brings his lifestyle to bear on the work. He mingles his unconscious loves and fears and adaptations with the words and images he synthesizes at a conscious level.

It is, therefore, quite impossible to say from a text alone how people will respond to it. Only after we have understood how some specific individual responds, how the different parts of his individual personality re-create the different details of the text, can we begin to formulate general hypotheses about the way many or all readers respond. Only then—if then. (Holland 1975, 12)

If we take Holland's arguments beyond the reading of a literary text to the viewing of a performance, his basic tenets still hold true: the spectator is an active participant in the process of decoding and constructing meanings from a performance. The process is, if anything, much more complicated because the spectator is reading twenty different sign systems at once, both actively and passively (i.e., the spectator can actively observe and listen, or she can close her eyes and tune out).

Holland's unique reader-response theory assumes that each spectator naturally seeks unity in any reading of a literary work. "A reader, as he synthesizes and re-creates a piece of literature, works; he transforms his own fantasies (of a kind that would ordinarily be unconscious) into the conscious social, moral, and intellectual meanings he finds by 'interpreting' the work" (17).

Poststructuralists, however, believe that reading a text is much more open ended; the text itself has plural dimensions, and each reader must discover or construct her own meanings (Selden 1989, 112).

Roland Barthes (1974) supports this notion. He believes that the reader gains meaning from a text not by his personal psychological bent and natural inclination to seek unity but, rather, by the text itself, which is open ended.

To interpret a text is not to give it a (more or less justified, more or less free) meaning, but on the contrary to appreciate what *plural* constitutes it. Let us first posit the image of a triumphant plural, unimpoverished by any constraint of representation (of imitation). In this ideal text, the networks are many and interact, without any one of them being able to surpass the rest; this text is a galaxy of signifiers, not a structure of signifieds; it has no beginning; it is reversible; we gain access to it by several entrances, none of which can be authoritatively declared to be the main one; the codes it mobilizes extend *as far as the eye can reach*. . . . (Barthes 1974, 5–6)

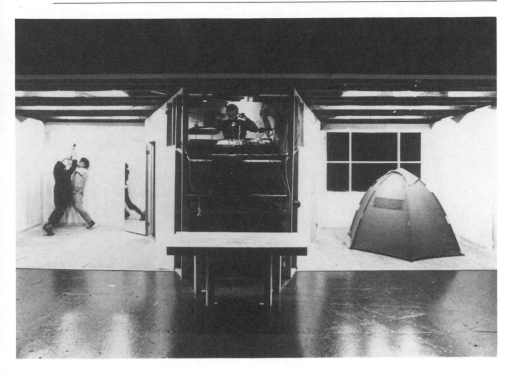

Fig. 2. Production: *Rumstick Road*. Director: Elizabeth LeCompte. Photo by Ken Kobland/Wooster Group.

The reader becomes the writer in the sense that she must construct meaning out of the open-ended signifiers of a work of art. It is true that not all works of art leave the same amount of room for open-ended reading. Thus, for example, a spectator at a postmodern theater performance is given the creative leeway to bring meanings out of the experience through an interaction with the seemingly disordered signifiers of the performance. For example, the setting for the Wooster Group's production of *Rumstick Road* (fig. 2) allows the spectator to choose where he wants to focus his attention at any given moment of the performance, a bit like a three-ring circus. "The Wooster Group initiates what could be described as an Einsteinian project that celebrates the multiplicity of perspectives and only one certainty: that the phenomenon will be different for each member of the audience" (Savran 1986, 54). A spectator, however, who attends a realistic production of a Tennessee Williams play will undoubtedly have less freedom of interpretation because of a more tightly proscribed, linear, unified, and closure-oriented production and cluster of signifiers. Nonetheless, at any performance the spectator is given an opportunity to work at constructing a private performance based on the existence of an open-ended performance text and on his personal bent, mood, location in the theater, and so forth.

I have presented a peek at only two of many reader-response theories. There is perhaps no value in discussing the specifics of several others. It might be more profitable to summarize how reader-response theories are beneficial to directors who overcode a playscript with their own ideas about what a performance means, all the while realizing that each spectator will be reading the performance text divergently.

> A text's meaning and significance [is] intimately bound up with the activity of the reader. . . . Texts are full of gaps, blanks, ambiguities, indeterminacies, which the reader must fill, close up, or develop. Some reader-response critics place an emphasis on the reader's contribution to a text's meaning, while others recognise that there are "triggers" in the text which direct the reader's interpretive activity. (R. Selden 1989, 121)

A director can, if he chooses, actively contrive triggers that lead spectators to construct meanings where he wants them to. To varying degrees, directors point readers/spectators in directions that shape or guide each spectator's reading.

## Signs and the Director

After a director has fully analyzed a script—or developed a theme or scenario for a nonscripted production—and has developed a production concept (if that is the director's method of operation), it becomes her task to orchestrate signifiers in order to communicate to the spectators her interpretation. The director overcodes the production with her vision of the performance's ultimate meanings. Directors make literally thousands of choices: they select individual signs and blend them into sequences of signs, which lead to large patterns of signs that ultimately produce a performance's meanings through each spectator's unique perception of the performance.

In the theater every object, every movement, every sound or noise, every smell, every color, every physical contact, every spatial relation-ship, is a sign. By virtue of its placement within the unique framework of the theater environment, everything has a special sign significance; meaning and communicative powers are heightened because every element has been lifted out of the context of everyday life.

In traditional dramatic performance the actor's body acquires its mimetic and representational powers by becoming something other than itself, more and less than individual. This applies equally to his speech (which assumes the general signified "discourse") and to every aspect of his performance, to the extent that even purely contingent factors, such as physiologically determined reflexes, are accepted as signifying units. (Elam 1980, 9)

## Transformability of Signs

Signifieds and their signifiers are highly transformable. This is particu-larly true in the theater, where everything is a sign by virtue of it being framed by the aesthetic codes of the theatrical event itself. Because of shifting contexts and/or given circumstances, the same object may stand for different signifieds at different moments in the performance. A plain chair may become a king's throne in one scene and a toilet in the next. The Chinese theater often uses a single property to signify a full range of places. A chair turned one way signifies a mountain; when placed on a table it signifies a city tower (Brušák 1976, 62). The Shakespearean stage structure itself can be used to identify a location as a forest in one scene and a banquet hall in the next, with no physical changes whatsoever. Jerzy Grotowski developed a whole theater aes-thetic based on the transformability of objects as a way of creating all aspects of the visual mise-en-scène. For his production of *Akropolis* he uses each object in multiple ways.

The bathtub is a very pedestrian bathtub; on the other hand it is a symbolic bathtub: it represents all the bathtubs in which human bodies were processed for the making of soap and leather. Turned upside down, the same bathtub becomes the altar in front of which an inmate chants a prayer. Set up on a high place, it becomes Jacob's nuptial bed. The wheelbarrows are tools for daily work; they become strange hearses for the transportation of the corpses; propped against the wall they are Priam's and

Hecuba's thrones. One of the stovepipes, transformed by Jacob's imagination, becomes his grotesque bride. (Barba and Flaszen 1965, 181)

Transformability extends to the playscript as well; each iteration of a playscript through performance may produce radically different sign clusters because of the specific choices a director makes in selecting which sign systems and complexes of signifiers to use, the order they are to be in, and so forth.

A fundamental principle of semiotics is the transferability of signifiers: a new context can allow a fresh connection between signifier and signified. The possibilities of interpretation are interminable: even a signifier of such awesome power can, in a new context, be assigned a new signified. This indicates that there is never any final Truth to be arrived at. We can never say that a particular signifier or string of signifiers (an entire literary work, for example) has been interpreted once and for all. To give it a final meaning (or to suppose that it has a final meaning) is merely to repress other possibilities of meaning. (R. Selden 1989, 80)

Richard Foreman is a master at using the transformability of sets, and especially properties, as a central component of his theater aesthetic.

Beginning with *Hotel China* many of the objects were more complicated, funkier, more idiosyncratic. My new perspective toward the psychic significance of objects allowed me to use the lamp in such a way that the lamp said, "I am a lamp, but it can also be a projectile that you hurl at your enemy. It could also be something that you can lay on its side and put ketchup on and try tasting to see if it tastes good." It could be any one of innumerable possibilities. (Foreman 1992, 80)

For several of Foreman's productions the performance text was developed through the actors' and director's/playwright's interaction with a variety of props that he brought to rehearsal, which the performers improvised with and transformed into myriad signifieds. Foreman capitalized on the ambiguous and changeable nature of signs as a way of presenting his highly imaginative yet quirky brand of Ontological-Hysteric Theatre.

## Foregrounding

Since several sign systems work simultaneously in a theater performance, directors employ foregrounding (highlighting, emphasizing)
as a technique to bring the spectator's attention to the most noteworthy signifiers at a given moment in the performance. At the next
changed moment a different set of signifiers may require foregrounding in order to compel the spectator to focus on a different set
of stimuli. All signs and sign systems should not produce equally
strong signifiers all the time, or the spectator would experience sign
overload and confusion. Some order of priority needs to be established
for literally every moment in the performance. To be bombarded with
uncontrolled multiple signifiers at every moment of a performance
would bring undifferentiated information overload to the soon-weary
spectator. Directors for the cinema and video use the camera to control
the focus of the spectator. Stage directors, lacking this focusing device,
orchestrate the foregrounding and backgrounding of signifiers and
sign systems. By thus guiding or channeling the spectator's receptors,
directors can insure some uniformity of perception (realizing that
there can never be 100 percent unanimity).

## Ostension

One of the unique features of a theater performance, which distin-
guishes it from literature and most other art forms, is that a performance does not describe action or events or objects but, for the most
part, shows them. This is the most primitive form of signification,
which is known in philosophy as ostension. If a child asks me what
a book is, instead of going through an elaborate, abstract description
of a book, I simply pick up the nearest book and say, "This is a
book."

> Semiotization involves the showing of objects and events (and the
> performance at large) to the audience, rather than describing, ex-
> plaining or defining them. This ostensive aspect of the stage
> "show" distinguishes it, for example, from narrative, where per-
> sons, objects and events are necessarily described and recounted.
> It is not, again, the dramatic referent—the object in the represented
> world—that is shown, but something that expressed its class. The

showing is emphasized and made explicit through indices, verbal references and other direct foregrounding devices, all geared towards presenting the stage spectacle for what it basically is, a "display." (Elam 1980, 30)

Semiotics is, in its totality, more complex than the few explanations offered above. For the purposes of this study, however, these reference points will serve as a beginning. My concern here is not to develop a complete understanding of semiotics for the literary or theater critic. It is, rather, to examine those aspects of semiotic theory that have practical and functional application for contemporary stage directors in the performance of their complex task of creating a theatrical work in a postmodern theater world.

## Communication in Performance

How does the complex process of communication take place in the theater? As we have seen, twenty sign systems constitute the vehicles for communication in the theater, and five communication systems provide the avenues for transferring signifiers into meanings. Directors who understand the complexities of the communication process in the theater have the potential to employ all the elements of communication inherent in a performance. The communication model in figure 3 gives directors a framework within which to make choices about the signifiers, sign systems, and cultural codes that can best be employed to help spectators construct meanings.

The following definitions provide a means of interpreting figure 3.

*Source:* The imagination of the playwright, director, designer, composer, performer, and technician.

*Transmitter:* The performers (voices, facial expressions, etc.), the mise-en-scène (setting, costumes, audio speakers, etc.), the audience.

*Signifier:* Spoken words, music, color, light, odor, movement, gesture, and so on.

*Receiver:* The spectator—her eyes, ears, nose, taste buds, skin.

*Meanings:* Cognition, emotions, spiritual awareness, aesthetic osmosis.

*Code:* The set of rules or guidelines that are understood by both the source (at the formation of the signifiers [encoding]) and the receiver (at the creation of the signified [decoding]).

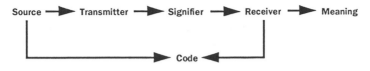

Fig. 3. Communication model

Although figure 3 appears to depict the transmission of a single sign, we have seen that there are pluridimensional sign systems working simultaneously during a performance and that many signifiers are emitted from these systems at each moment of the performance. Because of the diversity and richness of multiple sign systems, there can be no single meaning of a performance. Rather, there are multiple meanings, many of which are unique to each spectator.

At every theater performance, spectators absorb different stimuli generated by the complex sign systems according to where they are seated and where their sensors are focused from moment to moment. Spectators then sift through, consciously and unconsciously, the mishmash of signs differently because of their unique socioeconomic, educational, ethnic, cultural, geographic, and theatergoing backgrounds. They each construct different meanings that are consistent with their personal spheres of experience and knowledge and current emotional and psychological states.

For example, two spectators in an audience watching *Streamers* by David Rabe—a play about army life at the beginning of the Vietnam War—might construct profoundly different meanings if one spectator had served in Vietnam while the other had avoided the draft through an educational deferment or flight to Canada. Another pair of spectators sitting at the same production of *Streamers,* one a director and the other attending a live theater performance for the first time, would also likely construct fundamentally different meanings. In this case the director's meanings may center around her critical observation of the way the performers move about the stage or how the colors contrast sharply with one another. The theater neophyte may draw meaning from the heretofore never experienced live interaction between performers and himself as a spectator. To the experienced director this new discovery by the neophyte is not even something that comes into her consciousness (perhaps her years of attending the theater have jaded her perceptions in this regard). The director is giving priority to seeing how the production was directed. The neophyte may not know that a director even exists or what a director may have been expected to do. The primary meanings for the director (as audience member) may be that the production was poorly directed or that some aspect of the performance was particularly well staged or that the casting was all wrong, and so forth. Meanwhile, the neophyte's meanings might be grounded in his emotional involvement with the story and with the personal agony of the characters; he may have no cognizance of the quality of directorial effort.

At the same time there may be core meanings of the performance that are perceived by a majority of the audience, so that there is some degree of unanimity in the collective experience. Directors usually choose to approach a playscript (if there is one) as though it has some universal meanings. They then make choices based on their personal interpretation of what the script means (Pavis calls this the metatext), all the time planning the performance so that a majority of the audience will obtain core meanings through experiencing it.

## Audience as Signifier

Audiences not only interpret signifiers and construct meanings from the performance, they also produce signifiers that are read by performers, technicians, and other audience members. Individually, they cough, rattle programs, wiggle in their seats, and get up during the performance. Collectively, they applaud, shout bravo or boo, and, in cases in which they are asked direct questions by the performers, talk back. During performances at which spectators can easily see one another, the audience becomes a major signifier.

> As a spectator I see the event through all of our eyes and cease to see it only through mine. The simple stage [arena stage] reminds us of each other, as my counterpart across the circle mirrors my attention; from my mates I learn what the actor is doing even when he turns his back on me. (Huston 1992, 84)

This communication among the audience and the performers and technicians is part of the live theater experience. Some have argued that the theater performance communication loop is highly one-sided, but indeed there is circular communication: a dynamic interchange takes place between the performance and the audience.

What kind of information is being communicated to the spectator during a theatrical performance? Clearly, theatrical information consists of not just words but also sights, sounds, smells, and physical sensations. How signifiers are presented for reading by the audience is the ultimate responsibility of the director. A performance's meanings are drawn by the spectator from the orchestrated layers or grids of signifiers that exist because of the collaborative efforts of multiple artists (actors, designers, costumers, etc.), as well as other spectators. The director leads, guides, and supports the contributing artists' work in order to bring unity and therefore clarity to the signs present in a traditional performance or disunity and openendedness to a postmodern performance.

## Setting the Performance Parameters

Directors often place primary emphasis on the words and the story they are attempting to convey, choosing sets, costumes, performers, and colors that underscore this word-centered focus. Other communication systems, however, are becoming prominent in postmodern theater productions. Some directors, like Joseph Svoboda and Robert Wilson, emphasize visual sign systems; others, like Peter Sellars, often use music as a primary sign system; still others, like Ingmar Bergman in his production of *Madam De Sade*, choose costumes as the primary visual communication system. These directors are exploring how the foregrounding and backgrounding of the sign systems themselves (not just individual signifiers) can become a central part of the actual content and meanings of the performance.

One way of clarifying the options that are available to directors as they begin to work through a production concept—be it a scripted project or one created collectively from an idea or theme—is to visualize each performance sign system as a continuum between two extreme choices. At the left extreme is the decision not to use a particular sign system or to use it in the most marginal way. At the extreme right of each continuum is the decision to make a particular sign system a primary sign vehicle for the performance. In between these extremes are varying opportunities to use different sign systems to a lesser or greater degree. Figure 4 shows how this continuum might reflect a postmodern production of *King Lear*. The continuum indicates the level of commitment a director might make to a deconstructed production of *King Lear*. The kind of performance that would emerge from these directorial choices is one that would emphasize movement, sound, space, and intimate contact between performer and spectator. Masks might be used. There would be very little scenery, no elaborate costumes or color, and, perhaps most important, very little reliance

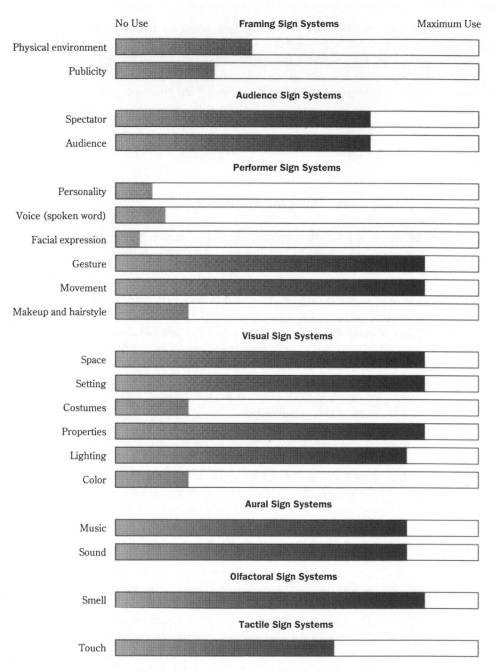

Fig. 4. Postmodern production of *King Lear*

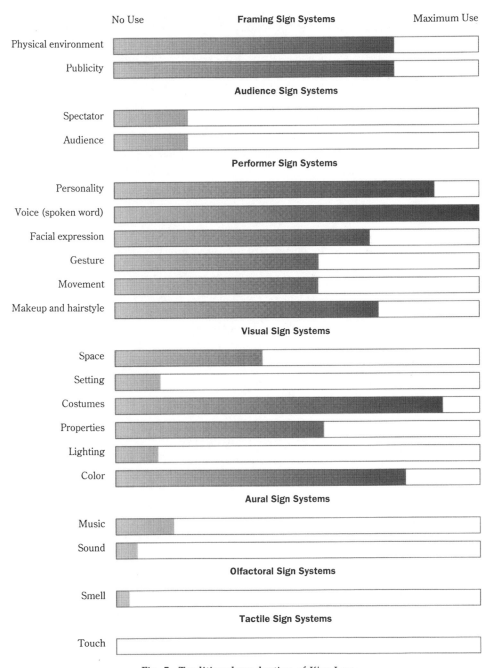

Fig. 5. Traditional production of *King Lear*

on the spoken word. The story would not be expressed primarily through dialogue (which would be severely cut). Instead, it would be conveyed largely through sight, paralexical sound, space, lighting, properties, touch, smell, and a carefully controlled and configured intimate performer-audience relationship.

A more traditional production of *King Lear* in a replica Globe outdoor theater would shift rather dramatically the choices reflected on the continuum (fig. 5). This production might have star performers playing the main characters. The spoken word, costumes, colors, properties, facial expressions, and performers' personalities would be the primary sign systems, while touch, smell, sound, setting, and an intimate performer-audience relationship would be much less important.

In comparing these two hypothetical productions, it is easy to see that the fundamental choices a director makes when deciding which sign systems to emphasize or deemphasize profoundly affect the style, content, and meanings of a performance. The choices depend on the director's own aesthetic interests and method of operating, the playscript or performance vehicle the director has chosen, and the meanings the director hopes the spectators will assemble. The emotional, spiritual, intellectual, and aesthetic impact of the performance will be shaped and perhaps even dictated by these core choices. The overall directorial style of a performance (or series of performances) will be identified by the sign systems the director chooses and the priority assigned to them.

## Summary

Contemporary theory has aided directors significantly by providing practical methodologies for translating playscripts into performances. Using the tools of semioticians, directors can understand how performances communicate meanings by examining the signifiers that are decoded by individual spectators. By defining the mise-en-scène as a dynamic dialectic among the playscript, director, performance, and audience, Pavis has supplied a framework for conceptualizing and actualizing the process of theatrical creation. Reader-response and reception theorists offer insights into how spectators read performances and how meanings are constructed by each spectator.

The remainder of this book will study how the individual sign systems function and how directors may use semiotics as a touchstone in transforming a playscript or performance idea into a production.

*Chapter 2*

# Framing Systems

Although it might be ideal to experience a work of art in its pure state, unencumbered by any outside trappings or influences, no work of art is ever experienced in total isolation. "Aesthetic perception is no universal code with timeless validity, but rather—like all aesthetic experience—is intertwined with historical experience" (Jauss 1982, 148). When a spectator reads a work of art she brings all her past knowledge and life experiences with her to the reading. According to Jauss, these prior experiences produce a "horizon of expectations" in each spectator that is shaped uniquely by the individual's values, knowledge, and experiences, which are formed into an aesthetic paradigm that constitutes her aesthetic model. This aesthetic paradigm and the immediate experiences she has before a performance or exhibition serve as "frames" or unique perspectives that influence how she constructs meanings.

If I travel to Paris to view a painting that is on display at a museum, for example, my viewing of the pure work of art (paint on canvas) is framed in several dimensions. First, my background as a college student with a minor in art history comes into play, informing my thinking with a historical perspective. Before my trip I read several articles and critical reviews about the exhibition, which develops preconceptions in my mind. When I arrive in Paris, I experience the city's architecture, colors, sounds, smells, food, and weather and I am fully enchanted. As I approach the museum by foot, I am exhilarated by its location in the city and its elegant surroundings, as well as its impressive architecture. Entering the unique space of the museum, I find it grandiose, cold, and crowded. Finally, I enter the room in which the painting is displayed and I am pleased to discover that it has been hung independently on a huge wall with lots of open space around it. I am disappointed, however, to find that the painting is dimly lit, covered with glass, and protected by a barrier that keeps me and everyone else from standing right next to it. Once I finally stand as close as I can get to the painting (but too far away to see it clearly), I have trouble concentrating on it because of the talking and jostling that goes on around me.

The overall meanings of the painting for me are profoundly shaped by both the historic horizon of expectation I bring with me and the multiple physical and psychological experiences surrounding the actual viewing. My prior knowledge and the immediate experiences can be considered clusters of signifiers (art history courses, critical reviews, the city, the museum building, the crowd), which I decode and construct meanings from according to my unique sociopsychological perspective.

## Theatrical Frames

When a spectator approaches a theater production he brings his own horizon of expectations to the event. A simple example is a theatergoer who has seen ten plays, all of which are highly realistic and linear. Since these ten plays constitute the total theatergoing experience of the individual, he has developed a horizon of expectation that leads him to expect all theatrical productions to be realistic and linear. If this spectator suddenly finds himself witnessing a production of the Onto-logical-Hysteric Theatre of Richard Foreman—a theater that routinely utilizes nudity, highly distorted sound, blazing lights that shine in the audience's eyes, bizarre juxtapositions of amplified spoken dialogue, unrelated music, and unnatural, frantic movement patterns (see fig. 13)—the spectator will have his horizon of expectation shattered, stretched, or reshaped. If the spectator accepts Foreman's production as legitimate theater, he will expand his horizon; if he rejects the event as a nontheatrical hodgepodge, he will likely keep his realistic, linear paradigm intact and fix his theater as a narrow activity that embraces all but one example of his theatergoing experience.

Beyond horizons of expectations, however, are numerous other experiences and sets of information that frame an event. Weather, publicity, type of theater, and the presence of a star performer are but a few frames that influence the reading of a performance. Whether these frames enhance or detract from the performance can be controlled to some extent by the director. It is impossible to manipulate the general education level of the spectators and each person's prior theater-attending experiences. For that matter, the director cannot know whether any spectators have read the playscript or seen a different performance of it before witnessing her production; however, she can manipulate some of the physical frames of a performance and can influence the audience's intellectual, historical, and aesthetic horizons through publicity, the kind and location of theater building, preperformance lectures or discussions, program notes, and the like.

> No longer do we necessarily approach theatre primarily as the physical enactment of a written text with our historical concern anchored in the interplay between that text and its physical realization. We are now at least equally likely to look at the theatre experience in a more global way, as a sociocultural event whose meanings and interpretations are not to be sought exclusively in the text being performed but in the experience of the audience assembled to share in the creation of the total event. . . .
>
> The way an audience experiences and interprets a play, we now recognize, is by no means governed solely by what happens on the stage. The entire theatre, its audience arrangements, its other public spaces, its physical appearance, even its location within a city, are all important elements of the process by which an audience makes meaning of its experience. (Carlson 1989, 2)

The frames for a performance are many; they vary according to the given circumstances of each performance and with each spectator. Spectators will bring their individual horizons of expectations to an event, including their knowledge and experiences of historical, social, and theatrical codes.

> Established cultural markers are important in pre-activating a certain anticipation, a horizon of expectations, in the audience drawn to any particular event. Multiple horizons of expectations are bound to exist within any culture and these are, always, open to renegotiation before, during, and after the theatrical performance. The relationship then between culture and the idea of the theatrical event is one that is necessarily flexible and inevitably rewritten on a daily basis. (S. Bennett 1990, 114)

These complex frames, these horizons of expectations, are negotiable. That is, the frames change as society changes and as the theatrical conventions change over time. What a spectator expects of a realistic contemporary comedy by Neil Simon is different from what a spectator expects for a postmodern production by Robert Wilson, is different from what an neophyte spectator expects from an unknown theater production, is different from what an Elizabethan spectator expected at Blackfriars or the priest expected at the Theatre of Dionysus, and so forth.

It is also important to note that audiences have very distinct horizons of expectations at different times. To have experienced a performance of Robert Wilson's *Deafman's Glance* in 1971 was undoubtedly different from witnessing *When We Dead Awaken* twenty years later. Likewise, witnessing a production of Eugène Ionesco's *The Bald Soprano* in 1950 had to have been a startling experience; today it would not be so. In the 1950s, Ionesco's work was shocking, bizarre, and incomprehensible to many in the audience, who brought a "realistic" horizon of expectations to the theater; today, Ionesco plays are easily acceptable and considered part of the modern repertory. Today's audiences also have begun to accept the postmodern aesthetic; fragmentary, nonlinear, nonclosure-oriented performances are working their way into the horizon of expectations of many adventuresome contemporary spectators.

> [If] the artistic character of a work is to be measured by the aesthetic distance with which it opposes the expectations of its first audience, then it follows that this distance, at first experienced as a pleasing or alienating new perspective, can disappear for later readers, to the extent that the original negativity of the work has become self-evident and has itself entered into the horizon of future aesthetic experience. (Jauss 1982, 25)

Any performance of a play will likely be informed by other productions of the playscript that a spectator many have seen or read about. Jauss calls this the "progressive understanding" of a text, while the Formalist school refers to this phenomenon as "literary evolution" (Jauss 1982, 32). It is hard to view a performance of *A Midsummer Night's Dream* without comparing it to Peter Brook's influential and dynamic production in 1970. If you saw Brook's production (or even pictures of it [fig. 6]) it is likely to have colored your reading of every subsequent production; it has for me. "All we can expect to achieve when studying the sequence of horizons and readings of a particular text is a 'fusion' of horizons: my reading becomes a focusing and ordering instrument in a complex perspective of horizons going right back to the contemporary reader of the text" (R. Selden 1989, 128). As time marches on, readings of a given playscript will change as new horizons of expectations are developed for each spectator and for a theatergoing society as a whole. "The understanding of the first reader

Fig. 6. Production: *A Midsummer Night's Dream*. Director: Peter Brook. Photo courtesy of The Shakespeare Centre.

will be sustained and enriched in a chain of receptions from generation to generation" (Jauss 1982, 20).

## Control of Frames

Directors vary in the control they exert over framing systems, as the following continuum indicates. Some directors consciously choose to frame their productions, to set on edge the audience's perceptive potential before a performance begins. Other directors ignore framing devices altogether.

Ignore
Frames

Control
Frames

The geographic location and kind of theater a performance is housed in are two of the most important frames. Knowledge and preconceptions about performance events, the performance company, the playscript (if there is one), and individual artists also provide clusters of signifiers. Even though some directors choose to ignore these frames, they do not disappear.

> Many of the audience's receptive processes are pre-activated by their anticipation of a particular kind of event. The nature of that anticipation is . . . inevitably variable. Furthermore, the horizon of expectations drawn up by the idea of the forthcoming event may or may not prove useful in the decoding of the event itself. A crucial aspect of audience involvement, then, is the degree to which a performance is accessible through the codes audiences are accustomed to utilizing, the conventions they are used to recognizing, at a theatrical event. Intelligibility and/or success of a particular performance will undoubtedly be determined on this basis. (S. Bennett 1990, 112)

Frames have an effect on the audience whether or not they are consciously manipulated by the director.

## Physical Framing Systems

All performances take place at a specific location—inside a theater or cabaret, in a park, on the street, in a warehouse, in someone's living room. Each location for a performance will touch spectators differently. An outdoor location is likely to produce certain preconceptions. Some spectators may be preoccupied with the weather—will it rain? Others may be exhilarated by the fresh air and natural beauty of the surroundings. Others may harbor negative feelings because they think performances should take place in a "proper" theater, not outside. Although the director does not always select the physical setting, he may choose to pick the environment, or manipulate it, in order to control its effect on the audience.

## Location

Semioticians view cities as "texts" whose meanings are expressed by signifiers that are decoded by the city's residents and visitors. One system of signs, for example, is the various geographical areas within a city: ethnic neighborhoods, business districts, slums, industrial concentrations, university districts, suburbs, art districts, parks, and lakes.

> Clearly, those theatres seeking to attract the attention and patronage of the general public will locate, whenever possible, near important nodes, along major paths, and perhaps close to prominent landmarks, while a theatre tied to a specific segment of the population will likely be found in a district congenial to that segment, either because the theatre was consciously placed there to share the connotations of the district or because, once established, it came to be associated with its district. Semiotics encourages us to consider the different connotations of one node, one path, one district as opposed to another and to ask what urban meanings are involved in the use of any particular location. (Carlson 1990, 48)

Where a performance is located within a city can influence the anticipated meanings of a theater experience. If I have tickets to see five plays in New York City—one on Broadway, one just off Broadway, one in Soho, one in Harlem, and one at some location I have never heard of—I will likely have preconceptions about the kinds of experiences I will have and the kinds of performances I will see, based on my understanding of the New York City "text" and the hierarchical strata of the New York City theater world. When I go to Broadway I expect to see an expensive, highly professional, commercial production. When I go to Soho I anticipate seeing a more experimental, or at least lower-budget, production. And when I go to Harlem I assume I will see an African-American performance. I may be completely wrong about these assumptions, but they nonetheless sway my thinking about the event.

In any city (and even in rural locations) directors often have a choice of possible locations for their production. If such is the case, a director can frame the very nature of the experience for the audience by where he locates the performance. Choices include outdoors or indoors, found space or a formal theater, and fringe or central district. Mainstream theater is most often located in arts districts or upscale business and commercial districts of cities, but marginalized theater groups often bring their theater to the ethnic neighborhoods: Chicano theaters, such as Teatro Campesino, perform in the casas or on the streets of the barrio or (in their early days) in the fields of the farm workers.

## Architectural Facade

The exterior architectural features of the theater itself, or the visual aesthetics of an outdoor location, contribute to the signification of a performance event. A large, monolithic, imposing theater that is set in an even larger arts center complex (such as the Kennedy Center in Washington, D.C., or the National Theatre in London) provides the spectator with a frame for a performance. At the opposite extreme, an old storefront in an industrial area of a city can also incite meanings as it frames an experimental theater production.

Not only the size but other aspects of the theater facade—how ostentatious it is, whether or not it has a marquee, its color, the graphics—all contribute to the framework of a performance. In the case of outdoor performances every aspect of the environment—flora and fauna, sounds, terrain, temperature, colors—offers signification and a special context that provokes intellectual, emotional, spiritual, and physical engagement with the impending event.

## Architectural Interiors

Theater spaces are designed with two purposes in mind: to provide an aesthetic environment in which to house the performance event and to provide places for performers and spectators.

> All theatre interiors consist of two essential areas: one is "the auditorium," which is designed specifically for the audience; the other, designed for the production, we know as "the stage." These two areas are entirely different, but cannot function fully if unrelated. Independently they have no life; together they produce a living theatre. It is therefore the sensitive interrelationship of the two that makes a theatre design either a success or a failure. All other areas

and all external forms must be additive to and enhance these inner functions. (Mielziner 1970, 14)

From the Greeks to the present day, however, most theaters have been built with more than a functional purpose in mind. Historically, theaters have been conceived of as special places that house both an audience and the performers in a setting that enhances the uniqueness and theatricality of the artistic event.

Theaters are designed traditionally to facilitate performers in a special space—a stage, with a separate yet connected space set aside for spectators. In addition, theaters are designed to accommodate current performance trends and the latest stage technology. In Shakespeare's time this meant a theater that accommodated quickly changing, multiple-scene playscripts. For the Restoration it meant a theater that allowed for an intimate performer-audience relationship, perspective settings, and an auditorium that facilitated the spectators' desire to see and be seen by one another. Each major period of theater history has its own physical theater style, depending upon the kinds of playscripts being written, the theater technology, and the kind, size, and expectations of the audience.

## The Lobby

Before a performance the audience usually assembles outside or in a lobby adjacent to the theater. The director may prepare the lobby in order to create a mood or environment that reflects the performance to come. Posters, models of the set, pictures of the cast, and sketches of costumes are standard items that often dress a theater's lobby. These items help the spectator become aesthetically, intellectually, or emotionally engaged in the production. They enable the spectator to make a transition into the world of the theater.

Directors often go a step further and create in the lobby the same atmosphere as that of the upcoming performance. Performers mingle with the audience or perform for them. For the Circle Repertory's production of *Balm and Gilead*, "even before the play begins . . . some of these derelicts are stumbling through the audience, selling lyrics for a sing-along, taking Polaroid shots of the spectators, nodding off in a corner" (Brustein 1991, 35). Often, special lighting and sound effects are used to tie the waiting place to the performance place. Props and/ or furniture similar to those used in the performance are situated in the lobby. Directors who carry this concept to its maximum create a complete miniproduction in the lobby as a preamble to the performance, or the performance starts in the lobby and moves into the theater.

## The Landscape

Similar techniques are used outside the theater, where audiences can be greeted with signifiers to frame the event. Elizabethan flags are flown for a Shakespearean production. Hot rod cars are parked outside the theater for a production of *Grease*. A marching band greets the audience of *Music Man*. A searchlight captures the mood of opening night.

The transition from a spectator's everyday world into the theatrical world is never instant and is often complex. By preparing the audience for an aesthetic experience as its members approach the performance place, directors help shift the preoccupation and focus of spectators away from family or business concerns to the impending event.

## Selecting a Performance Site

The following elements need to be considered in making a decision about how to physically frame a performance.

Theater location
    Country
    City
    Area of city
    Immediate environment
Theater facade and interior
    Architectural style
    Size of auditorium
    Size of performance space
    Proximity of performers and spectators
    Extent of technology available
    Size of lobby
    Availability of wall space or display cases in lobby
    Availability of sound equipment in lobby
    Adjacencies to lobby (art gallery, rehearsal hall, entryways,
       greenroom)

Architectural landscape
  Flagpole(s)
  Kiosk
  Lighting
  Landscape

Directors often have the opportunity to select or adapt the physical frames for a performance. In the best of all possible worlds a director will be able to choose from among several theater spaces. In order to maximize signification he will take several factors into consideration. For example, the size of the performance space (stage) and the auditorium needs to match the requirements of the playscript or theater piece. What size of cast is required? Does the play require room for dancing or stage fighting? Are there large crowd scenes? Is insularity, intimacy, or isolation a necessity? Is claustrophobia or the reverse—a sense of expansiveness—a key ingredient? What size of audience is expected? How many nights will the play be performed? Do spectators need to see one another? Will the spectators and the performers interact? Will the acting style be subtle or theatrical? Answers to these questions will guide the director as he determines which physical theater will best aid in the overall signification process.

If a director is assigned a certain theater, she may adapt the theater to provide the best possible environment for signification in her production. Stages can be extended into the auditorium for more intimacy. Stage curtains can be eliminated to create an expansive feeling. A balcony might go unused in order to make smaller a large auditorium. The audience might be seated only on the stage in order to turn a large theater into an intimate place (ignoring the auditorium altogether).

Another important consideration is whether or not there is enough appropriate technology (stage rigging, lighting instruments, sound systems and their control) and enough space to meet the scenic, sound, and lighting requirements. Some productions demand simplicity, while many contemporary productions that emphasize visual sign systems require elaboration. If the theater cannot accommodate the demands of the playscript or concept, the director must adapt his vision to meet the technical limitations of the theater.

The interior architectural style and decoration of the theater also strongly affects the framing of a performance. For example, it would be difficult to present a naturalistic production of Zola's *Thérèse Raquin* in a large Baroque-style theater with grand balconies, gold leaf gargoyles festooning the proscenium arch, and a bright red grand drape.

The contrast might disorient the audience. If a director must direct *Thérèse Raquin* in a Baroque theater, however, she can minimize the disruptive contrast by removing the red curtains, building a false proscenium to frame the production more appropriately, focusing the lights narrowly to keep the lavish facade in relative darkness, and dimming the houselights to take the edge off the reflective surfaces. On the other hand, this same theater might be ideal for a lavish opera—for which a grand setting would prime the spectators appropriately—or for a postmodern production that could focus on the contrast between the ornate and the minimal.

As these examples reveal, much can be done to adjust (downplay or call attention to) a theater's architecture and interior design so that the spectator can experience the appropriate environmental preamble to a performance.

## Intellectual, Historical, and Social Framing Systems

Powerful horizons of expectations are created by the knowledge individual spectators bring to a performance. Knowledge gained from experience as a playscript reader, theatergoer, or theater practitioner can lead to a deeper understanding of the performance qua performance—that is, as a theatrical entity itself. To understand (through experience) how difficult it is to read iambic pentameter so that it sounds both natural and poetic or to understand how a director deconstructed a playscript to suit his singular interpretation adds an additional layer of meaning and involvement (or, in some cases, detachment) for the experienced spectator. In addition, knowledge about the following aspects of performance will influence the meanings a spectator constructs:

The playscript (if there is one)
Other performances of the playscript
The director's work or reputation
The theater company's work, style, standards, and goals
The performers' work or reputation
The designers' work or reputation
Critical reviews of a performance (and quality of critics)

Each spectator comes to a performance with a different amount of information framing the experience. If an individual spectator is about to see her thirteenth different production of *Romeo and Juliet*, if she has read three negative reviews by critics she respects, if she is attending a theater that she frequents often because she likes the experimental nature of its productions, if she is seeing her husband play the title role of Romeo, and if her mother is the director, she will bring heavy baggage with her to the performance: this knowledge and its accompanying prejudices will play on her mind powerfully. If another spectator is going to the same performance for the first time, having never seen a play before, having never read *Romeo and Juliet*, having read no reviews of this performance, he will undoubtedly have a profoundly different horizon of expectation and, therefore, a different reading of the performance.

The same goes for spectators who watch different performances of a playscript at different historical moments in different countries.

> The horizon with which the first audiences received the play [Beckett's *Endgame*] is quite different from that of a more recent audience. Of course, not all members of audiences have entered the new "informed" horizon, but one should remember that Beckett's dramatic conventions have not only fed into the genre expectations of audiences but have also become part of a general "postmodern" consciousness which draws into its discourse ideas of the holocaust and the nuclear age. It is worth adding that the French horizon of expectations within which Beckett wrote was quite different from the English one. The work of Jarry and Ionesco, for example, had already disrupted the naturalistic expectations of theatre audiences. (R. Selden 1989, 132)

Awareness of a director's past productions and performance style is an important framing system for experienced theatergoers. Such individuals often make cult figures of their favorite directors. Strikingly inventive directors may become cult figures because of their well-publicized eccentricities. Postmodernists particularly receive this kind of audience support, although traditionalists stay away in droves from experimental productions by such directors as Robert Wilson (too slow), Martha Clarke (too jumpy), Richard Foreman (too intellectual), Philip Glass (too repetitive), and Peter Sellars (too bizarre). True believers in the postmodern aesthetic, however, attach themselves to these directors because of the surprises and challenges they present.

## Publicity

Spectators' horizons of expectations can be influenced through advertising, marketing material, and media coverage. They also receive important information from program notes, especially those of the director, designers, or performers.

> Advertising, reviews, commentary, discussions or extracts (particularly those presented on television or radio), prizes, and popularization of the author clearly work equally well on the theatre-goer. Scholarship, the teacher, and the professional critic all further serve to market the theatre product. Bad reviews can still limit the run of a production. More significantly, they often determine a very specific set of expectations in the audience and thus determine how that audience will receive the play. (S. Bennett 1990, 129)

Directors often help shape the publicity for their productions. If they leave the graphic designers and marketing staff to work in the dark, the marketing campaign is likely to neglect the director's special vision. Such an oversight can result in an unfavorable outcome. An audience expecting a pink comedy (based on the marketing director's interpretation) may discover that the director has chosen to emphasize the darker side of the playscript.

> So important has advance publicity become in the modern theatre, and so remote is it institutionally from most of those involved in the creation of the production itself, that there is often a danger that the community of readers, or the horizons of expectation of one, may be quite different from that assumed by the other, resulting in serious reading difficulties during the performance. Alan Schneider considered the audience's determination to see a different play than the one he was presenting the paramount reason for the disastrous American premiere of *Waiting for Godot* in Miami, and clearly, advance publicity made an important contribution to this. "The Miami audience," reports Schneider, "was being informed, in large type, that Bert Lahr, 'Star of Harvey and Burlesque,' and Tom Ewell, 'Star of The Seven-Year Itch,' were about to appear in their midst in 'The Laugh Sensation of Two Continents,' *Waiting for Godot*. The name of the author appeared only in very small print. My name, luckily, hardly appeared at all." (Carlson 1990, 20–21)

Elinor Fuchs believes that JoAnne Akalaitis's unconventional production of *Cymbeline* was misunderstood by the critics because she did not take a forceful stance in explaining it to them prior to the performances. "Her refusal to grind out advance publicity . . . with explanatory interviews may have damaged her cause with the press" (1989, 31).

The same problems arise if directors avoid involvement in the formulation of the program notes. The spectators can be prepared in an inappropriate way. A director who sees an advantage to informing the audience about his concept for the production, the play's history, its unique performance style, or its story line should either write the material or work closely with a dramaturge charged with that responsibility.

When spectators receive information about the director, designers, characters, setting, time period, and the like prior to performance, they develop a horizon or frame through which to view the performance. This information may be provided through publicity in posters, flyers, radio and television spots, newspaper stories, critical reviews, photographs, programs (including director's or other artists' notes), and biographies of the coartists and technicians; or through organized learning experiences, such as preperformance lectures, discussions with the artists, or play-reading study groups. Information gathered through any of these frames influences the spectator by setting up expectations that may play a vital role in the way the performance is perceived and how the audience responds.

I witnessed the first performance of the Living Theatre in America, after its return from Europe, which took place in New Haven at the Yale School of Drama a year after the Parisian May. At the beginning of *Paradise Now!* the actors intermingled with the spectators. And they recited, as if it were a litany, "We are not allowed to walk around naked, undress, and come onto the stage, and share grass with each other." "We are not allowed to make love in public, come up onto the stage, and make love together." The boys and girls from Yale—slowly, with reluctance, as if bewitched by a rat-catcher—went up on the stage and made love. But being aware that, after all, they were in a theatre, they performed their sexual acts in a difficult, uncomfortable, and elaborate Lotus position.

A year after its performances at Yale, the Living Theatre arrived at Berkeley with the same spectacle: the course of its action was common knowledge. The spectators were ready. At the moment the actors began their litany, the boys and girls in the audience had their jeans below their knees. When the words "We are not allowed to undress in public" were uttered, in a twinkling of an eye the entire audience was naked. After the spectacle, Judith Malina said to me with regret: "Very difficult, this Berkeley audience." (Kott 1980, 28)

As the Living Theatre discovered, once a production has a history it may well change an audience's horizon of expectation. A later audience may construct different meanings, whether the director wants them to or not.

Many directors want their spectators to get off on the right foot—to be prepared for the event they are about to experience. To the extent possible, they provide information and publicity that helps focus and ultimately unify the audience's overall experience. Directors cannot control all aspects of the publicity, however, and therefore are vulnerable to the vicissitudes of uncontrollable critics and word of mouth.

## Preperformance Time

Preperformance time can be used to prepare the audience for the distinctive event they are about to witness. The interior theater (auditorium and stage), the lobby, and the outdoor environment can be employed to indoctrinate the audience aesthetically. Of course, many directors do not focus energy or time manipulating these environmental or architectural framing devices. Nonetheless, these framing devices do affect the audience; they do not disappear. If the audience enters the performance space through an unattractive, bland, or distracting lobby, it may put them off; they may become disinterested or even disgusted. Unless a feeling of disinterest or disgust is part of a director's vision, it is likely to be an uphill battle to reengage the spectators' focus and interest.

Often, with very little effort, directors and designers are able to dress the lobby so the audience will enter the theater with a sense of heightened perception, looking forward to the impending special event. For example, when I directed Archibald MacLeish's *J. B.*— which takes place in a circus tent—the lobby was decorated as a street carnival. Wandering hucksters sold popcorn and balloons to spectators, musicians played circus music, a performer (as master of ceremonies) announced that the performance was about to begin and ushered the audience to their seats. In addition the lobby was decorated with signs and costumed performers to help locate the performance in its appropriate circus milieu. Also, the selection of the theater was ideal for this play; it was octagonal, with arena seating—the shape of a small circus tent.

Once the audience enters the performance space the director still has several options for further preparation of the spectators' reception of the impending performance. The director can choose whether or not the audience will see the setting as they enter the theater. "The condition of the stage set at the point of the audience's entry can provide an important first stimulus for the audience perception of the play. Where it is available for consumption, it acts as the initiator of the decoding process" (S. Bennett 1990, 142). As an example, Bennett points out that Tom Stoppard confronts the audience of *The Real Inspector Hound* with a body laying on the stage during the period before the performance begins. Obviously, the audience is confronted with a series of questions: Is the person dead? Is he a real person or a dummy? Who is he? Is he going to be a character in the performance? Who killed him? and so forth. The playwright and director (if she so chooses) will use the preperformance time to engage the spectators in a meaningful dialogue with the impending production.

Directors may choose the opposite effect: hiding the performance space from the audience in order to create a different kind of expectation.

> Diametrically opposed to this practice [of revealing the set to the audience] is the set concealed behind the theatre curtain. In this case the audience is unable to begin the decoding process based on literal evidence of the set, but is nevertheless reminded by the curtain (as well as by its likely counterpart, the proscenium-arch) of the theatrical frame. The curtain can also function to provoke the audience into speculation about the kind of set that will be revealed for the play they are about to watch. (S. Bennett 1990, 143)

The setting of the levels of light in the performance area can also frame the experience. Bright lights allow the audience members to see one another and serve to encourage them to observe and converse with one another, while dim lighting will deter socializing and encourage introspection, solemnity, or sleep.

## Postperformance Time

The meanings of a performance are framed by the events that take place following the reading of the performance as well. The kind and length of applause, style of curtain call (if any), discussion with other audience members, interaction with the director or performers (formally or informally), whether or not it's raining as spectators go to their cars, how tired they are, whether or not they go to dinner and dancing, whether they read the director's notes the next morning (if they failed to do so at the performance) all present an opportunity to add to, distort, or shift the meaning of the performance for each spectator. While it may be true that the director can only control a small part of the postperformance time, he can insist on an audience/cast/designer/director "talk" with the audience after individual performances as an extreme way of continuing to influence each spectator's reading of the performance text. Other options include special curtain calls, exit music, a gala party on the set or backstage, and the like.

# Summary

Although directors cannot control all frames, they can choose whether or not to use some framing devices to influence an audience's horizon of expectations and to communicate a performance's mood, spirit, style, and so forth.

> The level at which expectations are pitched at the outset has an often crucial influence on the way the "meaning" of individual signifiers as well as the total meaning of the performance is understood. These preliminary, or framing, devices belong to a higher order of sign than any individual signifiers, as they set the initial mood, the level at which all other signs are to be "decoded." They are comparable to the "keys" of musical notation. (Esslin 1987, 54–55)

As Esslin indicates, framing devices can play a crucial role in guiding the spectators' horizons of expectations and eagerness to read the performance. Where the theater is located, the ambiance of the lobby, the interior look and feel of the theater itself, and the style, color, graphics, and choice of words of the publicity all contribute to the mind-set of each spectator at the moment the performance begins. If they are excited, curious, and eager, the performance will be more keenly perceived than if they are confused, disengaged, or simply unenthusiastic about the event they are going to witness. Many framing devices can be manipulated by the director to influence an audience's attitude and anticipation about a performance before it begins and after it has concluded.

Using publicity and pre- and postperformance time as framing devices, however, is never an assurance that all spectators will receive the appropriate information. Indeed, many spectators will not read publicity in the newspaper, see television or radio spots, read the program notes or critical reviews, notice the photos or costume designs in the lobby, hear the preperformance music, read the playscript, remain for the postperformance discussion, or the like. While framing devices do shape the reading of a performance of some, or even many, audience members, these framing devices never govern all spectators. The performance itself will be the final signifier of meanings: frames and horizons of expectations prepare the spectators and help refine and focus their concentration, nothing more.

*Chapter 3*

# Audience Systems

Why do people go to the theater? For entertainment? For education? For spiritual stimulation? For intellectual awakening? To relieve stress? To have a religious experience? Indeed, people go for all these reasons, although they may see different productions for different reasons. A spectator may go to a production of *Love's Labor's Lost* to experience the beauty of Shakespeare's poetry. The same spectator may attend Robert Wilson's *Einstein on the Beach* expecting to be visually mesmerized or to be jolted or to be entertained or simply to be with other people—or for all of these reasons.

We go to live theater for "excitement, illumination, and fulfillment" (S. Selden 1969, 14). Excitement develops from having the senses stimulated beyond the normal, from calling into use all the receptive powers of the sensory system to read the performance. Illumination grows out of discovering something about ourselves and the world we live in that we did not see or understand through everyday living; the theater reveals the essence of our lives. Fulfillment comes from achieving a spiritual, emotional, or intellectual catharsis or high as the result of giving oneself over to the performance.

Spectators seek, then, myriad possible outcomes from a live theater performance. But viewers can have this same range of experiences by watching television or a movie, so what makes people want to come to the *theater*? One characteristic differentiates the live theater from performances of other media: the presence of both performers and spectators. What takes place between them live (unfolding moment to moment in present time) is the distinguishing feature of the theater. Where else can the spectator interact with and receive direct stimulation from a dramatic performance? "I thought that the effect of my plays on an audience should feel something like surfing. The audience was riding a wave of pile-up perceptions, which constituted the play, balanced on a wave of exhilarating, accelerating events" (Foreman 1992, 96). All the spectator's physical senses (hearing, seeing, smelling, touching, perhaps even tasting) can be stimulated by a live performance, and all the performer's physical senses can be engaged in an attempt to communicate with the spectators. The excitement of participating in a live event, in which performers and spectators are brought into communication with one another in a fictional world, sets the nerves and senses on edge and makes both performer and spectator feel alive and vital. "The audience and cast are evaluating one another during the progress of the play. The audience are responding to the play and the playing; the cast are responding to the audience's response to their playing. Responses flow backwards and forwards all the time" (Miles-Brown 1980, 40). It's a bit like living *inside* an exciting novel or poem, rather than being a reader looking on from the outside. The spectators are *in* the world of the play as it unfolds before their very eyes. To complete the circuit the performers tune in to the energy and vibrations of the audience.

Directors understand that audiences are composed of people who are looking for excitement, illumination, and fulfillment. One of their primary tasks is to fashion a production that engages the spectator on one or more of these levels. If a production fails to communicate in ways that touch an emotional, aesthetic, or intellectual core in the spectators, it will be, as Peter Brook says, "deadly."

## Influences on Reception

Many elements surrounding the actual witnessing of a theater performance can have a telling effect on the spectator's level of commitment and her expectations. Publicity, location of theater, type of theater company (professional, community, college), and frequency of theatergoing are frames through which spectators read a performance. These are just a few of the myriad influences that can sway the reading of a performance and its ultimate meanings for each spectator.

[It is a] necessity to view the theatrical event beyond its immediate conditions and to foreground its social constitution. The description of an individual response to a particular production may not be possible or, indeed, even desirable. But, because of that individual's participation in a given culture and the importance of his/her culturally-constituted horizon of expectations, and selection of a particular *social* event, it is important to reposition the study of drama to reflect this. (S. Bennett 1990, 184)

Chapter 2 presented an extended discussion of these framing experiences. There are, however, some personal experiences (or frames) that influence the audience's consciousness that are useful to review here.

## Anticipation

Susan Bennett (1990) considers this a "commitment to planning." Whether a spectator has been eagerly looking forward to a performance or dreading it, whether she holds a season subscription or is attending the theater as a first-time experience, whether she is traveling across town or internationally, will influence the expectations and personal value of attending a performance.

## Availability of Leisure Time

Is attending a performance squeezed into an extremely tight schedule? Is the spectator on vacation? Is the performance at the workplace, during lunch hour (S. Bennett 1990, 133)? The implications of time and its availability are no small factor in influencing the spectator's state of mind. If a spectator is in a rush, the reading is likely to be rushed. Having excessive leisure time, however, does not necessarily mean the experience will be positive. If a spectator is on holiday, even though there may be lots of time, his focus might be on events other than the performance.

## Cost of Admission

If a spectator pays two hundred dollars for a ticket to a Broadway gala, she has made a large personal investment. She is therefore likely to have significant expectations about the quality of performing, setting, costumes, and the like. It is imaginable that the spectator's judgment of the success and ultimate meanings of the event will be based on very high standards. On the other hand if a spectator stumbles across a street performance that is free, he may feel no commitment to the event; he has no vested interest and can easily walk away without losing anything. Cost means investment and therefore the possibility of added commitment and concentration on the performance.

### Social Relationship

Is a spectator attending a performance alone? With a first-time date? With a spouse who dislikes the theater? With a group of old college roommates? With a highly liked second couple? With the boss? With her parents? Each of these possible relationships charges the event with a special significance, and in cases in which there is a hidden relational agenda—desire to impress the boss or first date, rocky marriage, yearning to get reacquainted with college chums, or the like— the social relationship can detract from the spectator's ability to concentrate on the performance itself. A break in concentration caused by a dominating social agenda can strain a spectator's concentration and affect her ability to read signifiers.

## Meanings from Performance

The theater event itself offers multiple possible meanings to an audience. These meanings are hard to articulate because they are constructed by each spectator through impressions formed on several levels: subjective/objective, conscious/unconscious, and intellectual/ emotional. "Waves of auditory and visual vibrations emanate from the play and work upon hearts and minds to evoke emotions and thoughts. The design of the play creates a mosaic of feelings and ideas which constitutes a theatrical experience for the audience" (McMullan 1962, 35). Each spectator actively constructs his own meanings from individual perceptions and experiences as a member of an audience. Regardless of whether there is an audience of two or one thousand, each spectator will be influenced by the size, configuration, and reactions of the other spectators. "Although every spectator is individually a receiver, the way he is actually affected will vary according to the collective response of the audience as a whole" (Bassnett-McGuire 1980, 52).

Since a performance's meanings are assembled individually, the question arises about whether any single overarching meaning can be shared by all spectators in an audience.

Like the meaning of a dream, the meaning of the play is a metaphorical image. No matter how philosophical, logical, or real most plays seem, their reality, logic, or philosophy are parts of a larger meaning—a meaning which orders and patterns all these parts and may therefore be called a commanding image.

This commanding image is the essence of the playwright's communication. This essence, like the meaning of a dream, is a realization, a concept, a felt significance—expressed through the impact of the total form. (Clay and Krempel 1967, 25)

Any universally discerned meaning, however, will be only one of several final meanings of the performance; each total aggregation of meanings will be different for each spectator. If the director has a clear vision for the performance and believes that a single commanding image, theme, or meaning should be communicated to every spectator, then she structures all choices to develop that single idea. Still, there are no guarantees that every spectator will assemble the same meanings, and it is debatable whether or not tight control of meanings is achievable or even desirable.

Richard Fotheringham (1984) believes that the only way a director can hope to send a clear message is to know the audience (its size, socioeconomic background, age range, religion, etc.) and to understand the variables in the dimensions of theatrical communication. For Fotheringham the meanings of any performance are predicated on several key variables, namely:

The director's interpretation of the text
The actual conditions during a performance
    Performers' energy level
    Position in the performance run (early or late)
    Unexpected occurrences (accidents, rain)
What the audience knows about theater and the particular play
What the audience thinks about the performance company
The composition and countenance of the audience
    Socioeconomic background (and mix)
    Size
    State of each individual's mind
    Concentration level
    Willingness to interact

The success of a performance that has as its chief aim the communication of a core mood, thought, or experience and, ultimately, core meanings depends on the encoding of the pluridimensional signifiers with as much clarity as possible. Success also depends on how well the director understands the nature of the audience. The only way to try to get spectators to experience similar emotions, ideas, or meanings is to "present a performance in a context where a known social sub-group is present" (Fotheringham 1984, 35). The more homogeneous the audience, the more likely it is that the performance will have universally perceived meanings.

But in the postmodern theater, directors do not want to bring a single meaning to each spectator. Postmodernists believe that the world is encountered in fragments and that each person experiences it differently. There is, in their view, no universal meaning to a work of art. They juxtapose sights, sounds, space, and sentence fragments in odd aesthetic combinations that force each spectator to read the performance differently. Often there is no linear story to follow, only bits and pieces of information, impressions, and images. No matter how homogeneous the audience is, it is unlikely that all spectators will construct a single overarching meaning.

> Fundamental to our [Wilson's and Glass's] approach was the assumption that the audience itself completed the work. The statement is no mere metaphor; we meant it quite literally. In the case of *Einstein on the Beach*, the "story" was supplied by the imaginations of the audience, and there was no way for us to predict, even if we had wanted to, what the "story" might be for any particular person. (Glass 1987, 35)

The postmodern aesthetic assumes that each spectator will write his own story and meanings out of the visual images, music, voices, smells, and so forth. Each spectator randomly chooses to focus on and perceive different signifiers during the course of the performance. Everyone's story and meanings will be private and special, although they will be informed by the collective nature of the live performance experience.

## Audience as Sign System

When spectators come together they constitute a sign system for both performers and other audience members. That is, each spectator serves as a signifier for performers and other spectators to read.

> I began to observe more carefully how each member of an audience is influenced by the reaction of those around them. And it now seems to me that no member of any audience of reasonable size can ever see a play in isolation. Their reaction is always coloured by the reaction of those around them. And not merely coloured: according

to the nature of the audience the play will appear quite different, will indeed be a different play, in Bath or London according to the audience with whom we see it. How many of us realise that, while play and acting may not change, what was a bad play when we saw it in Cheltenham last Wednesday may be splendid if we see it in Manchester next Friday? (Jellicoe 1967, 9)

The audience contributes directly to the meanings of the performance by providing information in the following ways:

Physical features: age, gender, size, number of people, energy levels
Socioeconomic traits: ethnicity, race, education, clothing, familiarity with one another
Movement: gestures, applause, standing, sitting
Proximity: in the lobby, in the theater
Aural discourse: talking, paralexical sound (e.g., laughing, coughing)
Social interaction: eating, drinking

If I attend a performance at which the lobby and theater are jam-packed, each spectator is wearing a tuxedo or elegant dress, everyone is eating and drinking at a preperformance reception, everyone is wearing expensive jewelry, and almost everyone is speaking Spanish and knows one another very well, while I don't speak Spanish and don't know anyone and am dressed in casual clothes, the meanings I will receive from the performance, even if it is in English, will be profoundly affected. My feelings of inferiority in dress, lack of knowledge of Spanish, and dearth of friendship with other audience members may distract me from concentrating on the performance or force me to concentrate too much on my own inadequacies during the performance. Therefore, the meanings I walk away with may have almost nothing to do with the story, characters, or visual presence of what I have witnessed. In an extreme case the evening's experience and therefore meanings may have almost nothing to do with the performance itself. Alternatively, if I attend a different performance of the same production at which the audience is made up of casually dressed young people from a local high school and I am their teacher and the theater is only half-full, I will no doubt have an experience that will allow me more access to meanings derived from the performance itself.

Similarly, if I attend a performance at which several spectators arrive late, the spectator next to me falls asleep, several spectators leave at the first intermission and don't return, and several spectators cough or fan themselves with their programs during the performance, try as I may to overcome it, it is likely that the meanings I will construct will come in part from the audience's signification, not from the performers, scenery, costumes, music, or movement. In this particular case, the spectator's level of activity (or lack thereof) influences me to conclude that this performance is not worth watching, not emotionally stimulating, or not intellectually substantive, unless what is happening in the performance counteracts my reading of the audience's reading of the event.

The director cannot control the spectators, nor should he want to. But it is critical that he know what he wants them to take away from the encounter. A sense of unity? A clear story? A set of abstract impressions? Confusion? A feeling of having been assaulted? A private and personal insight? The director can make choices in preparing for a performance that will frame the experience for spectators in ways that reinforce rather than denigrate his vision and intended meanings.

## Theater as a Social Event

Attending the theater means going to a place where people congregate. In the parking lot, entrance way, lobby, and performance space, spectators come in contact with one another; they take part in a collective social event.

Throughout history the theater event has served different social functions. For the classical Greeks, performances had religious and ceremonial significance. During the Restoration, people came to the theater as much to be seen by others and for social interaction as to witness a performance. Indeed, during the sixteenth and seventeenth centuries it was quite common to have spectators sitting on the stage, not to see the performance better but, rather, to be seen at the performance better.

Attending the theater ranges from going to a carefully designed social occasion (gala opening, special fund-raising event, dinner theater) to routine attendance at a theater at which the spectator habitually arrives just before the curtain rises (or late) and leaves quickly after the performance.

Little                                    Special
Socializing                            Social Event

A director may fix the social importance of a performance event somewhere on the above continuum as a way of providing a context from which to influence the audience's sense of social engagement. If the director believes that the meanings of the performance can be enhanced by creating a highly socialized event, she may wish to frame the event in ways that support that decision. For example, if a director envisions a production of *Little Mary Sunshine* at an outdoor summer theater as a family festivity, she may invite the audience to have a picnic on the lawn prior to the performance. Conversely, if a director wants spectators to be alienated and analytical at a production of *Mother Courage*, he can break up couples and groups by not allowing them to sit together. Also the theater might offer no social amenities (e.g., lobby seating or refreshments) prior to the performance, thereby inhibiting socializing at the event.

Ariane Mnouchkine, noted for her interest in breaking the barriers between performers and spectators, sees the theater as a social gathering place. In Vincennes she converted three large cartridge warehouse hangars into a theater space known as the Cartoucherie.

Each hangar measures some 20 by 40 metres. The first acts as a reception area, with a bar. The actors take turns to serve and clean up, maintaining the principle that all should share, even in menial tasks. The bar offers rough red wine or beer for sale, together with sandwiches of coarse peasant bread. The second and third hangars are used for performance, including preparation, warming-up, costuming and making-up, all of which take place in an unscreened area open to scrutiny by spectators before they take their places. Mnouchkine herself is much in evidence, seeing to last-minute preparations. She claims that this openness is essential to establishing the right relationship with the audience: one in which the actors do not seek to dazzle, but invite participation. (Bradby and Williams 1988, 93–94)

Many theatergoers are drawn to the theater because of its social dimension—the opportunity to go out with friends or relatives, perhaps with dinner beforehand and drinks and dancing afterward. By purposefully framing a production to capture or negate the social aspects of the performance event, the director shapes the meanings of a performance before it even begins.

## Performer Communication

Performers communicate with the spectators directly (acknowledging their presence) or indirectly (pretending they don't exist). Some of the richest theater experiences combine direct and indirect modes of communication. In late twentieth-century America there seems to be a revival of audience participation. On New York stages direct audience participation has increased greatly; a "wild proliferation . . . has broken the boundaries between those who do and those who watch" (Gussow 1992, C2).

Direct communication takes place when performers interact with the audience, as when a performer speaks directly to the audience during a soliloquy or when performers touch spectators or ask the audience to sing along with them. Indirect communication occurs when performers act as though the world of the stage is a private or closed environment, as if there is no audience present: a fictional "fourth wall" exists between the performers and the spectators. One production in which performers were encouraged to communicate directly was Robert Kalfin's production of Carlo Goldoni's *The Mistress of the Inn*.

> Ms. [Tovah] Feldshuh's relationship with the audience is particularly winky and intimate. She draws applause from the women by telling them she adores making fun of men. She flirts with them, saying: "I really enjoy making men do everything I want—so do you." She fawns on the front row by confiding her plans. She peeks through the curtain at the beginning of the second act to notice "You're back." And finally, after vowing to change her ways, she throws the audience a bouquet of flowers, begging it to "remember kindly the mistress of the inn." (Brustein 1991, 142)

The director decides whether or not the performers will contact the spectators directly and, if so, how far they will be allowed or required to go. Can they invite spectators to respond verbally? Can they touch spectators? Can they invite spectators onto the stage? If direct communication is to be minimal, in what ways is the audience to be disregarded? The style of acting, the shape of the ground plan, the seating arrangement for the audience—indeed, the entire mise-en-scène—depend upon the director's decision about the performers' relationship to the spectators. For Robert Wilson's production of *Death Destruction and Detroit II* in 1987 he chose to surround the audience with four stages, one on each side. The audience found their seats by moving through an elaborate labyrinth of railings. Each seat swiveled so that all spectators could swing in any direction at any time to watch whatever portion of the action they chose (fig. 7).

Jerzy Grotowski wanted the audience to be both a witness and a participant in his productions. For *The Constant Prince* the spectators were asked to sit behind a barrier; they were forced to look over and down as if observing surgery in a hospital operating room. For his production of *Kordian* Grotowski wanted spectators to be a part of the performance space itself (in this case a hospital). Seating was dispersed; some spectators even sat inside the framework of bunk beds. The audience could not have been more closely involved: performers stood next to them, lay over them, and walked among them.

## Audience Communication

Live theater produces two-way communication. While it can be argued that more information flows from the stage area to the audience area than the reverse, feedback from the spectators to the performers and technicians (lighting and sound control operators) is nonetheless central to the total performance experience. What are some of the ways spectators communicate with the performers and technicians, and with one another?

*Size.* A full house (150 people in a small theater, 3,000 in a large one) can produce an electricity that energizes the performers. Minimal attendance is likely to be dispiriting to performer and spectator alike. For instance, a spectator may feel compelled to hold in check his boisterous laughter so he does not call attention to himself or disturb the quiet of the near-empty theater.

*Applause.* An audience's applause can range from being wildly enthusiastic and frequent to sparse or nonexistent.

*Talking.* Spectators talk among themselves if they are bored, or they respond to the performers when asked to (e.g., when asked to "sing along"). When unhappy, spectators may volunteer jeers and catcalls; when happy, offer cheers of endorsement ("Bravo!" "Author! Author!").

*Movement.* Spectators may come late and be disruptive or leave during the performance (and not return). Also, spectators may shift

Fig. 7. Theater: Schaubühne am Lehniner Platz, Berlin. Photo by Ruth Walz.

continuously in their seats, signifying boredom, or sit motionless or lean forward in anticipation—a sign of intense concentration and interest.

*Gestures.* Involuntary gestures such as sleeping or slouching send negative messages, while clapping, raising a fist in affirmation, or standing up provide great encouragement to the performers and other spectators.

*Sounds.* Coughing, shuffling programs, rustling candy wrappers, and shifting body position are all signifiers (even if inadvertent); a message is sent to the performers, technicians, and audience that all may not be well. Absolute stillness indicates the audience is deeply attentive (or asleep).

*Laughter.* Spectators' laughter in response to dialogue or the visual aspects of the mise-en-scène is a critical element in the success of a production. Plays that are intended to be comical must produce laughter from the audience or the performance will be judged unsuccessful.

Laughing, coming in late, and talking affect not only the performers and technicians; spectators are also influenced by these behaviors.

Actions are contagious. If some spectators begin laughing, others will also follow. If one spectator initiates a standing ovation, others will stand. If several spectators get up and leave the theater, others will also or at least be discomfited by the departures.

## Summary

Spectator behavior is influenced by such variables as preperformance expectations, seating, ability to concentrate, mood upon entering the theater space, individual personality, educational level, theatergoing experience, and inherent sociability. The director cannot predict or control individual preferences, prior experiences, or immediate perceptions of the audience, but he can either present a unified production with clarity and consistency of choices, thereby minimizing the impact of extraneous noise on the sign systems of the performance, or deliberately present a disjointed, ambiguous, and surreal production in which disunity and blurred vision and hearing are desired. Clarity and unity can bring unanimity to the individual perceptions of the spectators. On the other hand, confusion and disunity can challenge the audience to accept a new paradigm of theatrical experience.

> In the mesh of every successful performance, the signals from the script to the actor, and from the actor to the spectator and back again, complete a dramatic circuit of which the audience is an indispensable part. Drama needs an audience to throw the switch: no audience, no circuit; no circuit, no play. It is a short step to the next critical syllogism: bad drama, no current; and no current, therefore, no genuinely dramatic experience. (Styan 1975, 24)

Without question the audience emits and reads its own signifiers, which influence the construction of a performance's meanings.

# Chapter 4

# Performer Systems

Throughout history the performer has been the chief signifier in theatrical performances. Performers transmit information, and therefore meaning, through a number of different channels simultaneously. The performer's personality, delivery of words, gestures, movement, facial expression, makeup, hairstyle, and costume all work as separate sign systems that produce multivarious signifiers for the audience to read.

In the postmodern theater world the performer remains the primary signifier, although directors are stretching the definition of the traditional role of the performer. Live performers are sometimes replaced with human-manipulated or mechanical puppets (Wilson). Video walls and film projections bring live performers in contact with electronically produced human images (Svoboda). Performers' speeches are amplified to make them surreal (Foreman).

Directors experiment with performance styles to create exotic combinations of performer-produced signifiers. Ariane Mnouchkine directs Shakespeare in the exaggerated movement style of Kabuki theater. Josef Svoboda minimizes the centrality of the performer and places primary emphasis on visual and aural sign systems in his production of *The Minotarus*. Robert Wilson asks performers to exaggerate the pronunciation of words, phrases, sentences, or whole speeches to emphasize the otherworldly aspects of Ibsen's *When We Dead Awaken*. More and more, performers are asked to move away from realistic acting as directors search for novel ways to heighten and more thoroughly theatricalize the performance event. "I am not interested in the theatre where the audience becomes seduced by a kind of empathetic relationship to the actors" (Richard Foreman interview, in Bartow 1988a, 133). In some cases experimental directorial approaches put even more emphasis on the performer as the chief signifier than does the traditional theater, and in other cases the performer plays a diminished role to the other systems of signification in the theater.

The performer is an ideal sign. He is "a real human being who has become a sign for a human being" (Esslin 1987, 56). Furthermore, performers may also become signifiers of a whole class of individuals or of a race of people. For example, when a person takes on the role of King Lear he becomes during performance the signifier for an individual fictional character, King Lear. At the same time, the character Lear may become a universal representation of a class of people—old men, insane people, or kings.

> An actor appearing on the stage or screen is, in the first place, himself, the "real" person that he is with his physical characteristics, his voice and temperament; he is, secondly, himself, transformed, disguised, by costume, make-up, an assumed voice, a mental attitude derived from the study of and empathy with the fictional character he is playing: this is the "stage-figure" as the Prague school has dubbed him, the physical simulacrum of the character; but, thirdly, and most importantly there is the "fiction" itself, for which he stands, and which ultimately will emerge in the mind of the individual spectator watching the play or film. (Esslin 1987, 58)

Performers play a unique role in the signification process: they receive the primary focus in most performances and provide sources for communication through multiple sign systems. The sheer volume of signifiers that radiate from each performer produces the focal point for the performance's communication of information and meanings. During a performance it is impossible to isolate the performer's use of individual sign systems; nevertheless, it will be useful to explore the ways a director can manipulate individual sign systems to focus and enhance the performer's communication with the spectator.

Occasionally, contemporary directors choose to isolate or exaggerate one or more performer signs as a way of developing a unique production style. In one production, movement and gesture may take precedence over speaking. In another production, stationary performers may use exaggerated vocal and facial expressions to produce the most meaningful expression of a playscript. In yet another production, masks, gesture, and silence may be the main avenues for signification.

## Personal Qualities

Every performer is unique: each possesses a personal style, charisma, or élan. This special, almost indefinable, quality is heightened when a person transforms herself into a performer on a stage before a live audience. Try as they may, performers cannot fully divorce themselves from their individual selves. Likewise, the audience senses or experiences a performer's personal style and charisma as part of the performance experience. Spectators are charmed, entertained, engaged, or put off by a performer's personal style, regardless of what role he is playing or what the production is.

Part of the experience of attending a performance is the communication of the personality of the individual performer and of the collective, often conflicting, personalities of the ensemble of performers. All of this is present independent of the story line, given circumstances, and dramatic action of a playscript or performance piece. Performers who enjoy wide popularity create a special horizon of expectations for the spectator's decoding process. It is all but impossible for spectators to divorce the star performer from her personal aura; it intrudes on the performance and shapes the construction of the performance's meanings.

> Celebrities, almost by definition, substitute for this "someone" that we seem to know apart from the play. They bring something to the role other than a harmonious blend of features, an overdetermined quality that exceeds the needs of the fiction, and keeps them from disappearing entirely into the acting figure of the drama. Rather, their contribution to the performance is often a kind of collision with the role, sometimes hard to accept, but sometimes, too, loaded with the spectacular energy that an explosive crash can release. (Quinn 1990, 155)

Performers (particularly stars) by sheer dint of their personalities can transmit information that is complementary or antithetical to the intended meanings of a playscript or production. For this reason, casting a production is the most important set of choices a director makes.

When a director casts a play he pays attention to more than just the performer's physical and vocal characteristics. The director identifies the inherent personality of each performer and the potential effect of the performer on spectators—radiant energy, sexiness, moodiness, magnetism, evilness. If the major characters lack the right aura, personality, or sexiness, the performance may lack one of its most important ingredients: an audience that is enormously attracted to the performers' power to communicate. At the same time the director realizes "the personal, individual qualities of the performer always resist, to some degree, the transformation of the actor into the stage figure required for communication of a particular fiction" (Quinn 1990, 155). The extraperformance personal characteristics each performer brings to a role will become part of the stage character, even if they militate against an ideal character portrayal.

More important, directors take special care to find a mix of individual personalities that create the contrasts and conflicts inherent in a playscript's dramatic action. Electricity can be created onstage if just the right fusion of personal traits can be matched with the dramatic action of a playscript or performance piece. Enlightened directors also engage in color-blind casting by focusing their choices on whether or not performers can ignite the sparks inherent in the action and conflict of the play, rather than on the color of a performer's skin. Daring directors often make eccentric casting choices that are intended to bring new insights to a playscript, as when Peter Sellars cast Howie Seago, a deaf-mute actor, as Ajax in Sophocles' play.

Directors must decide whether to use nonperformers or stars, as represented on this continuum:

Nonperformers                                                    Celebrities

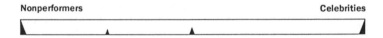

There are many choices between the two poles. A director might use young partially trained performers (theater students or apprentices) or well-trained, seasoned stage performers who have not achieved star status, or a mix of stars, trained professionals, and people off the street. The meanings of the performance and its quality and style of signification will be greatly influenced by the level of training and popular standing of the performers.

## Charisma

What are the elements that constitute a person's charisma? What special features endow certain individuals with a unique charm or power that can mesmerize an audience? Personal energy? A relaxed physical presence? An unusually attractive physical appearance? A warm and engaging voice? Penetrating eyes? A magical smile? Impenetrable concentration? The best answer is probably none and all of these things—and more. Directors identify these characteristics in individual performers and then cast the performers in ways that maximize the tensions, conflicts, and actions of the performance.

Beyond charisma, however, is the celebrity status that is often an outgrowth of a performer's personality and personal style.

> More particularly, certain actors acquire a public persona and this . . . can affect the audience's horizon of expectations. With the presence of a "star" on stage, the audience is inevitably aware of a double personality (for example Dustin Hoffman/Shylock) and it is generally the case, to a greater or lesser degree, that the audience is reading the actor's performance alongside the work being performed. (S. Bennett 1990, 162)

Celebrity status, then, is a complex signifier that becomes central to the meaning of the performance. When spectators went to the theater to see Lawrence Olivier they had certain expectations, many of which had nothing to do with the intended meaning of the playwright's script or the director's production. For example, when Olivier was cast in a secondary role, suddenly that role loomed larger in the eyes of most spectators than the playwright probably intended. The audience waited with great anticipation for Olivier to appear. When he finally entered the stage the audience's concentration was instantly heightened, their sensors became fine-tuned, and the intended meaning of the scene was probably distorted. What can the director do about a circumstance like this? Nothing—except recognize the special sign system that exists, independent of the play and its characters, in the communicative powers of the performer's personality, reputation, and popularity. No matter how much makeup is used or how skillful the performer is at adjusting his voice or physical appearance (and Olivier was a master of disguise), the star performer's unique qualities will shine through—and produce specific signifiers, signifieds, and meanings for the audience.

> The celebrity figure is an alternative reference, competing with and structuring the role of the stage figures as it promotes its own illusion. The sequence can be graphed this way:
>
> actor----------celebrity figure----------stage figure-----------audience
> (Quinn 1990, 160)

A clear example of the importance of a star to an audience's horizon of expectations is Elizabeth Taylor's appearance in *The Little Foxes* on Broadway. When she was absent from the performance "90 percent of the audience [turned] their tickets back and temporarily closed the theatre" (Brustein 1991, 223). In the spectators' eyes this performance was about experiencing Elizabeth Taylor, not *The Little Foxes*.

To avoid the distracting power of celebrity performers some directors, such as Richard Foreman and Robert Wilson, often use nonperformers. They cast people who have no formal acting, voice, or movement training and who have no acting experience. "What interested me was taking people from real life, nonactors, and putting them onstage to allow their real personalities to have a defiant impact on the conventional audience" (Foreman 1992, 32). Part of the thinking here is that nontrained performers break the audience's normal horizon of expectations and force them to experience a performance that is not filled with elegant voices, gracious movement, and overly charismatic people. Audiences are asked to rethink the role of the performer. They are asked to listen to words spoken by an amateur, to watch people who may be physically graceless and a bit awkward onstage—in short to see and project images of themselves as performers. They will be brought closer to being in the performance unless their horizon of expectations keeps them from accepting untrained performers and they therefore reject the experience as somehow invalid or just plain poor.

Robert Wilson's earlier productions almost exclusively used nontrained performers. Wilson is interested in creating natural performances onstage. He often casts interesting "character" types whom he has run across in real life.

> Naturalness (and the absence of visible effort) has always been the cornerstone of the performer's art in Wilson's theatre. From his earliest productions, he has attempted to help people find a way of presenting themselves on stage without selfconsciousness. . . . His performers were drawn from every background and social strata: a lady chicken farmer from Ohio, a gray-haired man he pursued through Grand Central Station because he bore a resemblance to Sigmund Freud, the six-month-old infant of one of his friends from Pratt, the handicapped, artist friends, his 86-year-old grandmother—very often the young and the old, those at the beginning and the end of the journey; closest to nature in either direction. (Shyer 1989, 9)

Creative casting means matching performers to roles in ways that heighten a performance's meanings. It also means the director must choose between the extremes of celebrity casting and novice casting, with myriad possibilities in between. Whether to cast a charismatic star or a neophyte is a directing decision that should come from the director's sense of a production's intended meanings. The choice of performers overcodes everything that will be communicated through the performer's multiple sign systems.

## Voice (Spoken Word)

Assuming that we understand the language of a playscript, when we read it we develop a personal understanding of what it is all about: we come to know its meaning as literature—we come to know it as a written sign system. This is how a director and his artistic collaborators develop a hypothetical performance (metatext); they first begin to envision the performance by experiencing the playscript as literature waiting to be performed.

Theater audiences, however, do not experience a playscript as literature. The collaborative work of the artists transforms the written playscript into a living performance. The audience experiences the performance as it moves through time. In simple terms this means that they only get one look and listen; they cannot reread a section of the performance as they can a script, nor can they instantly replay a scene as they can with a video. This time-boundness of the performance is especially critical in relationship to the performance's use of words.

First of all, spectators at a performance play a much different role in relationship to the words than does the reader of the playscript. Spectators do not interpret the words directly. The performer serves as an intermediary. The performer interprets the written words and colors them with his own meanings. The performer, through intonation, pace, loudness, and so forth, presents preinterpreted signifiers to the spectators. A spectator, in turn, reads the interpretation of the performer, who is attempting to produce the director's interpretation of the playwright's intentions. While all this sounds (and is) complicated, spectators, sitting at the performance, are not concerned about what level of reinterpretation they are experiencing. Spectators simply absorb as many signifiers as they can vis-à-vis the multiple sign systems that make up the performance—only one of which is the spoken word.

Most traditional directors, coartists, and technicians collaborate to present a clear and unified performance, one that captures the director's vision and presents it as unambiguously as possible. Since spoken dialogue is often a primary sign system, the more a director understands how the linguistic sign system functions, the more likely it is she will get the performers to interpret and speak dialogue in ways consistent with her specific vision.

Besides the denotative meaning of words and the straightforward articulation and pronunciation of the dialogue of a playscript or performance piece, there is a wide range of tonal and rhythmic elements inherent in the speech-making process that gives color and context-specific overcoding to spoken words as signifiers. Elam and various other authors label these elements paralinguistic. "Contextual constraints and the kinds of language-related behavior accompanying the utterance are essential to its correct interpretation by the addressee" (Elam 1980, 79).

The paralinguistic vocal elements that can be manipulated to encode spoken words are:

Loudness
Pitch
Inflection
Resonance
Articulation
Tempo
Rhythm

Performers use these seven paralinguistic elements to add interpretive layering to written words and to create the expressive and emotive qualities of human speech, two critical aspects of signification between performer and spectator.

Paralinguistic features constitute one of the most ancient objects of the actor's art. The rules of "declamation" or effective delivery are in effect controls on vocal "punctuation" (regulating articulation, pitch, tempo, loudness, resonance, rhythm control, etc.). The ability to control the flow of information and segment discourse in such a way as to maximize the attention and comprehension levels of the auditor is one of the actor's cardinal functions. The training that actors receive in articulation, breathing (and thus tempo and rhythm control) and "projection," i.e., the achievement of audibility without the concomitant vocalization "shouting," comprises, as it were, a set of more or less obligatory secondary paralinguistic rules specific to the art. (Elam 1980, 81–82)

Performers' vocal qualities help define in their characters such traits as health, masculinity or femininity, personality, and temperament. In addition, of course, the ever-changing vocal qualities of a performer reflect the moment-to-moment emotional state of the character. By manipulating the variables of the paralinguistic process, directors can help orchestrate the vocalization of a character's traits, emotional state, and relationship to other characters.

The use of the human voice for spoken words and as pure paralinguistic sound can be quite startling. Directors such as Robert Wilson, Richard Foreman, and Andrei Serban have experimented widely with the use of the human voice, including its electronic manipulation, and have produced a richer, more powerful vocal vocabulary for the theater.

Directors have several primary choices to make about the use of the spoken word that can be represented as continua. The first is whether or not to use the language of the audience or to choose a foreign or abstract language.

Native                                              Abstract
Language                                            Language

The second most important question is whether or not to make the spoken word a high or low priority in the use of sign systems for a production.

No                                                    Only
Spoken Words                                  Spoken Words

At the extreme left would be a choice to present a mime performance; at the far right would be a reader's theater or radio performance in which only spoken words and other aural signifiers would be employed.

The director's third choice is whether or not to employ natural speaking characteristics or an artificial, exaggerated, or electronically amplified style.

| Natural Speech | | | | Artificial Speech |

Once a director has decided where to place her production on these three continua she can then make more detailed or subtle choices related to the use of the spoken word. In order to understand more fully the kinds of choices postmodernists have made in their attempt to expand the use of the voice to communicate, it is useful to contrast traditional vocal techniques (most often used for realistic productions) with postmodernist practices. In most traditional productions, directors strive to insure that every spectator hears every word that is spoken: the dialogue is delivered in a realistic style, the performers project their natural voices without aid of amplification, standard practices of articulation, emphasis, and tempo are adhered to, and the like. Postmodernist often decry these practices and create their own vocal aesthetics, deliberately choosing distortion, juxtaposition, non-sense sounds, and inarticulateness.

## Loudness

Sound levels are rated in decibels (dB). The human ear can hear over a wide range of loudness levels, from barely audible (20 dB) to harm-fully loud (130 dB). Performers must be loud enough to meet the minimum hearing requirement of the spectator sitting farthest from the stage. Concomitantly, the performer's volume should not cause the spectator pain. Within this broad range of loudness levels, per-formers and directors are free to experiment—to find the best possible combinations of loudness and softness throughout the performance.

In traditional verbal discourse, loudness is used as a signifier through emphasizing syllables, words, phrases, or whole speeches. Increased loudness applied to a syllable is termed an accent, to a word is a stress, and to a phrase or sentence is emphasis. An increase or decrease in the loudness level is a signifier of special attention to an individual word or group of words. For example, a substantial in-crease (or decrease) in the loudness of a word, relative to all the other words in a sentence, can alert the spectator that this word is the most important word (or idea) in a character's utterance. The same holds true for the accented syllable or the emphasized phrase, sentence, or paragraph. The accenting of syllables is particularly important to the performer who is speaking verse. Accented and unaccented syllables carry the rhythm of the dialogue in a controlled and patterned way.

The general loudness level of a character is an indicator of her personality and temperament. A character who speaks loudly all the time signals self-assurance, brashness, or a hearing impairment. Another character who speaks calmly at a normal volume presents a picture of someone who is well mannered, highly rational, or boring. A character who speaks very quietly may be shy, ill, or sultry and sexy. The message of each of these signifiers (consistent vocal levels) is highly dependent on context: a whisper will convey sexiness only if it is spoken by a sexy person or in an intimate situation, such as a bedroom or the back seat of a car.

During a performance, significant variations in the volume of a character's speech are a signifier of his emotional state or intensity of motivation. The dramatic action of the performance is often highlighted by modulating the loudness of characters' speeches. The director, vocal coach, and sound technician can orchestrate the use of loudness as a communicative sign system. In today's theater, directors are aided by electronic sound reinforcement equipment that gives them even more flexibility and options for adjusting sound levels that go beyond the normal range of human voices.

Many postmodern directors amplify the spoken word as an integral part of their performance aesthetic. Amplification allows for a greater range in volume than can be produced by the unaided human voice; it also allows for highly unique employment of the spoken word. For example, it is possible to have a quiet whisper amplified to a point of painful loudness. A shout can be reduced to a whisper, or an echoed whisper, or a reverberated whisper, or a variety of other imaginative possibilities. The introductory stage directions to Richard Foreman's playscript for *Lava* provide an example of how a playwright/director prescribes vocal amplification.

All that can be heard at first is the scratching chalk on the blackboard, as a deep and ominous VOICE comes from giant loudspeakers hung over the table.

Below the speakers stands an oscilloscope, displaying the active graph of the deep VOICES's [sic] speaking as it continues throughout the play. Just before the VOICE begins speaking the text, through other speakers at the side of the stage, another VOICE is heard reading off a series of random numbers, from one to nine. This VOICE recurs, as indicated in the text of the play, always going through the same random sequence. In this case, the numbers fade as the text proper begins. (Foreman 1992, 319)

Foreman not only amplifies most voices on and off the stage so that he can increase greatly the range of loudness and softness for the human voice, in *Lava* he also graphically displays the modulations in loudness levels by placing an oscilloscope onstage so the audience not only hears the volume changes but also sees them. He calls attention to the nonlinguistic aspects of the spoken voice as a signifier in its own right. For Foreman the volume changes become the content as well as the means of signification.

## Pitch

In simplistic terms, pitch refers to the musical note that the voice produces at a discrete moment of speaking or singing. All performers are capable of creating a variety of pitches, but those with substantive voice training have the ability to use an even wider range of pitches in creating a character.

As with loudness, pitch is a tool for emphasizing the most important syllables, words, phrases, or sentences during the act of speaking. Pitch is arguably the most useful tool for expressing precise shades of meaning. Changes in tempo and loudness are most useful in expressing general emotional states, but pitch is the best way of communicating finely tuned thoughts or logical arguments. Pitch is also a way of establishing certain character traits: age, masculinity or femininity, and temperament. When casting the play, the director chooses performers who have contrasting and complementary pitch ranges. A carefully chosen pitch range not only insures a variety of aural compositions but also provides signifiers, or "markings," for individual character traits.

Each performer has a single pitch that she uses much more frequently than all the others, known as the modal pitch. The chief means of providing emphasis when speaking is to go up or down from the modal pitch. In singing, voice type is classified by modal pitch and vocal range; adult male voices are bass, baritone, and tenor, while female voices are contralto, soprano, and so forth. While speaking voices are not as clearly classified as singing voices, directors often identify performers' vocal ranges for purposes of comparison when casting a play.

Variations in modal pitch communicate specific information to an audience about the character or the given circumstances. For example:

A change of emotional state can produce radical pitch changes. Excitement brings a rise in pitch, sorrow lowers it.

A person's physical state can produce pitch variations. Sleepiness or physical exhaustion often lowers the modal pitch, while peak energy results in a higher pitch.

The normal modal pitch difference between adult male and female speakers is four full tones on the musical scale. The male vocal cord length is generally longer and therefore vibrates slower, producing a lower tone.

There is a radical difference between prepubescent children and adults. The normal pitch may shift as much as a full octave as children mature.

When casting a production and working with performers, directors listen for the modal pitch of the performers and find ways to make optimal use of it. Directors ask questions such as: What modal pitch is appropriate for each character? What pattern or contrasts of modal pitches would be useful for signifying the differences among characters?

Even more important than the modal pitch of a performer is his pitch range. The range of a voice is identified as the number of notes between the highest and lowest pitches used during speaking (or singing). Well-trained performers possess a wide pitch range, which enhances the range of their emotional expression. For traditional productions, performers need to produce a broad spectrum of pitches because of the roller coaster emotions they are often called upon to enact and because of the demand for extraordinary clarity of expression during the performance (there is no chance to repeat dialogue). This is also true for verse plays, in which the richness of language and rhythm places greater demands on the performer. "A relatively small change in pitch, stress and timbre of the way in which 'melt' is spoken in Hamlet's 'O! that this too too solid flesh would melt,' can make all the difference between exasperated disgust at being 'too too solid,' and palely interesting melancholy" (Miller 1986, 41). Directors, vocal coaches, and the performers themselves shape the use of pitch modulation so that at every moment of a performance it aids the performer's communication with the spectator. Performers who have trained voices with dazzling pitch ranges are often chosen because their voices carry the potential for sonorous signification.

### Inflection

Directors also consider how the variation in pitch usage can be orchestrated to help communicate the conflicts and tensions inherent in the play and the meanings and connotations of the words as signifiers in the communication process. Inflection is the use of pitch changes without a pause or break: the voice slides or glides up and down the scale. Inflection is used to achieve three major results: to provide stress to an accented syllable in a word, to indicate whether or not a sentence is a question, and to indicate the general emotional level of the speaker.

Adding stress to an accented syllable is often done by raising the pitch (usually combined with an increase in loudness). The same holds true for words in sentences, which are rarely spoken in a monotone. In normal speech the most important words are given a higher pitch, and the single most important word is given the highest pitch of all.

The relative pitch level at the end of a phrase or sentence can tell the listener whether the speaker is asking a question or making a statement. The spectator cannot see punctuation. The performer, however, can indicate to the listener that she has just made a statement by lowering the pitch at the end of the sentence. The reverse holds true for questions, in which the pitch rises. There are exceptions to these guidelines—for instance, there is usually no pitch rise at the end of a question that begins with an interrogative (who, what, when, where, why, which). Nevertheless, in general, upward slides express questions, incomplete thoughts, or some form of indecision. Downward slides usually express the completion of a thought and/or a strong emphasis. A double slide (up then down; down then up) often expresses confusion or uncertainty.

The general raising or lowering of a performer's voice for a sustained period of time is an important indicator of his emotional or motivational state. A sustained raising of pitch usually indicates excitement or an increase in intensity of purpose. A sustained lowering of the modal pitch indicates a major shift in a character's internal equilibrium.

Some contemporary directors experiment with the use of pitch ranges and inflections—often trying to jolt their audiences—by asking the performers to break the normal horizon of expectations concerning the use of the voice in the theater. Many Richard Foreman plays, for example, are performed by untrained actors "who speak their lines flatly, without inflection" (Kirkpatrick 1988, 157). For the first six years that he worked with his company Foreman's performers "could speak with authority, but were asked not to reflect the normal emotional content of the line so that the word quality itself could be heard ringing throughout the text, not swamped by the emotional thrust of the actor's performance. Empathy, [Foreman] felt, obscured what was happening in the spoken language" (Foreman 1992, 35). In many of his productions, Foreman is attempting to have the audience concentrate on the purity of the language itself; he is not interested in having the performers lay heavy vocal signifiers on top of the literal meanings of the written text. The words are central, not the emotive capability of trained performers' voices. This is obviously another reason why Foreman nearly always uses microphones onstage: so the performers can be heard while speaking in normal tones. Projection requires (or forces) more use of emphasis and coloring.

The collaboration between Robert Wilson and Heiner Müller produced a desire to have dialogue read in a flat or deemphasized way.

> Dismissing every theory of modern acting with a sweep of the hand, Müller told the student actors, "Just read it as if it didn't matter." As with CIVIL warS Wilson urged on the cast a cool, flat manner of delivery ("too expressive" was a criticism they were to hear again and again). . . . Wilson believes that this seemingly contradictory mode of presentation enhances rather than diminishes their impact: "When you've got a hot text and you want it to be really hot, you have to be very cold. If you perform it in a hot way, what you're going to get is . . . nothing." (Shyer 1989, 131)

Wilson also believes that the electronic manipulation of the human voice adds layers of signification that communicate directly the alienation of the human being in the postmodern world. This alienation is expressed in Wilson's production of *Death Destruction and Detroit*.

> The person becomes "Persona." The speech rings out as if through the mask of an ancient theatre actor. The electronic alienation, connected with a neutral, emphasized speech, allows for the appearance of a person as a medium, as a placement of speech and gesticulation. Thus an impression is being created that it is not the person who speaks the language, but that the language is using the person to be spoken by it. (Wolfgang Max Faust, quoted in Shyer 1989, 236)

Electronically manipulating the spoken word, downplaying the normal use of pitch and inflection, and casting performers who have no formal vocal training are ways of using language and the spoken word to break stereotypes and either minimize or call special attention to the text of a performance.

## Resonance

The overall quality of the speaking voice is dependent on the resonance of the voice—that is, the richness, color, and vibrancy of sound that the total voice mechanism produces. Resonance is produced primarily by three major cavities in the head: the mouth, the nasal chambers, and the pharynx (the cavity in back of the nose and mouth and above the larynx). Through the flexing and adjusting of these three chambers, the quality of voice resonance can be enriched. Resonance is also produced by the chest cavity. Jerzy Grotowski experimentally trained his performers to use their entire bodies as resonators. "This is obtained by using simultaneously the head and chest resonators" (Grotowski 1968, 154). His performers produced some of the most powerful and resonant voices ever heard in the theater.

The importance of resonance for directors comes during the casting process, when they determine if a performer's voice can match the quality of the character she may play. Resonating chambers vary greatly between human beings in terms of their size and flexibility, but the following are standard vocal quality types that directors often look for:

Rich (round and deep)
Nasal
Breathy
Hoarse (chesty)
Thin
Strident (harsh or screechy)
Falsetto

Each of these basic voice types is a signifier of certain culturally coded character types. When casting, directors look for performers who are capable of reproducing the encoded signifiers of certain character traits. Not all characters on the stage should have perfectly resonant and rich voices.

With the aid of modern technology, directors are manipulating electronically the resonance, voice quality, location, and direction of both individual and group voices to create unnatural (and sometimes unintelligible) sounds and speech.

"Everything is processed through a sound mixer which controls the levels of the various signals. We also have a computer that enables us to separate voice signals and send them to different speakers around the house." This capability has made possible some of Kuhn's [Robert Wilson's sound designer] most arresting sonic inventions. The voices of the actors may occupy different areas in the theatre or jump suddenly from one spot to another. . . . Perhaps the most extraordinary of all was the moment in the Dutch CIVIL warS when the tiny figure of William the Silent sat in the hand of the world's largest woman, reading the Edict of Nantes while his voice traveled in a nearly perfect circle around the perimeter of the auditorium. (Shyer 1989, 236)

Other directors such as Grotowski and Andrei Serban have scorned the use of electronic manipulation yet have attempted to foreground the vocalized text through the use of specially trained performers with extraordinary powers of resonance, pitch range, inflection, and energy. Grotowski's performers' "voices reached from the smallest whisper to an astonishing, almost cavernous tone, an intoned declaiming, of a resonance and power I have not heard from actors before" (Seymour 1963, 33–34). Serban's production of three Greek tragedies (*The Fragments of a Trilogy*) reflected similar experimentation. These productions used various combinations of Greek (ancient and modern) and Latin to create a language that was unintelligible to American audiences. Words were "spoken, chanted, shrieked, whispered, and sung mainly in ancient Greek, to focus attention on the emotive possibilities of sound, not on the meanings of words" (Novick 1986, 15).

Jerzy Grotowski's Polish Laboratory Theatre was the seat of intensive experimentation with performer training during the 1960s. He emphasized the use of the body and voice as the means of primal communication with the audience in an intimate setting. For his production of *Shakuntala* the performers composed artificial ways of speaking that gave the allusion to conventional sacral incantations and liturgy and yet often went contrary to the everyday meaning of the words themselves (Burzynski and Osinski 1979, 19). A review of Grotowski's *Akropolis* suggests the range of vocal signifiers present.

The means of verbal expression have been considerably enlarged because all means of vocal expression are used, starting from the confused babbling of the very small child and including the most sophisticated oratorical recitation. Inarticulate groans, animal roars, tender folk songs, liturgical chants, dialects, declamation of poetry: everything is there. The sounds are interwoven in a complex score which brings back fleetingly the memory of all the forms of language. (Barba and Flaszen 1965, 181–82)

Grotowski's theater experimented with Artaudian principles: he was attempting to develop a new language of the theater that was primal, a language that had little to do with literal meanings, especially through words. Grotowski used the voice to express a language of sound effects, of resonances, of deeply felt emotions, and of primal urgings—unrealistic, unamplified, and deeply human.

## Articulation

For traditional productions, performers attempt to speak words clearly and naturally so that the audience understands what they are saying. Proper articulation involves the intricate manipulation of vocal folds, soft palate, hard palate, tongue, jaw, teeth, and lips. The articulation of consonants and proper production of vowel sounds is of primary importance to the vocalization of lexical signifiers.

A director's concern with articulation comes first during the casting process, when performers are tested for clarity of articulation under a variety of conditions; second during the rehearsal period, when performers work to find their character's particular articulation; and third during the performance, when the performers strive to be heard at all times by every spectator in the theater. Here again electronic support has aided the performer's ability to be heard in every corner of the theater.

As a contrast to the traditional desire for performers to be articulate, Martha Clarke asked the performers in her production of *Miracolo d'Amore* to produce inarticulate sounds and speech that were at one point intended to mimic a scraping noise being produced by one of the performers through physical means. Clarke was seeking ambiguity and androgyneity for the performers, each of whom was "disguised above all by his or her voice. The voice [was] artificial sounding, without any connotation of gender" (Nadotti 1988, 120). By breaking with the tradition of having performers articulate their spoken words clearly, Clarke produced, through physical and vocal manipulation, a performer who signified "a macabre, postsexualized body that abolishes the principle of unity and imposes the overturning of values and signs" (Nadotti 1988,120).

## Tempo

Speed, pause, and duration are all components of tempo. Tempo is the rate of speed at which syllables, words, phrases, sentences, and speeches are spoken. The basic components of tempo are the duration (or quantity) of time expended in speaking each syllable or word, the number of pauses, and the length of each pause.

Normally, by holding one syllable longer than the other syllables in a word, a speaker can emphasize that syllable. In a like manner a speaker can emphasize a word by holding it longer than the other words in a phrase or sentence. Emphasis, then, is achieved by extending the duration of a syllable or word beyond that of less important syllables or words.

Just as punctuation is used in writing, pauses in speaking are employed to separate complete ideas, which are spoken as individual phrases. The relative length of a pause helps to identify further the significance of what has just been said or what is to come next. The use of the pause is one of the most effective techniques for achieving and holding attention. Harold Pinter, Samuel Beckett, and Robert Wilson have turned the pause into one of the most important dramatic elements of the modern and postmodern theater; whole worlds of ideas get communicated between the words and lines of dialogue rather than through them. The following are some of the functions of pauses:

Give special emphasis to people's names or special places
Make distinctive ideas or thoughts stand out
Set up the punch line for a joke (timing is everything)
Indicate major transitions in thinking
Heighten tension
Indicate uncertainty
Create a surreal atmosphere

Tempo is a major force in communicating with the audience. Directors and performers must see that the tempo of each character's speech helps to emphasize the most important words, phrases, and speeches. Furthermore, they can utilize speech tempo to help identify

the basic psychological attributes and emotional states of the characters.

## Rhythm

By its simplest definition, rhythm is a regularly recurring accent, a
cadenced pattern. Webster defines it as "an ordered recurrent alterna-
tion of strong and weak elements." Under performance conditions
rhythm and tempo are nearly impossible to separate. Rhythm is the
pattern of accented and unaccented syllables, words, and phrases and
the use of pauses in speaking.

The most observable rhythm in dialogue is contained in
playscripts written in poetic form, the most common being those of
Shakespeare and his contemporaries, who wrote primarily in
unrhymed iambic pentameter. Well-trained performers and directors
have studied scansion (the analysis of metrical patterns) and are
therefore familiar with the special guideposts that verse plays supply
for performers.

While prose dialogue does not have the clear and consistent metrical pattern of verse, it often contains distinctive, ever-shifting rhythmic patterns that add to the communication of the performance and
aid performers in the creation of their characters. Rhythm is perhaps
the greatest tool for the reinforcement of the mood and emotions of a
character or scene. The ever-increasing pounding of the drums in
Eugene O'Neill's *Emperor Jones* and Tennessee Williams's *Suddenly Last
Summer* reveals how prose can be intensely rhythmical. In both works
the rhythm of the drums is captured and reflected in the dialogue.
Rhythm also plays a significant role in differentiating various accents
and dialects; different cultures have different rhythms that are reflected in the sound of their spoken language.

Directors orchestrate the rhythm of the play not only through its
dialogue but also through other sign systems such as movement, music, and light. The rhythmic center of most traditional performances
is, however, realized through the speech of the performers. Speech
can be manipulated through electronic technology to create striking
and startling rhythmic effects. For Wilson's production of *The Golden
Windows* Hans-Peter Kuhn "created a [sound] loop of Miss Nicklisch
saying 'buzzard' and made it beat like a drum. The play is very calm
and this section really jumped out of it. It's really like a piece of a
cappella music" (Shyer 1989, 238).

## Shifting Horizons

The horizon of expectation for the spoken word in the traditional theaters of the 1960s through the 1980s centered on the well-articulated, well-projected, richly and resonantly delivered speaking of dialogue, unaided by amplification of any kind.. In the postmodern theater, linguistic utterances are manipulated by directors and their collaborative artists in ways that break the traditional theatergoer's horizon of expectations. The spectator may discover that dialogue is spoken plainly by novice performers, downplaying the delivery (overcoding) of the text so that the words as words become the central signifier; or the spectator may encounter supertrained actors who have vocal capabilities that are nearly inhuman, such as those of Grotowski, Serban, and Brook; or the spectator may experience a performance in which modern aural technology becomes itself a dominant signifier as performers' voices are manipulated, distorted, echoed, or looped to produce spoken words that are unnatural, inhuman, unrecognizable, or simply more clearly heard than would be possible without technological support. It seems contradictory that postmodern productions use language and the speaking of words in polar ways: in one production the words as signifiers are less important and the vocal quality itself is foregrounded; in another production the words are highlighted by minimizing the vocal overcoding of the performer; in yet another production all spoken words are amplified, sometimes to allow the performer to speak more naturally (quietly without projection) and other times to produce highly unnatural sounds through distortion, special effects, or the disorienting placement of the source of the sound. Each of these methods, however, is in keeping with the postmodern aesthetic of reflecting the disjointed, self-referential, and otherworldly nature of contemporary culture and society.

## Facial Expression

Facial expression is an everyday sign system. We read people's faces all the time: "You look tired." "Have you been exercising?" "I don't see any humor in that." In the theater, facial expression becomes an even more important sign system because the audience looks more intently at the performer for physical clues concerning the subtextual meaning behind the words being expressed.

The natural appearance of the performer's face is a powerful signifier. At first sight the performer's face may communicate a sense of
beauty, sexiness, terror, stupidity, race, gender, ethnicity, health, age,
ugliness, intellectual capability, or slyness. The meanings, however,
can be very different to different spectators. Traits such as beauty,
ugliness, and intelligence lie in the eye of the beholder, for there are
no cultural codes that clearly define facial aesthetics in any concrete
way. Historical periods, differing cultures, and individual taste make
it impossible to codify facial meanings scientifically.

Faces are not masks. They are ever-changing; they reflect time of
day, mood, physical pain, and health, to name just a few sensations.
The dynamic rather than static quality of facial expression makes it a
valuable and manipulable tool for directors and performers. Yet precisely because facial expression is a natural part of our everyday expression, it seems that traditional Western performers and especially
their directors have exerted very little direct control over its use as a
sign system. Facial expression naturally has a one-to-one relationship
with the emotional intensity of a performer; the face automatically
forms the appropriate expressive configuration to match the inner
emotion. It might be appropriate to say that good performers have
naturally expressive faces.

It is commonplace for performers to train their voices and bodies
to become more expressive, but it is rare for them to train their faces
in a similar manner. James Penrod, however, believes that the face can
be trained. He encourages performers and directors to be aware of the
expressive and communicative potential of the human face and to find
ways of enhancing its use. Through careful study, he maintains, performers can learn the cultural codes that various expressions signify.
Penrod recommends that performers work with a mirror.

> Try to determine the expressive values of each facial movement as
> you make it. Does raising the eyebrows express surprise or a sense
> of superiority? Does lowering the eyebrows express displeasure of
> some kind or does it merely denote thinking? Do downcast eyes
> suggest shame or thought? If the eyes are moved sideward and
> downward does it suggest contempt or shyness? If the mouth is
> opened wide is it expressing fear or great joy? If the teeth are firmly
> clenched and the lips pressed tightly together, does this express
> determination, defiance, or anger? (1974, 48–49)

Penrod recognizes that the same expression (e.g., lowered eye-
brows) may convey different meanings when expressed by different

performers. Earlier analyses of facial expressions tended to be more rigid. During the nineteenth century, for instance, François Delsarte developed an extensive system of bodily movements. One part of his system was a very specific codification of facial expression.

In the play of the physiognomy every portion of the face performs a separate part. Thus, for instance, it is not useless to know what function nature has assigned to the eye, the nose, the mouth, in the expression of certain emotions of the soul. True passion, which never errs, has no need of recurring to such studies; but they are indispensable to the feigned passion of the actor. How useful would it not be to the actor who wishes to represent madness or wrath, to know that the eye never expresses the sentiment experienced, but simply indicates the object of this sentiment! Cover the lower part of your face with your hand, and impart to your look all the energy of which it is susceptible, still it will be impossible for the most sagacious observer to discover whether your look expresses anger or attention. On the other hand, uncover the lower part of the face, and if the nostrils are dilated, if the contracted lips are drawn up, there is no doubt that anger is written on your countenance. An observation which confirms the purely indicative part performed by the eye is, that among raving madmen the lower part of the face is violently contracted, while the vague and uncertain look shows clearly that their fury has no object. It is easy to conceive what a wonderful interest the actor, painter, or sculptor must find in the study of expression. Hence, the eloquent secrets of pantomime, those imperceptible movements of great actors which produce such powerful impressions, are decomposed and subjected to laws whose evidence and simplicity are a two-fold source of admiration. (A. Gueroult, quoted in Zorn 1968, 17)

Delsarte developed a series of drawings of the lips, nose, face, and eyes that codify specific meanings for individual facial parts. He saw eye expression as having three components: the optic (direction of glance), the pupil (its size), and the eyebrow. Combinations of these three components serve as signs with specific meanings or emotions. Figure 8 provides Delsarte's codification of eye expressions.

A director determines how important facial expression is for his production by locating a point on this continuum:

In order to determine the quantity, level, and style of facial expression the director asks several questions. How far away will the majority of the audience be from the performers? Is the production naturalistic? Are there constantly shifting emotions, and, if so, which sign systems will be of primary importance to signify these shifts? Are exaggerated or absurd expressions desirable? How will makeup be used? Will masks be used? How facially dexterous are the performers? Answers

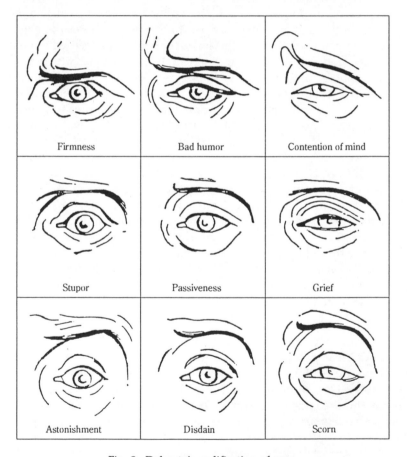

Fig. 8. Delsarte's codification of eyes

to these questions and others will help shape a decision about how a director will use facial expression within the mise-en-scène.

One critical feature in determining the level of facial expression used is the relationship of the performers to the audience. Intimate theaters allow more easily for facial expression to be employed as a primary means of signification; in very large theaters, distance keeps many spectators from being able to read faces meaningfully.

Perhaps the most intriguing work on facial expression in the modern theater was done by the Polish Laboratory Theatre under the leadership of Jerzy Grotowski. He worked with performers to perfect their ability to use facial muscles to create exaggerated, immovable expressions. Grotowski's performers were capable of using extreme muscular control and contortions to create human facial masks. For his production of *Akropolis* the performers created rigid archetypal death masks using only their facial muscles (Bradby and Williams 1988, 118). In the final scene, which takes place in the concentration camp oven, the performers' facial expressions are frozen in supreme agony. This ability to use facial muscles to simulate masks is also required for performers in the Kathakali and Malayan theaters (unlike performers in most Asian theaters, who employ real or painted masks) (Richie 1970, 209). Likewise, JoAnne Akalaitis capitalized on highly orchestrated facial expressions and movements for her lusty and passionate production of *'Tis Pity She's a Whore,* which produced "an involuntary revelation of their hidden, coarse hungers" (Rich 1992, C14).

The observation of facial expressions as signifiers is to be expected. Spectators will naturally examine performers' faces, seeking clues about their characters' physical and psychological nature. Directors may choose to highlight the use of facial expression by employing exaggerated facial muscles, distorted makeup, or masks.

## Gesture

Gesture refers to the sign system that uses the performer's body as the signifier. The performer's body—its size (short or tall, small or large), body type (thin or overweight, muscular or flabby), and composition (short or long legs, small or big bones)—is a signifier. A performer's presence can appear menacing, sexually enticing, funny, disgusting, or insignificant depending on the visual signifiers perceived by the audience. When casting, directors consider how a performer's body type acts as a signifier (or series of signifiers).

Gesture refers to communication through the body and its parts. A performer moves her arm, hand, and finger to point to someone she sees in the distance. This gesture serves as a sign. "Gesture can be read as language in its own right, and Artaud in fact saw gestural or *kinesic* as the fundamental code of the theatre. . . . " (Bassnett-McGuire 1980, 48). In classical mime and visually oriented postmodern performances, gestures (usually coupled with movement) are leading signifiers of the performance.

In most Asian theaters, gestures are highly codified. In Japanese Noh, Bunraku, and Kabuki theaters, precise gestures signify precise meanings. The Kathakali dance theater of India incorporates perhaps the most systematized gesture and movement sign systems of all. Here every small turn of the head or slight finger movement conveys a precise meaning. But for all these theaters a specific code must be understood if the spectator is to comprehend all of the performance's detailed meanings.

Even in theaters that lack a specific, detailed codification system for gestures, a performer's body and his gestures can send more meaningful information to the audience than do his spoken words. In fact, gestures can provide insight into a scene's subtext that override the denotative meaning of the words being spoken. "Body language may carry a more immediate wallop because of its strong potential to evoke sensuous associations of personal experience. When both verbal and nonverbal communication occur, body language often contradicts verbal language" (Hanna 1983, 7). For example, if a woman is telling a man "I am here to protect you" yet is advancing toward him with tightly closed fists held in a striking position, the male character and audience are likely to think that the woman is indeed going to harm him. This ability of gesture to reinforce or contradict the meaning of words makes it one of the most important sign systems in the theater.

As a matter of fact, most people express themselves in bodily reactions and attitudes before they do in speech. They reveal themselves first by their movements, by their mannerisms of face or of body. They express themselves by what they do or refrain from doing. And only then, as a general rule, do they add vocally their more detailed reactions. In normal situations, for example, people lean toward an object or a person that interests them; they turn away when they are disgusted or have lost interest; they become visibly tense when they are worried or frightened. They slump in their chairs, straighten their shoulders, shake their heads, or brace themselves for a shock, depending on what is going on in their minds. They suggest in their whole bodily attitudes their joy, their anger, their embarrassment, their indecision, or their despair. That is to say, they *communicate* directly with anyone who is watching; and, in a general way, the watcher knows what they are thinking and what they are likely to do.

If this is true in real life, it is all the more so on the stage. The spectator cannot guess what you as an actor are thinking and feeling; he must have some outward indication of your intentions; he knows only what he sees and hears. If he merely hears an important dramatic idea, but never "sees" it, his impression is so much the weaker.

An actor can rarely communicate his station in life, his age, his habits of mind, or his emotional nature by his voice alone. His movement and posture are his calling card. They tell who he is, where he has been, and what he represents; and they speak quickly, clearly, and directly. (Albright 1959, 25–27)

Gestures as signs do not have the precise meanings ascribable to the written word. Most individual gestures (at least in American society) do not have a single meaning. "The gesture does not exist as an isolated entity and cannot, unlike the word or morpheme, be separated from the general continuum. One cannot, therefore, tabulate a gestural 'lexicon' in which kinesic paradigms may be conveniently set out" (Elam 1980, 71). Nevertheless, Peter Brook's production of *Ubu* attempted to incorporate simplified and heightened gestures as a way of communicating precise meanings.

Gesture and mimicry in *Ubu* are played big throughout, as are actors' movements in relation to each other. All draw on easily recognizable signs we use in the course of our daily lives. Gestures which say, without words, "Get lost!" or "I don't give a shit"— appropriate backing for Ubu's *merdre* ... are nothing other than signs circulating in society and which, reworked in performance, presuppose that most spectators are familiar with them. (Shevtsova 1989, 293)

Brook has spent much of his life experimenting with gesture, movement, and sound in an attempt to find a more universal (nonlinguistic) language for the theater. For him gestures can be encoded to communicate specific meanings.

Martha Clarke moved from the dance world to the theater, bringing with her an intense focus on gesture and movement as signifiers.

Fig. 9. Production: *Vienna: Lufthaus*. Director: Martha Clarke. Photo by Gary Gunderson.

Critics frequently comment on how touched they are by the striking visual images Clarke's performers create onstage. For example, in her production of *Vienna: Lufthaus* a performer appeared with boots on his hands and created a variety of evocative images (fig. 9). The climax of this scene was when he kinkily mimed both partners in the act of making love. The performer "twisted his arms to suggest the orgasmically writhing legs of a woman, then doubled over in such a way that his head appeared to be buried in her crotch" (Copeland 1988, 14). Clarke's focus on gesture and movement has allowed her to align the dance and theater worlds.

In most cases gestures are read in a context of multiple signifiers. Gestures often precede, or are executed simultaneously with, the speaking of dialogue, a movement through space, or a facial expression. Gestures, therefore, are decoded from a context of overlapping signifiers.

One of the most important results of Delsarte's study of bodily movements was his conclusion that gesture is much more important than the spoken word (which reinforces Elam's theory).

> Gesture must always precede speech. In fact, speech is reflected expression. It must come after gesture, which is parallel with the impression received. Nature incites a movement, speech names this movement. Speech is only the title, the label of what gesture has anticipated. Speech comes only to confirm what the audience already comprehends. Speech is given for naming things. Gesture asks the question, "What?" and speech answers. Gesture after the answer would be absurd. (Delsarte, quoted in Zorn 1968, 159–60)

Delsarte worked out a system of hand gestures indicating how hands can be used to communicate very specific attitudes, emotions, or information. He found that at least nine specific messages or meanings are communicated by discrete hand gestures (fig. 10).

Delsarte's attempt (among others) to codify gestures is useful for directors who orchestrate performers' bodies and gestures. "Due to the complexity of the hand's anatomical structure and its articulation possibilities, there are, in the movements of the fingers alone, infinite possible modifications of form and behavior" (Barba and Savarese 1991, 132). While Asian theater historically incorporates intricate, coded hand gestures in its theatrical sign systems, in the West only recently has theater for the deaf come to the fore for both hearing-impaired and nonimpaired spectators. "This theatre is fascinating for those spectators who do not understand the sign language alphabet because of the pure dynamics of hands speaking in silence, just as we Occidentals are fascinated by the Indian *mudras* without understanding what they mean" (Barba and Savarese 1991, 132–33).

Directors are faced with a series of choices surrounding their use of gestures in a performance. The following continua represent the polarity of choices.

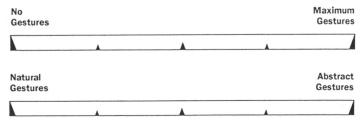

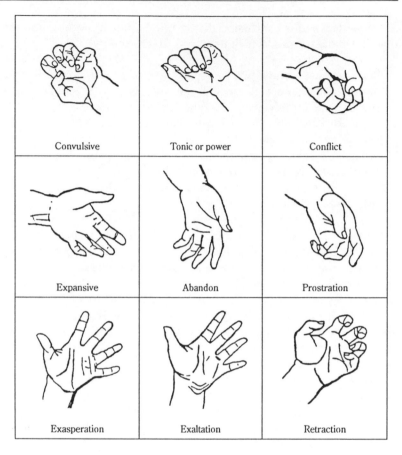

Fig. 10. Delsarte's codification of hands

In making these critical choices, the director begins to define the amount and kind of visual signification that will come from the performers.

Some directors—such as Jerzy Grotowski, Martha Clarke, Andrei Serban, Robert Wilson, and JoAnne Akalaitis—are experimenting with gestures in order to find ways of making them a more consequential signifier for audiences. Wilson is noted for the meticulousness with which he rehearses performers' gestures and movements. He often demonstrates for a performer exactly the gestures he wants her to make, and he asks her to repeat them precisely. "He gives you the gestures and the walk . . . and from those you create the character. So it's a paradox. You're completely mechanical. You're completely free" (Richy Müller, quoted in Holmberg 1990, H36).

Gestures also contribute to the audience's perception of a performance's and director's visual style. Especially for a period play, in which the manners and social customs of the times are quite different from those of today's audiences, gestures are useful as signs to indicate the manners of the time, if the director chooses to create the original world of the playscript. A codified system of manners, movements, and gestures exists for each major historical period and for each unique culture and society. The director who chooses to present an "authentic" production of a period play researches the customs of the day and works with the performers to make the historical gestures a part of their characterizations. Because exact historical accuracy may not be required or desired, a director may select a few critical gestures that capture the flavor of the period instead of reproducing every gestural custom of the era. The following description of a late Renaissance bow reveals how complicated and precise gestural codes can be:

> The left foot was drawn backwards with leg and foot turned outward slightly and the knee straight. Both heels remained on the ground, and the body and head were held erect. Then, without pausing, the gentleman bent both knees and bowed forward from the hips. The head followed the line of the body without the chin's sinking into the chest. As the knees bent, the weight of the body moved partially to the back foot so that this weight could be evenly distributed to both feet. The knee of the back leg was turned out slightly as the knee bent; if this movement were exaggerated, it looked ugly. Throughout the bow, the front and back heel remained on the ground if the knee bend were slight; if the knee bend were deep, the back heel was raised, thus keeping the weight of the body partially on the ball of the back foot. In a very deep bow, the back knee nearly touched the floor; the body returned to an erect position at the completion of the bow, and the weight moved to the front foot, thus releasing the back. (Russell 1980, 179)

This example is just one small part of a complex behavioral code from the late Renaissance. What about eating habits? Methods of walking and sitting? Courting rituals? Dueling rituals? When these cultural codes are incorporated into a production that is designed to reflect accurately the historical period of a playscript, they contribute to the perception of both style and meaning.

A performer must not only learn the social graces and customs of the time but adapt them to the character he is playing. For example, a character who disdains all formal manners and court procedures may either not bow before the king or do so only slightly—in a way that communicates his displeasure at having to bow to anyone. Another character, a sycophant, might go overboard with his bow: he does everything he can to impress the king. And so it goes—the performers each find the appropriate gestures, within the context of a strict social code, to express their character's individuality.

Postmodern directors also use gesture as a chief means of signifying the style of their work. The performers in Wilson's productions are asked to mimic his personal style of gesture and movement (fig. 11). Wilson "takes himself through every character's physical life. It's always him. And the gestures are limited to his gestural style. But it causes tremendous focus. It all converges" (Stephanie Roth, quoted in Hafrey 1991, H5). Grotowski's theater is typified by highly physical gestures that in many productions produces a tense, agonized style of physical portrayal. His performers' "typical gestures hide their faces—behind crooked arms, coattails, umbrellas, hats, by a bent back or by a turn. They are alone; they refuse communication" (Brecht 1970, 184). Ariane Mnouchkine is noted for an athletic yet highly stylized gestural code: she is well known for incorporating Kabuki movements and gestures into productions of Shakespeare. Alternatively, for her production of *The Kitchen* she asked the performers to work in a restaurant kitchen, then, "by means of mimed gesture and heightened movement, they could present on stage an image of the frantic rhythm and growing tension of kitchen work. The result was a powerful theatrical metaphor for a working life of any kind" (Bradby and Williams 1988, 86–87). Richard Foreman created a postmodern Gothic style for his production of *Fall of the House of Usher:* "The use of abrupt and exaggerated gesture [produced] a sort of expressionist updating of Gothic melodrama. Waving hands and running feet advertise horror at every moment, an evident attempt to replicate the pervasive dread of Poe's original language" (B. Holland 1989, 45).

The mode or style of a production that a director chooses affects the kinds of gestures to be used. Is the production a classical tragedy? Farce? Melodrama? Sophisticated comedy? Naturalistic tragedy? Postmodern collage? Or absurd comedy? In defining the mode or style of the production, the director implicitly chooses to use a certain style of gesture. The differences in gestural style for a classical tragedy, naturalistic tragedy, or postmodern tragedy are significant, the first being grand, the second natural and subdued, and the third frenetic,

Fig. 11. Production: *Death Destruction and Detroit*. Director: Robert
Wilson. Photo by Ruth Walz.

disjointed, or even slow motion. At the other extreme, farce requires
yet another style of gesture.

> The incongruous juxtapositions, mechanical confessions, staccato
> repetitions, brisk reversals, and violent directness of farce all call
> for short, sharp, quick rhythms punctuated by laughter, not
> thought. In its movement and gesture farce is true to its origins and
> employs the speed, energy, physical variety, and broad gesture
> required to hold the attention of popular audiences throughout the
> history of theatre. (Harrop and Epstein 1982, 168)

Richard Foreman works hard at breaking traditional horizons of
expectations in order to get the spectator to see differently. He uses

unexpected gestures as one of the chief means by which to bring the audience into a new mode of perception. "I frequently give the performers positions that put the body in a state of tension. Or I do the opposite; I give them positions that suggest a degree of relaxation inappropriate to the situation. Both options break through the shell of normal behavior" (Foreman 1992, 40).

Peter Sellars employs nontraditional gestures and movement in his productions of Mozart's operas as a way of heightening signification. Sellars has a special "way of expressing the nuances of Mozart's scores with the hand gestures and body language of his performers" (Sterritt 1989, 10). In an attempt to find a postmodern equivalency to the eighteenth-century world of Mozart and to break the formal production style of the traditional opera world, Sellars seeks to find a visual equivalent to the human voice (which dominates traditional opera) through a heavier focus on physical gesture. "When his characters twist themselves into odd postures and positions, as they do particularly in 'Don Giovanni,' they seem to be straining against the confines of physical reality itself" (Sterritt 1989, 10).

Each of these directors has found a personal way of communicating their theatrical, postmodern aesthetic by foregrounding the gestural sign system and finding, through the work of their choreographers and performers, theatricalized and dynamic visual languages. Each director's use of gesture is stylistically different, yet their independent explorations have led them to conclude that gestures truly do speak louder than words.

The use of gesture, then, is a complicated and sophisticated business. Directors and performers must employ gestures that communicate the period and style of the performance at the same time they reveal the individual personality, emotional state, and motivations of their characters at every changing moment of the performance. More important, the distinctive style of the performance and director is embodied in the gestural gestalt of the production as a whole.

## Movement

Movement refers to the sign system that employs the performer's body as it moves through space as a signifier of meanings. It is impossible, however, to separate the perception of movement signs from gestural signs. During performance, movement and gesture provide a context for decoding each other. Yet there are certain properties of movement that can be isolated for analysis and use by directors.

Movement's three chief communicative properties are its ability to reveal each character's individual personality and motivation, its ability to reflect and reinforce the essential dramatic action of the performance, and its ability to help define the style of a production.

Movement (combined with gesture) is a primary means of portraying individual character traits. Performers who understand the communicative properties of movement, and who develop flexibility, strength, and grace, are able to employ this sign system in powerful ways.

> People's movement behaviour can be observed systematically, and it is useful for the artist of the stage to learn something about the best procedure in observation. The purposeful assessment of a person's movement should begin at the moment one first sees him. A person's entrance through a door, his walk up to the first stop, and his carriage in standing, sitting, or any other position can be of great significance. It is the task of an artist in creating a fine and lucid characterisation not only to bring out typical movement habits, but also the latent capacities from which a definite development of personality can originate. The artist must realise that his own movement make-up is the ground on which he has to build. The control and development of his personal movement habits will provide him with the key to the mystery of the significance of movement. (Laban 1960, 94)

This is also true for the director who, when guiding the work of the performers, oversees the use of movement as a series of signifiers that make up a complex sign system.

The director needs to ask the question: How important will the movement sign system be for communicating my vision of this production? Two basal continua represent a broad range of choices.

After the director locates her production on these two continua there are other questions she needs to ask: How fast or slow? How natural or abstract? How curved or angular? Should there be harmony or discord in movement patterns? Should the movement follow or counter traditional movement codes? How will the performer's movement mesh with the movement of sets, lights, costumes, and the audience? Will dance be incorporated? What movement skills must the performers possess? How will gestures and movement work together? Many of these questions can only be answered through the casting and rehearsal process, for only after experimentation is it possible to know definitively what kind, style, and frequency of movement will work in a performance.

## The Elements of Movement

Movements consist of several physical components:

Direction
Speed
Duration
Intensity
Rhythm

Performers and directors manipulate these five elements to provide signifiers for spectators to decode.

### Direction

All movement has direction: forward or backward, left or right, up or down, diagonal, parallel, or perpendicular. In everyday life these directions are relative (contextual): they are based on an observer's position and relationship to the one who is producing the movement. In the theater, movement is often less relative or ambiguous, especially in a theater with a proscenium stage in which the audience sits out front. Even in thrust or arena theaters there is a relatively fixed relationship between the audience and the stage space. No matter what the performer-audience relationship is, however, cultural codes for movement exist.

A performer can move in any direction at any given time. Each movement in a specific direction is a signifier; it is an opportunity to communicate with the audience. There are, however, no denotative movement codes that apply in all circumstances. For example, in many traditional theater productions it is thought that when a character moves forward (toward the audience) he makes a stronger statement than when he moves backward (away from the audience). In such productions moving diagonally toward the audience is considered more powerful than moving diagonally away from or perpendicular with the seating of the audience. It is also believed that to move from the spectator's left to right is stronger, since this is the way we read. Yet many postmodernists disavow the code value of these guidelines. Richard Foreman resists traditional stage poetics: he does not use one of the most powerful movements in the theater, the diagonal, at all. "I usually tell the actors I do not allow diagonal crosses onstage. If they have to get from upstage right to downstage left, they must do it by walking straight down and then making a right turn, rather than making the simpler diagonal cross." He does this "to create a simple, strong readable grid of right-angle relationships, to create clarity like brilliant moves in a game of chess" (1992, 47).

In traditional productions it is thought that the direction of a movement affects the messages being received by the audience. If a character continually backs away from interactions with other characters, the audience will come to believe that she lacks courage or determination. Or if a character moves forward to the very edge of the stage to deliver a speech, the audience is likely to sit up and take more notice of the words. Foreman purposefully negates anticipated movement patterns, however, in order to project his counteraesthetic.

> When directing, I'm actively engaged in deciding, from moment to moment, whether the staging should reinforce the overt meaning of the text, or if it should contradict it in some way. Sometimes it's as simple an issue as whether an actor should move toward or away from an object. Suppose an actor looks at a cabbage on a table and says, "Oh, this is a beautiful cabbage." If he says the line walking toward the cabbage, it conveys an emotional effect that simply reinforces his statement. If he says the line while backing away from the cabbage until he bangs into the opposite wall, it gives the cabbage itself more importance; maybe he has difficulty dealing with the awe the cabbage's beauty arouses in him. (1992, 50)

### Speed

All movement has a speed—fast, medium, or slow (or any degree in between). The speed of a movement signifies the personality or emotional state of a character. To move very slowly backward signals caution, fear, or illness, depending on the context (the moment-to-moment circumstances). To jump forward suddenly signals fright, surprise, or eagerness. The overall speed of an entire production can also be a primary signifier of a performances' meaning. For instance, Ariane Mnouchkine's production of Arnold Wesker's *The Kitchen* was characterized by a highly physical, ebullient movement style (Bradby and Williams 1988, 85). Mnouchkine wanted to create the atmosphere of a working kitchen, and she found the appropriate metaphor in an intensified movement style.

*Duration*

The duration of any movement is a result of its speed and distance. A quick movement that covers a long distance across or down the stage implies a powerful motivation or emotional state. A very short, slow move might be a sign of sneakiness, old age, or danger, depending upon the context. Most productions call for a variety of movement durations, which grow out of the natural ebb and flow of the tensions and the dramatic action of the playscript.

Some directors experiment with exaggerations of tempo. Robert Wilson, for example, is noted for stretching out time by having the performers move in extreme slow motion.

> As one critic wrote, by slowing down the ordinary in our lives Wilson manages to "extract from it all the light it holds." No one has shown such a gift of light as Sheryl Sutton [an actress who appears in many Wilson productions], whose elegance, ease and absolute concentration can transform the simplest gesture into something compelling and peculiarly beautiful, whether it be lifting a glass of milk, rising slowly from a chair or—as in *Einstein on the Beach*—simply crossing the stage in liquid slow motion. (Shyer 1989, 10)

On the opposite end of the continuum is much of the work of Richard Foreman. "There is speed in our culture, and I want to reflect both the exhilaration and the neurosis such speed injects into our lives" (Foreman 1992, 21). While many of Foreman's productions employ hyperactivity as a primary signifier, he also experiments with the opposite by using complicated tableau/move/freeze/tableau sequences that produce a disjointed yet consistent movement pattern throughout the performance. "The actors [in *Angelface*] spent much of the evening standing in tableaux. They would hold for five or six lines, and then there'd be a slight shift of bodies, and they'd hold for another five or six lines. Another slight shift, five or six lines more" (69). In this case rate of speed and duration were used to produce a mechanistic, highly stylized movement scheme.

## Intensity

Every movement has an inherent level of intensity that goes beyond speed and duration. Intensity grows out of the emotional state or personality profile of a character or the tension created by the dramatic action. To move with force, with extreme muscular tension, or with intense concentration can do much to underscore the dramatic action. Andrei Serban's production of *The Marriage of Figaro* focused on intense, sustained, and frenetic movement as a core signifier of the performance. Crazed characters literally rolled on and off the stage on roller skates, in a wheelchair, in a grocery cart, and on a skateboard. The mise-en-scène was "wildly eclectic, artificial, stimulating" (Steele 1985, 10).

## Rhythm

Rhythm was described earlier as a regularly recurring accent—a rhythmic pattern. Rhythm in movement is relatively easy to produce or observe but hard to describe. Rhythm is usually either symmetrical or asymmetrical, and it is normally modulated by its tempo.

Each movement in a performance—be it walking, running, sitting, jumping, dancing, or whatever—possesses and emanates a rhythmic pattern and tempo that signifies a character's personality and/or her emotional state at the moment. Directors and performers use rhythm and tempo to define character and to underscore the flow of the dramatic action.

The total performance is made up of conflicting and intersecting rhythms and tempos that originate from the individual characters and the ever-changing tensions and relaxations inherent in the dramatic action. Also, the rhythms and tempos of the movement of the characters are interwoven with the rhythms and tempos of the spoken dialogue, music, scene changes, and the like (more on this later). The composition and unification of a performance depends on the director's ability to weave these patterns of rhythms and tempos together, thereby heightening the dramatic action and, simultaneously, intensifying the spectator's emotional and spiritual involvement.

Directors sometimes use contrapuntal rhythms to heighten the dramatic action of a performance. This can be done by juxtaposing conflicting rhythms from two different sign systems. Such was the case in Peter Sellars's production of *Marriage of Figaro,* in which music and movement contradicted each other: the dancers writhed to a silent rock beat, while the orchestra performed a stately march (MacDonald 1991, 709). By presenting this contrast, Sellars foregrounded movement rhythm in order to heighten the spectators' awareness of the inherent rhythms of the music. He jolted the audience into recognizing the rhythm of the music by displaying the contrasting movement of the dancers, who were clearly out of syncopation with the aural signifiers.

## Movement Defines Character

Movement produces signs that communicate specific information about the characters:

Nationality/ethnicity
Environment
Temperament/personality
Age/health
Profession
Sex (masculinity/femininity)
Historical period

### *Nationality/Ethnicity*

Different cultures and time periods reflect patterns of social customs, clothing, and temperament that are, in turn, reflected in the way people move and interact.

### *Environment*

A person's environment has an enormous effect on how he moves, gestures, and interacts with others. Weather (rain, snow, temperature), location (church, beach, school), and social milieu are critical in determining the kind of movements that are appropriate for a character at any given moment of a performance. One of the reasons Robert Wilson uses people he finds in the streets is because he likes their realistic movement that has been shaped by social and environmental conditions. He wants to capture their natural rhythm, posture, and movement; he transports them onto the stage, where he often slows them down so the audience can observe more closely the beauty and individual personal imprint that can be revealed through a close look at movement and gesture.

### Temperament/Personality

Characters often possess strong temperaments and personalities. Lady Macbeth is fiercely determined and purposeful. Hamlet is melancholic and contemplative. Falstaff is mischievous, aggressive, and childlike. These different temperaments and personalities can be reflected, and indeed projected, by the use of individualized movements.

### Age/Health

Careful observation of different age groups and health levels in people reveals a rich range of movement patterns and energy levels. A precise orchestration of performers' movements can pinpoint the age and health of each character in a performance.

### Profession

Certain professions demand unique kinds of physical activity. Movement reveals the imprint of an occupation on a character's physical presence. Athletes, housewives, ministers, truck drivers, musicians, and garbage collectors each spend their days repeating certain physical activities; this repetition stamps each individual with a special kinetic energy and pattern. The director guides the performer to find and repeat this energy and pattern realistically or in an exaggerated fashion as a means of communicating a character's occupation.

### Sex (Masculinity/Femininity)

How a person moves is one of the first signs of masculinity or femininity. In particular, period productions that attempt to present historically accurate movement style require different gender-related movement patterns.

> [For women] much stress was placed on dance as an appropriate training for female deportment; particular attention was given to

the holding of the head since this was the part of the body that
would first draw the attention of the courtier. The dancing master
also taught the lady the correct art of walking: to "put her feet close
to one another, the toes outward . . . sedately and in a straight
line." (Russell 1980, 206)

*Historical Period*

If a production is attempting to re-create the social customs or manners of the play's historical time, movement can be of great service.
Even if the director is changing the prescribed historical period, movement can help communicate the new historical time. For example,
when Ariane Mnouchkine placed her production of Shakespeare's
*Richard II* in Japan and directed it in the style of Kabuki theater, the
movement style was totally different from that of a production attempting to recapture the conditions of the original production. In her
production, movement was a dominant signifier of the altered historical circumstances and the performance's style. Peter Sellars is known
for juxtaposing contemporary movement patterns with period opera
music as a way to get and keep the spectator's interest and to remind
the audience that, although they may be watching a Mozart opera
written in the eighteenth century, they live in a postmodern world.
"Ultimately, you have to recognize that the theatre exists only in one
tense—the present" (Sellars, quoted in Kettle 1990, 44). Sellars attempts to merge the past with contemporary cultural codes; he puts
history in touch with the postmodern age. He does not want the
audience to forget who, where, or when they are.

## Communication through Movement

Typical movements are standing, walking, running, sitting, kneeling,
lying down, turning, dancing, jumping, fighting, falling, reaching/
touching, and manipulating objects. Performers enact these physical
actions during the course of a performance in ways that are consistent
with their characters and the director's chosen style. Each movement
becomes a signifier when seen in the context of the complete mise-en-
scène.

Many scientists are of the opinion that there are no meaningless
movements. The meanings of the individual movements, however,
can be known only within the framework of a movement pattern

and dramatic context. Looking at movement the way a scientist does can be valuable for artistic re-creation. Scientists often break a person's total movement pattern down into isolated elements noting the frequency and dynamic characteristics of certain kinds of movements. In developing a characterization, you must eventually decide upon specific kinds of action and join them together into a pattern expressive of your view of the character. Like the scientist you can analyze movement to reveal a communicative pattern, and then select isolated elements of movement to create character in a specific dramatic context. (Penrod 1974, 117)

The director, working with performers and a movement coach, explores a wide range of possible movements for each character and for the production as a whole and selects and arranges specific movements that help reveal individual character traits, the performance's style, and its overall meaning.

The amount and style of movement will vary greatly, however, because each director must decide how much emphasis to place on movement as a means of communicating to the audience. When Robert Wilson directed *King Lear* he instinctively designed individual movement patterns for Lear's three daughters.

As he showed the three actresses playing the king's daughters—Goneril, Regan and Cordelia—how to enter for the scene in which Lear divides his kingdom among them, the direction was technical and formal: how fast to walk, how to cock the head, how to hold the fingers. Taking a sheet of paper, the director drew three lines: straight (Goneril), zigzag (Regan) and curved (Cordelia). "Your walk is your character," he said. "I can't explain it, but I can draw it." He can also do it. The basis of much of his direction is his ability as a performer, and as the actors watched he mimed each walk. (Holmberg 1990, H7)

For Wilson, and other postmodernists, the movement of the characters is a part of the pattern of movement of all the visual elements, which aid in revealing the dramatic action of the playscript or performance piece and, more important, the meanings of the performance itself.

While directors of traditional productions use movement as a means of signification, postmodern directors often highlight its use, challenging the audience's horizon of expectations through exaggeration, slow motion, hypertension, tableau, mechanization, or absolute stillness, thereby contrasting or contradicting entrenched codes. In many postmodern productions, movement and other visual elements are the dominant sign systems—something that rarely happens in traditional theater, in which words are often the focus of the director's, performers', and audience's work.

## Makeup and Hairstyle

People draw conclusions about another person's health, demeanor, mood, and personality by reading his face and hair. "You look so healthy" (you have a tan). "You look ill" (your eyes are red and swollen). "Did you just wake up?" (your hair is a mess). "He looks untrustworthy" (he has greasy hair and a mustache). "You look younger" (you dyed your hair). Many people go to great pains to make themselves look as youthful, healthy, affluent, and stylish as possible, often using makeup and hair treatments to achieve this goal. The same holds true for signification in the theater: makeup and hairstyle constitute a sign system of enormous importance.

> Like speech and body movement, makeup is part of an actor's craft, and the actor who neglects his makeup risks failure to project visually the precise and carefully drawn character-concept he has in his mind. His body is his sole means of visual communication with his audience, and neglect of a single visual aid will certainly lessen the possible impact of his performance and may spell the difference between success and failure. (Corson 1975, 3–4)

Directors must ask two primary questions about the possible use of makeup and hairstyle. Should they be used as a signifiers? Should they be realistic or abstract or else some gradation or combination of these extremes? Since these questions are not easily answered by a simple "yes or "no," they are best represented as continua.

The range of choices is bountiful. It is possible to use no makeup for some characters and extensive makeup for others or to use mildly abstract makeup for some characters and highly distorted makeup for others. Makeup artists, of course, argue that makeup should be an important element of every production.

> Designing makeup should be as much a part of actor preparation as movement and diction. The audience focuses on the performer's face for vital clues as to the character's age, life style, feeling, life experiences, and the like. An incredible amount of information can be conveyed by well-designed makeup, enhancing the performer's body and voice. (Arnink 1984, 12)

## Communication of Persona

Makeup and hairstyle provide specific information that helps identify a character's persona:

Ethnicity, nationality, and/or race
Environment
Profession
Temperament/personality
Health
Age

### Ethnicity, Nationality, and/or Race

Productions are peopled with all sorts of characters from every conceivable heritage, race, and country. In fact, these backgrounds are an integral part of the given circumstances and the dramatic action of a play. The director asks: Is the ethnic or racial heritage of a character important to the play's ultimate meaning? If so, how can makeup and hairstyle be encoded to heighten communication? For example, when Ariane Mnouchkine directed *The Terrible but Unfinished History of Norodom Sihanouk* she used extensive makeup, including false, protruding teeth, bronze skin, and black, glossy hair to turn her French performers into Cambodian-like people (Bradby and Williams 1988, 110).

*Environment*

Skin condition and color are greatly influenced by all aspects of the environment. If a person lives in the Southwest and works outdoors all day, the look (and feel) of her face, hands, and hair will be significantly different from that of a person who lives in a gray, rainy climate; or is wealthy and frequents spas and beauty salons; or has just come in from windy, -20 degree weather.

Makeup and hairstyle can be adjusted to communicate the changing circumstances of the performance. If a character has just awakened, his hair might be messy. If the same character is drunk, his makeup might be smeared or reddened. If another character has been running, her face and hair might be wet. When environmental circumstances change, adjustments in makeup and hairstyle signify these changes.

Whether an environment is realistic or otherworldly also determines makeup choices. When Richard Foreman directed *Woyzeck* his goal was to create an environment of desolation and emptiness. He concocted a world inhabited by zombies, a "ubiquitous chorus of dull-witted people [who were] made up in ghoulish white with red eye sockets" (Kalb 1990, 71).

*Profession*

The nature of dramatic action is such that it often places a character's profession at the focal point of his actions and choices. For JoAnne Akalaitis's production of *Cymbeline* the Queen wore a flaming red wig and kimono as a means of identifying the Oriental style of the production, the inflamed nature of the character, and her royal stature.

*Temperament/Personality*

If a character possesses a flamboyant and outgoing personality (like Falstaff or Big Daddy), makeup aids in signaling this trait—exaggerated features such as a large nose or red hair might be employed. In some highly stylized productions, such as melodramas or Kabuki theater, characters represent types (virgin, hero, bad guy). Postmodern directors often employ masklike makeup and exaggerated hairstyle to depict distorted aspects of the human condition. In most plays, however, characters constantly shift their energy and emotional states—one moment happy, another moment terrified, yet another moment worn out. Performers can change their makeup and hairstyle during the course of the performance to signify shifts in emotions, actions, or tensions.

## Health

Makeup in particular but also hairstyle can communicate a character's state of health. From a person's physical appearance we can see whether or not someone is ill or well, tired or energized. Plays focusing on health issues such as AIDS (*The Normal Heart*), pestilence (*The Plague*), and hypochondria (*The Imaginary Invalid*) present opportunities to use makeup as a way of keeping the audience informed about the progress of a character's illness.

## Age

Makeup and hairstyle help set the age of a character. It is rare for the cast of a play to be perfectly matched with the age of their characters. In professional repertory theaters in which a company of performers play a variety of roles in a number of plays, makeup and the use of wigs can stretch the age range of the company.

Makeup and hairstyle are not isolated sign systems. Like all the sign systems of the theater, they interact with other systems. Several sign systems convey messages about age, health, and emotional states. Movement of the body, costume, loudness of speech, choice of words, and others can all signify fifty years old, of Chinese descent, dying of cancer, and damn mad about it.

## Material for Signification

The design elements that makeup artists and coiffeurs have at their disposal are color, line, shape, texture, and composition. The materials they use to encode the performer are makeup (greasepaint, pancake), pencils, powder, putty, crepe hair, wigs, latex, artificial blood, and tooth paint. Makeup artists and coiffeurs work with these design elements and materials in order to adjust, shape, and color the complexion and hair; this encoding provides meanings for the spectators.

Makeup and hairstyle can be used to reflect more than just character traits. Emotional states, dramatic action, given circumstances (time of day, weather conditions, time period, place), and performance style can also be communicated.

Postmodern directors often range widely in their employment of makeup and hairstyle. They may use no makeup or, more typically, employ makeup extensively and abstractly. It is not unusual to see blackface, whiteface, exaggerated eyes, ears, noses, or abnormal hair color. To change the natural appearance of performers in order to call attention to their mechanical, pathological, otherworldly, ephemeral, or historical uniqueness, directors have taken cues from such diverse areas as vaudeville, the circus, silent movies, high fashion, melodrama, puppetry, and Asian theater to produce stunning visual images of people who arise from the extremes of the imagination and dreams. In most cases these directors choose to signify a dehumanized, disjointed, fantastic, or topsy-turvy world.

## Summary

A theatrical event without performers is difficult to imagine. Performers can be puppets, animals, or mechanical devices, but the vast majority of theater performances have human performers interacting with human spectators. While there are many other sign systems at work in most performances, live performers remain the theater's chief signifiers, even for most postmodern productions. The performers' personalities, the way they interpret (and therefore deliver) the dialogue, the way they move and gesture, how they manipulate their faces and use makeup and hairstyles, all provide signifiers that are interpreted by the audience. For most theater performances the primary focus of spectators is on the performers: what they do and say and how they look and move renders the core meanings. Developing a vision of the ideal performance and then, through casting and rehearsals, getting the performers to create that vision onstage is the special province of the director. As we have seen, many directors have redefined the role of the performers, asking them to employ boldly theatrical and often abstract gestures, vocalizations, movements, makeup, and the like as a means of communicating the directors' postmodern visions.

# Chapter 5

# Visual Systems

One of the intriguing aspects of live theater is that it takes place in three-dimensional space. A study of theater history reveals a constant shifting and evolution of theater space for both formal and informal performances. In all cases, however, the spectator becomes part of the theater space, which for contemporary audiences can range from a formal proscenium arch theater to an outdoor setting to a converted garage, loft, or barn. Yet no matter where a performance takes place there is always some form of visual setting that serves as an environment or backdrop for the performance's action. Trees, lawn, and sky provide the setting for outdoor performances; black walls and exposed lighting provide the setting for many experimental or laboratory performances; and elaborate scenic backdrops or three-dimensional scenery support most professional productions. Performers usually wear clothing and makeup chosen to reflect their character's personality and socioeconomic status. Performers' bodies, furniture, and properties festoon the stage. Natural or sculpted light illuminates the performers and visual elements of a performance. And each of these visual components normally radiates one or more colors.

These components—space, setting, costumes, properties, and lighting—are the visual sign systems of the theater event. A performance is visual art: viewing its components provides an aesthetic experience in and of itself. Mood, location, historical or geographic context, style, and emotion are communicated through the visual sign systems of the theater. Several postmodern directors have found that the visual sign systems of the theater are the most consequential signifiers. "Often I've developed the visual aspect of the performance to a point where it becomes the major emotional element affecting the audience" (Foreman 1992, 147). When all the visual elements unite with the performer's sign systems, and with the framing and aural systems, the full impact of a performance is experienced by the audience.

## Space

A spectator who enters a theater enters a specific space. A spectator's perception of the theater space—its length, width, height, shape, and feel—is part of the total experience of the performance. There are, however, other dimensions that affect the spectator's experience. How is the space entered by the audience? How is it divided? Are the spectators separated from the performers? Where do the performers enter the space? If there is a stage, where is it located? How large is it? Is it elevated or sunken?

Each director answers these questions differently. Peter Brook, for example, calls for an empty space.

> An empty space entails the elimination of all that is superfluous—the polar opposite of the constant wastage and excess which exists in life, where we are bombarded by thousands of impressions incessantly. Theater doesn't reproduce life, it suggests it by clearing away and freeing up the space around the action. . . . In a space swept clear of all superfluities, it is possible to inhabit several different "times" at once. (1992, 107)

Richard Foreman calls for a gymnasium for the mind.

> The playing space is an environment for the text to explore, a gymnasium for a psychic, spiritual, and physical workout. It's an exercise room, a factory, an examination room, and a laboratory. If the mise-en-scène does not pay homage to all this, it castrates the full body of the theatre. (1992, 54)

Josef Svoboda calls for a massive space.

> His use of space, light, projections, colors, kinetics, mirrors and form have startled and amazed. He is a magician—a transformer of space who sees not merely a script or the actor, but an audio-visual-kinetic totality in which all elements of theatre combine to express a single idea. (Aronson 1987, 25)

Jerzy Grotowski calls for an intimate space.

> For each production, he claimed, "the essential concern is finding the proper spectator/actor relationship for each type of performance and embodying the decision in physical arrangements." (Braun 1982, 195)

Spaces and spatial arrangement have a profound effect on the type of experience the audience will have. Two extreme examples of theater spaces are the proscenium theater and the environmental theater.

> In the orthodox theatre, including so-called open stages, such as arenas, thrust stages, and caliper stages, the stage is brightly lit and active; from it information flows into the darkened auditorium where the audience is arranged in regular seats. Feedback from the house to the stage is limited.
> Environmental theater encourages give-and-take throughout a globally organized space in which the areas occupied by the audience are a kind of sea through which the performers swim; and the performance areas are kinds of islands or continents in the midst of the audience. The audience does not sit in regularly arranged rows; there is one whole space rather than two opposing spaces. The environmental use of space is fundamentally collaborative; the action flows in many directions sustained only by the cooperation of performers and spectators. (Schechner 1973, 37–39)

As figure 12 shows, theater space can be used in very different ways to give unique experiences to the audience. In a proscenium theater the audience is separated from the performer by the proscenium arch. There is communication, but it is mostly one-directional; it allows for little intimacy but offers a deep and broad visual perspective. Although they sit next to one another, the spectators do not actually see one another—just the backs of heads. Nor do the spectators sit within the scenographic environment. Robert Wilson's emphasis on visual communication has led him to use proscenium theaters exclusively. "I like the formality and distance of a proscenium theatre. My work is usually conceived in terms of a two-dimensional space where one side is hidden. You don't see the ropes or the lights. . . . I can't see in other kinds of spaces, my eye goes all around and I can't see the actor for someone scratching in the audience" (Quoted in Shyer 1989, 164).

In an environmental theater, spectators are mixed in with performers: they are within the scenographic environment; they share the same space; they can touch and feel, as well as see and hear, not only the performers but also one another.

> In Grotowski's productions not only has the proscenium arch been abolished, not only do actors address the spectators directly, walking and sitting among them; but all division between stage

**Proscenium Theater**

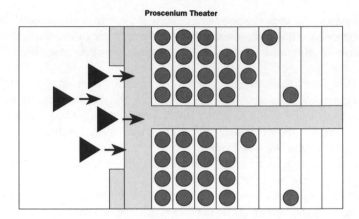

**Environmental Theater**

 = Performers;  ● = Audience.

Fig. 12.  Performer-audience interaction in proscenium and environmental theaters

and auditorium has been eliminated. . . . At the Thirteen Rows the duality of stage-auditorium has been substituted by uniform theatre space. The whole auditorium, as well as the original stage area have become the acting space. (Burzynski and Osinski 1979, 13–14)

The audience's experience is not necessarily better in one type of theater than another, but the encounters are vitally different. Wilson and Grotowski are seeking opposite experiences for their spectators, and they employ space specifically to aid the spectator in constructing meanings.

Numerous other arrangements of space for performance are possible, including:

Apron stage
Thrust stage
Arena stage
Surround stage
Found space: streets, parks, churches, lobbies, etc.
Converted space: enhanced nontheater space
Circus/carnival/parade space
Sporting event spaces

Apron, thrust, and arena stages bring the spectators in view of one another and allow for greater intimacy. In these spaces the audience remains outside the stage environment—they are looking on.

A surround stage places the audience in the center of the theater space; the action takes place on a stage or multiple stage spaces that surround the audience (see fig. 7). The audience is inside the stage environment but not part of the world of the setting. The spectator is still looking into the world of the performers.

Found space is any existing space that is taken over and used for a performance event without alteration. No scenic environment is placed in the space. A church houses a medieval mystery or morality play. A street corner hosts an improvisation. Guerrilla theater is staged in front of a nuclear power plant. A Midsummer Night's Dream is performed in a forest. Found spaces usually result in the mixing of performers and audience; there are no specific seating areas. Indeed, spectators may be asked to participate in the performance event. Physical contact between performers and spectators or between spectators and spectators is likely.

Converted spaces are found spaces that are transformed by adding designated seating and/or architectural or scenic pieces that help locate the action of the performance. A street becomes a converted space by adding a medieval-style pageant wagon, a scenic tent, or by hanging banners that define the locale of the performance. Garages and lofts are converted into theaters by adding scenic pieces and/or movable platforms and chairs. For Ariane Mnouchkine's production of L'Age *d'Or* a cartridge warehouse hanger "was transformed by piling tons of earth into dunes, covered with hessian matting. The audience sat on these slopes, moving from space to space as invited by the performers. No other scenic elements were used" (Bradby and Williams 1988, 97). Even a proscenium arch theater can be converted by taking out the traditional seating or by putting the audience on the stage and building a stage in the auditorium. For his production of *Agamemnon* in 1977 at the Vivian Beaumont theater Andrei Serban had two sets of spectators, a group in the auditorium and another assemblage on stage sitting on bleachers that "continually move[d] to change the acting space" (Kissel 1977, 237).

A converted space is usually more fixed than a found space: the audience sits here, the performing area is there, this piece of scenery will show that the play takes place in seventeenth-century Italy, and so on.

> The scope of the environmental designer's responsibility extends to organizing the total space, selecting materials, determining construction technique, and considering the associational and intrinsic value of each aspect of design. The traditional division of space into lobby, stage, technical areas, backstage and auditorium is, in this kind of theatre, no longer considered to be immutable, but is subject to organization and reorganization according to a particular production concept. Traditionally, spatial arrangements are imposed on a production, as in theatres with fixed seating. The environmentalist, however, feels that aesthetic considerations should determine movement and performer-audience arrangements.
>
> Typically the environmental designer's impulse begins with architectural and engineering considerations because he has to serve a new kind of physically oriented actor, an actively participating audience and a concept that views space, time and action in terms of an immediate living experience. Therefore, the designer is concerned with the total disposition of space and its related problems— not only problems of production, but also those involved with building codes, safety, comfort, public services, and the peculiar engineering and construction difficulties that arise when a whole complex of theatre experiences are placed under one roof. Thus, in the environmental production, the interaction and negotiation between performers and audience require a sharing of facilities which implies not so much stage design but architecture. In essence, the designer becomes a hybrid architect-designer who conceives of a totally new theatre for each production. (Rojo 1974, 20–21)

Circus/carnival/parade spaces are special performance spaces, for each defines a unique audience-event relationship. A circus normally consists of fixed seating that encircles a one-, two-, or three-ring performance space. Multiple events taking place simultaneously split the spectators' focus and provide a high state of sensory stimulation. The same multisensory stimulation takes place at a carnival, but spectators at a carnival move from booth to booth and can be highly selective in their focus. A parade, on the other hand, calls for relatively fixed seating (on both sides of the street) while the multisectioned event passes in front of them. The spectators experience sequential sensory stimulation: they focus on a portion of the parade as it passes by while experiencing residual signification from the part that has just passed and anticipating the part that is about to come.

In all three instances—circus, carnival, and parade—the spectators are in a special space and environment that affects the amount of aural and visual signification they experience. There are usually so many stimuli that the spectators must select those portions of the event they find most interesting.

Sporting event spaces are highly specialized spaces for hosting athletic events. The natatorium with its swimming pool and bleachers, the football stadium with its athletic field, the sports arena with its basketball floor or ice hockey rink are all highly structured spaces that can be converted for theater performances. The rigidity of the sporting events spaces, however, forces the director and designer to match the playscript or performance piece to the fixed dynamics of the space.

Because space dictates much of the sensory impact of a performance on the spectator, directors seek out the most appropriate space possible for each production. Answers to the following questions shape a director's final decision about the use of space:

Should the audience and performers be separated?

Are the spectators observers of or participants in the event?

Will the audience be required to touch, smell, or interact with the performers?

Will the spectators sit still (in one place) for the entire performance, or will they be asked to move about?

Will the performers have direct eye contact with the spectators?

Will the spectators be inside the environment of the performance, or will they be outside looking in?

Will the entrances and exits for the spectators be the same as those used by the performers?

How many entrance and exit locations are needed?

What is the emotional or psychological feel of the space?
What is the spiritual feel of the space?
Should the space feel open or closed?
Should the space feel warm (friendly) or cold (hostile)?
When should the audience enter? Well before the performance
    starts? Right at the moment the performance starts? After the
    performers have entered the theater space?

The elements of space that can be manipulated by directors and designers are mass, volume, dimension (two- or three-dimensional), and shape (circular, square, rectangular, wide or narrow, deep or shallow, high or low, closed or open). Directors and theater designers have the opportunity to make the theater space an active and primary signifier of the performance's meanings. Examples of their predilections abound. Robert Wilson chooses massive two-dimensional space. "There are three basic things that Bob does. There's the back wall, the floor and then the elements within that. It's a very classical use of stage space. Very horizontal, integrated, lack of decoration. Wing and drop, very little departure from that" (Tom Kamm, quoted in Shyer 1989, 165). Richard Foreman "has stated that his use of space can be described as 'cubistic' insofar as the conscious rationale behind his manipulation of space, performers, and objects is to 'tilt things' or display a variety of angles and perspectives" (Davy 1981, 41). "Grotowski's overtly manipulative spatial design [for *Dr. Faustus*, 1963] was intended specifically to provoke and dismay the spectators into authentic human reactions, the actors' aggressive physicality and raw emotionality taking place literally inches from their faces" (Bradby and Williams 1988, 120). In each case the director has chosen to use space in divergent ways but has succeeded in affecting his audience's reading of the performance; the space provides both a message and a frame for the other visual sign systems.

The three major choices that a director makes when defining space for a production can be represented by continua.

Open
Space

Confined
Space

Traditional
Theater

Nontraditional
Space

Audience Separate
from Performers

Audience Mixed
with Performers

After the director locates her use of space on these three continua she is ready to experiment with proxemics, picturization, and blocking. Once she has developed guidelines for these spatial elements, she will be able to explore the other visual sign systems.

## Proxemics

The first step toward designing the production's mise-en-scène (after defining the theater space) is to determine the nature of the space in which the performers will move by developing a ground plan of the stage space. The ground plan determines the movement possibilities for the performers as well as the potential spatial relationships possible between performers or among groups of performers. The physical distance between people relates to social, cultural, and environmental factors, and changes in physical relationships among performers are part of the way in which information is conveyed to the spectator. Proxemics is the study of space as it relates to physical distances between people, and the production ground plan is a key factor in determining the proxemic probabilities for the performers. The ground plan includes a pictorial representation of entrances and exits; an outline of the location of the set (or set pieces); the location of windows, doors, etc.; the floor area (the performer's space), stairways, ramps, etc.; platforms or pits; trapdoors; the location of furniture and freestanding props; and the location of curtains or other masking material.

According to Edward Hall (1966) there are three types of space: fixed-feature space, semifixed-feature space, and informal space. Fixed-feature space defines the parameters of the acting area: the location of the permanent walls, columns, doorways, fireplaces, windows, platforms, stairways, and so forth. Semifixed-feature space identifies those objects in the stage environment that have size, shape, and substance but that can be moved during the performance: furniture, props, and scenery pieces. All the scenic effects and furniture in a production can be semifixed-feature space if there are different settings for multiple scenes. The third type of space is informal space. This is open space; it has no structural definition.

An example of fixed-feature space is the Elizabethan theater, which has an open-thrust acting space, a fixed level above, and two entrances, one on each side of the stage. Furniture and scenic pieces were kept to a minimum in Elizabethan times, and the playwright often created a change of scenery through dialogue. An example of a semifixed-feature space is the stage of a multiscene production for which every scene has a different setting and furniture. Informal space is the space that flows around the walls, doorways, and furniture of a room; the trees, fences, and water fountains of a park; or the counters, escalators, and cash registers of a department store. This is the space through which the performers move.

A director uses proxemics in his dynamic and ever-changing manipulation of space and spatial relationships among the setting, objects, and performers. A stage space that is compact and cluttered with objects and performers signifies very different tensions, relationships, moods, and meanings from one that is vast and contains only one chair and one performer.

## Picturization and Blocking

Signification in the theater takes place when spectators observe stage "pictures" in either a static or kinetic format. That is, spectators observe onstage frozen moments as well as an ever-flowing sequence of stage pictures that result in constantly changing signification.

The placement of static performers and scenery is termed *picturization*, while the movement pattern of the performers is called *blocking*. The chief functions of picturization and blocking are:

To allow the performers to be seen by the spectators
To move characters on, around, and off the stage
To communicate through visual composition (static and kinetic, realistic and abstract)
To communicate character relationships, motivations, and emotions
To focus communication by providing emphasis
To represent the performance's style kinetically

How performers move onstage and how their characters form patterns of spatial relationships among themselves and with the scenic elements reveal much about the tensions and alliances outlined in the dramatic action of a playscript. Peter Brook is noted for creating simple yet powerful stage pictures. For his production of Chekhov's *The*

*Cherry Orchard* there was a special quality to "Brook's carefully composed groupings, which have the artful posed air of Victorian photographs, or might suggest paintings, a Manet picnic, or one of those Russian genre interiors" (Barnes 1988, 364).

In nonlinear theater pieces, picturization and blocking may appear highly abstract or symbolic and yet reveal significant nonliteral meanings. Postmodern theater often relies on pictures, visionscapes, abstract movement, and video and film images to provide the primary means of signification. Robert Wilson and Josef Svoboda use the power of stage architecture, movement of performers, and modern technology to produce aesthetically vibrant kinetic productions. For Wilson's production of *Hamletmachine* he created highly unique movements.

An independent choreography [was] made up of slow, ritualistic entrances and simple actions and gestures: a man hitting his head on a table, three women scratching their heads in unison, a man leaning over a wall, another hopping across the space on one leg, a woman turning in a swivel chair—all of which were activated by the sound of Japanese wood blocks. (Shyer 1989, 129)

A look at the semiotics of distance and spatial relationships of traditional theater is perhaps the best way to begin to understand how picturization and blocking may play a commanding role in any theatrical production.

*Spatial Relationships*

Edward Hall identified four major classifications of distances that are meaning-bearing signifiers of people and their social interactions. The four distances are intimate, personal, social, and public. Hall further defines the four spatial relationships by subdividing them into close and far phases. These classifications can guide directors in developing the static placement and movement of performers in and around the stage space. Directors must realize, however, that the codes of the theater are different from everyday life. Hall's four distances must be adjusted to fit the unique circumstances of each theater and each production. For example, distances that might appear intimate in a tiny theater could read quite differently in a large outdoor performance space.

Hall observed that the type of spatial relationship a person establishes with another is based on variables such as personality (shy, self-confident, aggressive), emotional attitude at the moment (amorous, angry, lonely), territoriality (Is the location neutral, mine, or yours?), and relationship to other people (mother, employer, athletic opponent, stranger). Armed with an understanding of a production's given circumstances, characterizations, and dramatic action, the director moves performers about the theater space in ways that signify meanings. The distances that characters keep from one another and from the audience and the way both enter or exit are signifiers. Spatial relationships provide rich information about each character, including her relationship to other characters and the shifting emotional tensions produced by the dramatic action.

Spatial relationships between spectators and performers and between spectators and other spectators produce signifiers. In this regard there is a quadruple dynamic working during a performance. One reference point involves the distances among the performers within the playing space. A second involves the distances between the performers as a group and the audience as a group. A third dynamic exists between individual performers and individual spectators. The fourth concerns the distances between the individual spectators and other spectators. At a given moment I (as spectator) see/experience the distances among performers, the distances between performers on stage and me as a member of the collective audience, the distances between me (from my exact location) and each individual performer (in their exact locations), and the distances between me and each individual spectator. All four of these distance dynamics exist simultaneously throughout the constantly changing performance and provide signifiers to be read and interpreted.

Hall offers a detailed explanation about how people share space and what it reveals about them and their relationships to other people. His observations are worth quoting at some length here, because they reveal a code through which people may decode spatial signifiers.

> *Intimate Distance—Close Phase* (touching)
> This is the distance of love-making and wrestling, comforting and protecting. Physical contact or the high possibility of physical involvement is uppermost in the awareness of both persons. . . . In the maximum contact phase, the muscles and skin communicate.
>
> *Intimate Distance—Far Phase* (6 to 18 inches)
> Heads, thighs, and pelvis are not easily brought into contact, but hands can reach and grasp extremities.

*Personal Distance—Close Phase* (1¹/₂ to 2¹/₂ feet)

The kinesthetic sense of closeness derives in part from the possibilities present in regard to what each participant can do to the other with his extremities. At this distance, one can hold or grasp the other person. . . . Where people stand in relation to each other signals their relationship, or how they feel toward each other, or both.

*Personal Distance—Far Phase* (2¹/₂ to 4 feet)

Keeping someone at "arm's length" is one way of expressing the far phase of personal distance. It extends from a point that is just outside easy touching distance by one person to a point where two people can touch fingers if they extend both arms. This is the limit of physical domination in the very real sense. . . . Subjects of personal interest and involvement can be discussed at this distance.

*Social Distance—Close Phase* (4 to 7 feet)

Intimate visual detail in the face is not perceived, and nobody touches or expects to touch another person unless there is some special effort. . . . Impersonal business occurs at this distance, and in the close phase there is more involvement than in the distant phase. People who work together tend to use close social distance. It is also a very common distance for people who are attending a casual social gathering. To stand and look down at a person at this distance has a domineering effect.

*Social Distance—Far Phase* (7 to 12 feet)

This is the distance to which people move when someone says, "Stand away so I can look at you." Business and social discourse conducted at the far end of social distance has a more formal character than if it occurs inside the close phase. . . . A proxemic feature of social distance (far phase) is that it can be used to insulate or screen people from each other. This distance makes it possible for them to continue to work in the presence of another person without appearing to be rude.

*Public Distance—Close Phase* (12 to 25 feet)

At twelve feet an alert subject can take evasive or defensive action if threatened. The distance may even cue a vestigial but subliminal form of flight reaction.

*Public Distance—Far Phase* (25 feet or more)
>Thirty feet is the distance that is automatically set around important public figures. . . . The usual public distance is not restricted to public figures but can be used by anyone on public occasions. There are certain adjustments that must be made, however. Most actors know that at thirty or more feet the subtle shades of meaning conveyed by the normal voice are lost as are the details of facial expression and movement. Not only the voice but everything else must be exaggerated or amplified. Much of the nonverbal part of the communication shifts to gestures and body stance. (1966, 117–25)

Hall's basic distance relationships provide a starting point for developing a working methodology for directors in blocking or picturing traditional productions. A director's hypothetical mise-en-scène ought to contain a vision of the characters moving around the stage space in relationship to other characters—their intimacy or lack thereof, motivational intensity, emotional state, and attempts to dominate or be submissive. Directors need to take cognizance of the distances that exist between performers and individual spectators as well. The reading of spatial relationships not only depends on the relationship between performers but also on the distance between those performers and individual audience members. This is especially important if the audience members are sitting literally in the playing space.

>To transfer Hall's comprehensive analysis of behavior directly to the stage is a catastrophic mistake. A stage differs from real life in a way that is essentially proxemic. . . . The fundamental relationship of the theater is not between two actors, but between the two of them and those who watch: when the contract of mutual responsibility is broken, the stage dies and the theatre is void. The stage is a vicarious simulation, looping through the behaviors not only of those who perform but of others who do not. (Huston 1992,113)

Many directors believe that the physical relationship of performers to one another and their constant adjustments through movement must be motivated by the dramatic action of the playscript or performance piece in order to be justified. They believe that without such motivation the characters' movements will confuse rather than clarify communication between performers and spectators by providing false signifiers. A few innovative directors, such as Peter Sellars and Martha Clarke, however, are using movement in more abstract and unpredictable (unmotivated) ways. In their productions characters may move in aesthetically extraordinary ways so that basic distance relationships between characters may not appear logically motivated by the story or dramatic action. Such experiments are often startling to the audience but also beguiling. "When working solely with movement, I go into a completely abstract vein" (Martha Clarke interview, in Bartow 1988a, 58). For her production of *The Garden of Earthly Delights* ten dancers moved about the stage creating an illusion of unreality, which was solidified when they "celestially somersaulted through the air on cables" (Bartow 1988b, 12). Such movement defies reality and challenges the audience to experience abstraction itself as a signifier.

*Reasons for Movement*

In life people move to and fro for reasons. When a child climbs the stairs there is a reason; perhaps she is determined to learn how to "conquer" these formidable steps, perhaps she is angry with her parents and wants to get away from them, or perhaps she wants to see what Daddy is doing making all that noise upstairs. In most theater performances physical activity is also motivated by human impulses. Directors generate signifiers through performers' movements that are rooted in the characters' impulses and motivations. But these movements do not have to be realistic. Directors can create abstract kinetic patterns that produce a rich mosaic of signifiers that may or may not bring unity to all the visual components of the mise-en-scène. For example, if the director and designers choose angularity as one of the guiding motifs of the production, they will implement this goal in the ground plan, sets, costumes, lighting, and properties for the production. The director will then guide the placement of the performers and their movement (as signifiers) to reflect the angularity of the other visual elements.

Picturization and blocking, then, are highly complex components of a performance's visual sign systems that act as signifiers for spectators about characters' personalities, motivations, and emotional states and the playscript's dramatic action. For postmodern productions, movements are often more abstract, inharmonious, bizarre, or at odds with normal audience expectations. In such cases abstract or eccentric movement simply becomes part of the performance's meanings.

*Performer Visibility*

It would be ideal for all the spectators to see all the characters' physical features all the time. As a practical consideration, however, this is not possible. If a spectator sees the front of a performer's body and head, he is unable to see the performer's back. In an arena, environmental, or street performance one spectator may see the front of a performer, while another will view his back. Even in a proscenium theater, in which all of the spectators are facing one direction, there will be differences in perception because of the relative distance and variations in angle from different seating locations.

There is no way, then, that a director can keep all the performer's physical features in full view of all the spectators all the time. Directors, however, try to place performers so that the appropriate visual sign systems engage all of the spectators enough of the time to provide sufficient stimulation to keep them fully engaged and to insure some unanimity of experience.

### Entrances, Exits, and Required Activity

Performances that are based on a playscript have certain required character placements and movements built in. Characters are required to enter or exit the stage from specific locations at specific points in the dialogue. For example, Hamlet must enter the stage early enough to see his uncle, Claudius, praying; if Hamlet does not witness this event, the play's action cannot proceed. Also, a character may need to be at a specific place on the stage at a specific point in a performance. The Imaginary Invalid must be in bed when the doctor arrives, or the scene loses its point. Most playscripts have dozens, if not hundreds, of required placements, movements, and activities. Directors and performers may find ways of justifying these required physical placements or movements within the context of a character's personality and the production's dramatic action, or they may choose to ignore these requirements in order to present a disjointed or peculiar series of stage pictures untethered from motivational expectations.

### Visual Composition

A theater performance is a kinetic sculpture with its own aesthetic value and meanings, which are separate from the linguistic and aural sign systems. We could liken this to a silent mime or dance performance, in which the visual experience alone provides the event's meanings. Keeping this in mind, directors encode the performers' placements and movements in order to represent emotions and conflicts and to create an overall visual aesthetic statement. The impact of this statement might be intellectual, emotional, or spiritual or, more likely, a combination of all three. Just as a great painting moves its perceiver, the performance's mise-en-scène, when properly orchestrated, provides profound insight into the event's meanings.

## Defining Relationships, Motivations, and Emotions

Except for required character placements and movements, most picturization and movement come about naturally as a requirement of a production's dramatic action and given circumstances. By guiding character placements and movements, directors provide precise signifiers of character relationships, motivations, and emotional shifts, which are, in turn, interpreted by the spectators. If all movements and picturizations are the outgrowth of individual characters' human impulses, and if they are consistent with the playscript's or performance piece's given circumstances and dramatic action, the communicative potential will be fully realized. If, on the other hand, a director chooses a poetic, mystical, or abstract visual scheme for her production, the visual aesthetics will be markedly different. For example, Wilson's *CIVIL warS* "rests in a timeless landscape in which Ninjas fly through the air, giraffes talk and the Monitor and the Merrimac do battle; the world's tallest woman crosses a cabbage patch with a dwarf in her hand, children fly a hot air balloon down the Grand Canyon and Madame Curie rides her bicycle in an underwater flower garden." These disjointed, fragmented visual images "become a pageant of human civilization, a parable of a race fated either for apocalypse or redemption" (Coe 1985, 4).

## Emphasis

The placement of performers on the stage and their movement about the stage have important technical consequences. Placement and movement are two of the most forceful techniques for achieving emphasis onstage (semioticians call this foregrounding). Emphasis is here defined as the locus of the audience's attention at any given moment of the performance. In other words, the element of the mise-en-scène that receives the attention of the audience can be said to have achieved emphasis (just as quotation marks and italics can give "emphasis" to the word *emphasis*).

Directors pay close attention to the use of emphasis in the theater. Without a conscious attempt to maneuver the focus of the spectators, directors may find that each spectator is paying attention to a different aspect of the performance: one is looking at a special lighting effect, another is listening to the words of the protagonist, another is looking at another spectator who is fidgeting in his seat. If this kind of diffused focus prevails throughout a performance, each spectator will leave the event with a very different perception of the performance's meanings. While there will never be complete unity of perceptive experience among the spectators, the director, if he so chooses, plays an important role in minimizing the diffusion of focus and loss of sign perception by consciously employing techniques to focus the attention of the audience on selected characters, places, or things.

Body position: Performers who are facing full front (or facing the majority of the audience, in the case of environmental or arena staging) are more likely to receive emphasis than those who are turned away.

Positions of performers relative to one another: Two or more performers will share equal emphasis if they have the same relative position on stage—for instance, if they are positioned full front or are turned one-quarter toward one another.

Acting area positions: On a proscenium stage the performer positioned in the most centralized area or the one that is closest to the audience is more likely to receive the spectator's attention.

Levels: As a guiding principle, if performers are placed at different levels onstage, the one above all others is most emphasized.

Isolation: Isolating one performer from the other performers onstage emphasizes the lone individual.

Environmental amplification: The central element of a stage setting can draw attention to a performer who is positioned in front of or adjacent to it.

Other methods of achieving emphasis are:

Eye focus: If all the performers onstage are looking at one performer, the spectators will also look at that person.

Color: If one character's costume is bright relative to the other costumes, it will achieve emphasis.

Lighting: The use of special effects in lighting—area color and/or varying intensities—can produce emphasis.

Movement: A moving character will be emphasized.

Speaking: Spectators normally focus their attention on the character who is speaking.

There are many ways to manipulate the attention of the audience. The examples described above, however, are of little use to nontraditional directors who employ juxtaposition, layering, and montage to create idiosyncratic patterns of signs. Postmodern directors may in fact create a nonemphasized production in which spectators are expected to watch and listen to whatever attracts their attention. Indeed, Richard Foreman encourages each spectator's eyes to roam the total mise-en-scène.

I like to assume that the spectator is watching the entire stage at all moments of the play, so I try to make a stage picture in which every inch of the stage dynamically participates in the moment-by-moment composition of the piece. I might carefully adjust the tiniest detail, far away from what seems to be the focus of attention in a scene, because I want to maintain the compositional attention across the entire panorama of the stage. (1992, 55)

Most nontraditional directors believe spectators create their own meanings through a process of personal foci, associations, and preferences. "Theater people should accept the fact that their work will always arouse multiple associations, that theater is not a matter of simple, direct, conscious communication" (Hornby 1987, 33).

As we have seen, space is central to the performance's meanings. Directors know that the size, shape, and configuration of the theater space dictates a performance's mise-en-scène. The setting, properties, costumes, and lighting will each be constrained or liberated by the mass, volume, and shape of the performance space. Some postmodern directors even look outside the traditional theater space for an appropriate place to bring a concept, script, performers, and audience together. For others the proscenium stage is chosen but used in imaginative new ways. In either case, however, space is seen as a pivotal element in the dialectical relationship between the performance and its spectators.

## Setting

While the director and designer(s) share responsibility in making decisions about the layout and design of the environment and space for the performance, the director remains the final decision maker. Because judgments about the arrangement and use of space affect so many future acting-related decisions, the director must be the final architect of the production's space. Directors who emphasize the visual sign systems in their performances often form a close relationship with a single designer: "JoAnne Akalaitis and Douglas Stein, Andrei Serban and Michael Yeargan, Peter Sellars and Adrianne Lobel, Martha Clarke and Robert Israel. The ideas they evolve are symbiotic, with the designer assuming as much responsibility for the directorial interpretation as the director does for the design" (Brustein 1991, 232–33). Some visually oriented directors, such as Robert Wilson and Richard Foreman, simply design their own mise-en-scènes. It is interesting to note that Wilson began his career studying architecture and fine art, while Foreman was a scene designer in high school. It is little wonder that their theater aesthetic evokes landscapes and visual collages as governing signifiers.

The set designer either takes the director's concept or vision (if she has one) and develops a visual design that is intended to reflect the meanings of the playscript or performance piece or else works with the director to evolve a single vision. The relationship between the designer and the director can be represented by a continuum. At one end is the director who has a specific vision for the mise-en-scène. This director may design the production himself or ask a designer to simply draw up his preformed ideas. At the other end is the director who has little knowledge of (or interest in) the theater's visual elements, or who has such faith in her designer that she trusts his independent judgment. This director delegates responsibility for the setting or environment to the designer.

Director                                                         Designer
Designs                                                         Designs

Even though we happen to be talking here of the set designer, the same continuum applies to the director's relationship with the other designers.

The relationship between the director, designer, and playwright is often complicated. At times it may involve a power struggle.

A man writes a play. It contains an implied vision of the world he has created. Another man, the director, reads it. He conjures up another vision. A third man is given the same play. In him, yet another vision of that world is evoked. He is then told to "design it"—that is, to take his vision, coalesce it with the visions of the other two men, and materialize it.

Since each of the three men in this process—the writer, the director, and the designer—tends to be creative in his own right, it is foolhardy to expect the three separate visions to combine as one. The playwright, according to the unwritten rules that govern play production, relinquishes *his* vision of the work as soon as the director creates *his*, and the designer, if he is worth his salt, brings his own distinctive view of the whole. From the outset, three visual conceptions of the work compete for precedence. As soon as performers are brought into the equation, additional notions of style, shape, and color arrive with them.

Which vision ultimately dominates depends on the weight and influence of the respective collaborators. An established director with a clear personal view can usually call the tune. Sometimes, if the strongest member of the triumvirate is the playwright, he can insist on the supremacy of *his* vision. More often than not, because a certain kind of politesse tempers all power struggles, the designer's conception is compromised by the needs of the director and the preferences of the playwright. Sometimes, where a star designer is involved, the director gratefully accepts his visual concoctions and adapts his production accordingly. (Marowitz 1986, 42–43)

Charles Marowitz operates on the left side of the designer-director continuum; he believes the director's vision is paramount and that designers work to render the director's vision, not their own.

While the director is responsible for the mise-en-scène of the performance, there is a wide range of working methodologies that can produce the desired outcome. Which methodology the director chooses depends on the following variables:

The extent to which the director has a well-tuned visual aesthetic sensibility

Whether or not the playwright is involved in the development of the performance

The quality and forcefulness of the designer(s)

The relative importance or centrality of the visual aspects of the production. Is the emphasis on the acting? The verbal elements (reader's theater)? The spectacle?

The technical capabilities of the theater/performance space

The extent to which the coartists develop a trusting relationship

The visionary experience and skill levels of the designer(s)

It is the director's responsibility to get the most from each of the collaborative artists; by treating each one as an individual, the collective result is likely to be of high quality.

### Determining the Environment

What is the purpose of a theater environment or stage setting? Is it possible to have a theater performance without an environment or setting? How does a setting or environment serve as a signifier? How does an environment help a spectator construct meanings?

A stage setting or theater environment, properly conceived and executed, exposes the core meanings of the performance. "A setting is not just a beautiful thing, a collection of beautiful things. It is a presence, a mood, a warm wind fanning the drama to flame. It echoes, it enhances, it animates. It is an expectancy, a foreboding, a tension. It says nothing, but it gives everything" (R. E. Jones 1941, 26). The setting or environment presents dramatic action in visual form: it is a signifier of the performance's meanings. Josef Svoboda is particularly well known for emphasizing the significative supremacy of a production's visual elements.

> In a Svoboda production, the design is equal to the script and the performer. Svoboda has compared scenography to a section of instruments in a symphony orchestra with the director as conductor—design, like the woodwinds, can blend in, dominate, luxuriate in "solo," or fade out altogether as the situation demands. (Aronson 1987, 25)

Not all productions have elaborate sets. Some performances are staged with no setting or environment (other than the unchanged theater space or found space). A director decides how much importance to give to the scenic elements or environment of each production. How much scenery is needed to support the work of the performers and the signification of the dramatic action? Often this question can be answered properly only after addressing further questions: How much technical machinery is available for shifting the scenery (revolves, wagons, flying, trapping)? What is the budget for materials, supplies, and workers? What is the size of the work force available to construct, rig, and paint?

## Purpose of the Scene Design

A performance environment can communicate the following information:

Historical period of the performance
Geographical location (country or city)
Exact place (battlefield, bedroom)
Level of society of the characters
Time of day
Season of the year
Weather conditions
Mood or atmosphere
Emphasis
Visual style

Here again the director has the opportunity to make choices about the importance of different scenic elements. The options available range from using no scenery to using scenery to communicate as many messages as possible. This suggests the following continuum:

**No Communication**            **Complex Communication**
**through Setting**                    **through Setting**

At the far right is a production that uses visual elements as a primary sign system. Here a setting might communicate mood, historical period, location, time of day, season, social level, or the setting might be a dominating, abstract, kinetic, and poetic landscape or sculpture. In the middle of the continuum is a production that might use the set to communicate mood, location, and social level, leaving, for instance, the historical period, time of day, and season unstated. Near the far left is a production that uses scenery to communicate only one element, perhaps mood or place.

Peter Brook uses space to make a profound, understated proclamation. For *The Cherry Orchard,* which was produced in the large, somewhat decayed Brooklyn Academy of Music's Majestic Theatre, Brook used "a few pieces of furniture, some screens, mainly Persian carpets." In the last scene, when the family was leaving, the huge carpet was rolled up, revealing "the bare floor, the kind of simple, telling image for which Brook is famous" (Kissel 1988, 363). For *A Midsummer*

*Night's Dream* he utilized a white box on a white stage—nothing more. For *Carmen* he created a "bullring carpeted with gravel and earth" (Rich 1983, 124). *Mahabharata* had a "deceptively simple setting—the three bare walls of the proscenium, framing a sandpit, a river, and a small pond" (Brustein 1991, 139).

> Similarly, Ariane Mnouchkine employed elemental scenery for *Les Atrides*. Guy-Claude François, the designer, sets the [Greek] cycle in a bare, dusty yard enclosed by a low, chipped concrete wall. It is a kind of corral in which some sort of violence has already taken place: stock-car racing, perhaps, or the breaking-in of wild horses or young bulls; but more likely, to judge from the stains on the walls, mass-execution of enemies without trial. (Ratcliffe 1991, H5)

At the opposite end of the scenic quantity spectrum lie Foreman, Wilson, and Svoboda. Except for rare experiments, such as his production of *Woyzeck*, Foreman eschews empty spaces. "At times I have considered working without sets and props, in an empty theatrical space without the burden of an elaborate physical production. But then I realize that such a naked space does not allow the text to ricochet between levels of meaning, which is my obsession" (1992, 65). Foreman's physical theater is designed to assist in altering the "experience of 'seeing' itself" (Davy 1981, 38). He cannot accomplish this goal through empty space.

Robert Wilson is a landscape artist who believes that the sovereignty of the theater rests in vast yet stark visual images.

> Those privileged to see [Wilson's] *The Forest* were rewarded with a wealth of dazzling, exquisitely executed dream images which remained imprinted on the mind's eye long after the curtain fell; the splitting of the sun into planets, revealing a beached monster on the sand while a child played with a model of a small city; factory workers laboring on huge ladders near massive gears as Gilgamesh smoked in his chair, attended by eerie domestics and a weary lion; the golden Enkidu in his cave, accompanied by an armored knight, a figure in doublet and hose, a man cooking himself in a vat, an outsized porcupine; the slow-motion seduction of Enkidu by a lipstick-stained whore as animals and trees paraded across the stage in stately procession; the rock and ice landscapes of the concluding acts, where the two men joined battle with a dragon. It was a piece designed with such beauty that each stage picture constituted a work of art, reinforcing Wilson's position as one of our greatest visionary artists. (Brustein 1991, 30–31)

## Set Designer's Responsibility

The elements designers use to create stage designs are the same as those employed by artists who draw, paint, or sculpt: line, form, mass, color, unity, balance, rhythm. In oversimplified terms directors and designers orchestrate these elements to produce complex layers of signifiers that are assembled into meanings by spectators as the performance moves through time.

> The chief difference between the art of an easel painter—which is what I started out to be—and that of a scenic artist—which is what I ended up as—is that the scenic artist practices an interpretive art which deals in four dimensions at the same time, the fourth being the dimension of time-space. No matter how pictorially interesting a stage set may be as the curtain rises, its life consists in its continuing development in relation to the movement of the play. The setting may change in pure composition as a result of the shifting movements of the performers. Sometimes it may even change shape before the spectator's eyes. The dramatically effective setting is never static. There are hundreds of picture planes and angles of vision in the theatre, and the stage picture must be satisfying to each member of the audience at all times. Color is not just what has been painted on the canvas but what spotlights or projections can do to it. A three-dimensional plastic setting can shift, as if by magic, to a flat two-dimensional design.
>
> The prime mission of the scenic artist is to establish style (always in conjunction with the director). What is the manner of presentation we are about to witness? The designer must create signposts and symbols, clues and innuendoes, that will communicate instantly to the audience and provide a key to the personalities on the stage. Sometimes this must be achieved in a split second between the rise of the curtain and the first word spoken by the performer. Mood, light, form, color, and even subliminal sound may be the means at the scenic artist's hand. (Mielziner 1965, 18)

The set and space help unify the total performance experience, with all its various sign systems. Will the set help the performers? Complement the costumes? Challenge the visual aesthetics of the audience? Encourage the appropriate movement and picturization? Mesh with the lighting? Fit the space? Reflect a deconstructive vision? The director and designer(s) must insure that the setting and the other visual components of the mise-en-scène merge to form a well-conceived unity or, if desired, that they diverge and clash, bringing discord.

## Designing the Environment

Theatrical environments have style and form. Should the set and furnishings be naturalistic, realistic, romantic, highly abstract, or a mixture? The range of stylistic choices can be represented on a continuum:

Absolute
Naturalism

Radical
Abstraction

Using this continuum, the director and designer begin to locate the visual style of the design. They discuss the playscript or performance piece and the hypothetical performance in terms of the degree of naturalism or abstraction of the setting. Between the left and right extremes lie naturalism, realism, abstract realism, romanticism, impressionism, expressionism, dadaism, postmodernism, and other styles. While directors and designers may not talk in terms of "isms," they do talk about the relative realness or abstractness of a production.

Beyond style there are other important choices that the director and designer make about the environment. Should the set be light or dark? Monotone or multicolored? Small or large? Short or tall? Thin or thick? Narrow or wide? Angular or curved? Ornately decorated or barren? Monolevel or multilevel? Raked or flat floor? These choices will affect both the overcoding of visual signifiers for the spectators and the set's practical usefulness for the performers. Answering each of these questions points the director and designer toward a visual conception.

## Translating the Design into the Set

After the set has been designed it must be transformed from a two-dimensional drawing or a three-dimensional model into a setting on a stage. The director, designer, and technical director have a broad spectrum of technologies, tools, and materials to choose from when transforming a design into a set. The postmodern age has brought to the theater new materials, surfaces, textures, colors, and aesthetic tastes that are reflected in the mise-en-scène. In the not too distant past sets were constructed of wood, steel, canvas, and paint, but today sets are built from every conceivable material, including special metals, rigid plastic, molded plastic, Styrofoam, and glass. For example, when Richard Foreman was having difficulty producing the alienation affect he wanted the audience to experience, he "erected a large glass wall between the actors and the audience as a tactic to remind the spectators that the play was something to be *observed* rather than entered" (Foreman 1992, 269). For Robert Woodruff's production of Brecht's *Baal* at the Trinity Rep, Douglas Stein, the designer, created "a punk high-tech environmental setting, a compound of neon, cellophane, and vinyl" (Brustein 1991, 196).

The postmodern theater has also seen a rise in the use of visual technologies: projected scenery (slides or film), video walls, laser lighting, and holographs. These technologies have led to tantalizingly provocative visual stimulation unheard of only a few years ago. For instance, the new Laterna Magika Theatre in Prague, designed by Josef Svoboda, is a computerized, projector-infused, high-tech junkie's dream.

> Laterna Magika was an attempt to find a modern means of dealing with the theatrical possibilities—combining film and still projection with live performers, Svoboda and his collaborators hoped to transcend time and space, to depict inner thoughts and external reality simultaneously. An image in a character's mind could be projected, characters could move fluidly from interiors to exteriors, mood could be created as easily as a representation of a room. (Aronson 1987, 96)

Svoboda's production of *Minotarus* consisted of a completely enclosed proscenium stage; it looked like an inverted gray-wrapped package. At the back was a square hole out of which three dancer-performers emerged and receded. The scenery was a continuous projection of mostly abstract images that reflected the movement patterns and tensions of the dancer-performers and the continuous, powerful, rhythmic, electronic music. It was a technically awesome computer-orchestrated, visual and aural creation of the highest order, a style of performance and design Svoboda terms "stage kinetics." "I wanted to develop a 'psychoplastic' stage. . . . From the beginning my idea was movement and change—change, change, change. When actors change they need a new ground plan for almost every situation" (Svoboda, quoted in Aronson 1987, 94).

Richard Foreman has placed television monitors onstage to provide multiple (and often competing) images. He also uses projected images, the most notable and consistent of which is the projection of printed words. "By presenting written material in his theatre, Foreman provides a reading experience for the spectator that overlaps the aural experience—two modes for experiencing language occurring simultaneously" (Davy 1981, 147). Foreman also uses low-tech black-boards as a means of juxtaposing written words with spoken words. In using printed or projected words as scenery Foreman adds an additional layer of discourse to his mise-en-scène to serve a variety of changing functions: alienating, questioning, contradicting, or reinforcing other visual or aural signifiers.

A technical director's creativity involves in part her ability to find the right material and media to create three-dimensional sculptures or two-dimensional painted, printed, or projected scenery. She must select and manipulate construction and rigging materials, tools, and media from a colorful palette of technical options if the director's conception and designer's work are to appear in full perfection on the stage and if it is going to emit the appropriate signifiers. The technician's expertise contributes to the encoding process in ways that are not always understood or appreciated.

For productions that call for many projections or much shifting of scenery the director, designer, technical director, and computer programmer (in many cases) choreograph the movement of scenery. Shifting scenery or images—especially if it is done within the spectator's view—is an integral part of the mise-en-scène. A director's vision of the performance must include the movement of the set or the use of electronic projections, video, or film.

It is clear that postmodern directors and designers use the setting in more kinetic, expansive, and primal ways than do their traditional counterparts. Words are either nonexistent, minimally employed, or in a tug-of-war with potent visual signifiers. Employing the extremes of simplicity or hyperkineticity, these directors see visual communication as pivotal to their quest to affect audiences psychically and spiritually. The look and feel of the setting frame and signify the magical, emotive, and intellectual forces of the postmodern theater.

## Costumes

Costumes constitute a unique sign system of special complexity. Costumes are decoded by spectators at the cross section of a multilayered grid; that is, they are put into action as signifiers by performers who impose personalized movement and gesture on them. At the same time, costumes as three-dimensional pieces of art are always read in and through an environmental context of space, setting, lighting, and proximity, each of which can fundamentally change the spectator's readings by presenting competing volume, mass, color, rhythm, distance, and the like. These competing, contextualizing sign systems can dominate, and therefore radically alter, how a costume is read—as when a strong red light consumes a white costume or when a black costume on a black performer is placed in front of a black curtain with no movement. Because costumes intersect so meaningfully with almost all the sign systems of the theater, directors and designers must consider not only their mass, shape, color, and line but also their relationship to the particular person (body, personality, energy level, movement capability, and style).

Besides these complexities costume designers have an additional responsibility. Although all the costumes they design are part of an integrated costume system, each costume reflects the status and personality of individual characters (except for productions that use a monodesign). The director and costume designer, then, must conceptualize not only the look of each costume individually but also take special notice of how the individual and collective costumes work as linchpins to hold an intricate web of overlapping signifiers together (either loosely or tightly) at each changing moment of a performance. This is complex stuff: if not handled carefully, unification of the entire mise-en-scène may vaporize, leaving a disjointed, confusing, hazy, or compartmentalized mishmash of individual visual signifiers.

## Determining the Design

First, the director determines the importance of costumes in the hierarchy of sign systems within a production. How much signification will the costumes be asked to deliver? A director can dress all the characters in basic black because she wants the performer's movements and words to be the primary sign systems or because she wants to make a significant statement about "blackness" through the costumes. Alternatively, a director can rely heavily on costumes to provide not just a single signifier but, instead, a richly layered set of signifiers. This suggests the continuum:

No or Neutral
Costumes

Primary or Elaborate
Costumes

At the center of this continuum might be the use of costumes as signifiers of the personality, ethnicity, emotional bent, profession, age, and relationship among characters (perhaps leaving the set designer to depict the geographic location, season, and weather).

When Peter Brook wanted to emphasize poetry and language in his production of *Oedipus* by Seneca at the Old Vic, he dressed the performers in black sweaters and slacks or unadorned black dresses. For *Akropolis* Jerzy Grotowski used "stark and anonymous costumes (made of sacking), with wooden clogs as footwear" (Bradby and Williams 1988, 117–18). In his early years Richard Foreman chose to let chance dictate costuming as a sign system.

> For the first ten years, the actors wore in performance whatever they happened to show up wearing on the first day of rehearsal. The costumes were, in effect, found objects. If their clothes had to be cleaned, I asked the actors to wear something similar, so that all through rehearsals they looked as they would in performance. I felt that was important, because as I was staging the play I'd decide where they would stand based on what they looked like—the "weight" of their visual presence—and if an actor wore a red shirt one day and a green shirt the next, that would play havoc with my decision making. (1992, 71)

On the other end of the continuum lie Robert Wilson, JoAnne Akalaitis, Ariane Mnouchkine, and Peter Sellars, who use costumes as a major sign system for most of their productions.

The director and costume designer have a number of questions to answer once they have determined the relative importance of the costume sign system within the production as a whole. Should the costumes be realistic or abstract? Nonhistorical or historically correct? Monotone or multicolored? Should there be one costume per character or multiple costumes? Finally, the director needs to determine which of the following kinds of information he wants communicated to the spectators through the costumes.

Historical period
Geographic location (country, state, city)
Personality of the character
Ethnicity/nationality of the character
Socioeconomic conditions
Mood or atmosphere
Time of day (and changes in time)
Season of the year
Weather conditions
Shifting emotions of character
Pageantry

Profession/occupation
Femininity/masculinity
Age
Period
Style
Visual emphasis

Depending upon the nature of a playscript and the director's vision for its stage realization, one director may choose to use costumes to depict all of these elements simultaneously, a second director may choose costumes to achieve visual emphasis and mood, a third may want to focus on communicating a unique personal style, and so forth.

Once some of the preliminary decisions about costume designs have been made the designer explores fabric choices for each costume as well as for the production as a whole. Different fabrics serve as signifiers: rough fabric signifies poverty or barbarism; smooth and shiny fabric signifies wealth, royalty, or sexiness. Other costume choices are whether or not to use hats, jewelry, eye wear, or wigs. Every choice leads to a heightened or subdued importance of costumes in the total signification scheme.

Another critical consideration is the relationship of the costumes to the rest of the mise-en-scène, especially the setting. Should the signs from these different sign systems be contrasting, harmonious, or discordant? For one production it may be desirable to have the costumes mimic the style, shape, and color of the setting. Another production might call for a contrast between the costumes and setting. Peter Sellars is noted for providing jarring visual contrasts in his productions, although most directors work to find harmony between the setting and costumes. Richard Foreman's continuous quest to create visual disharmony and psychic tension in his productions led him to contrast the frenzied, cluttered settings and a disjointed assaultive verbal text with the simplest costume of all, nudity.

I wanted to split the audience's attention between the fact of confrontational nudity and the nonerotic strangeness of what went on in the language, and to invoke doubleness inside the spectator so he or she could experience and appreciate the war of attentions coursing through his or her consciousness. (1992, 89–90)

In Foreman's production of *Rhoda in Potatoland* (fig. 13) we see the conflicting signifiers of a frenetic mise-en-scène. A cluttered setting, bright lights, performers in clothing, and a reclining nude woman

Fig. 13. Production: *Rhoda in Potatoland*. Director: Richard Foreman.
Photo copyright © 1993, Babette Mangolte.

form an interdependent cluster of signifiers for spectators. Foreman's
individual costume choices become part of a rich grid of signifiers. The
bright lights (which are clearly foregrounded) and the nude women
lying on a diagonal draw attention at this frozen moment. (The actual
spectators may have found different focal points, however, if aural
signifiers were operating at this moment in the performance.)

Directors use costumes as signifiers in very different ways. One of
the most interesting uses of costumes to depict historical periods
comes from the Wooster Group's production of *L.S.D.* (which includes within the performance a reading from Arthur Miller's *The
Crucible*). Some characters wore seventeenth-century dress, some
wore 1950s clothing, and others donned contemporary street clothes
(mid-1980s). "The attire does not give the piece the accuracy of a
costume drama but puts historical difference on the stage.... The
contrast between costumes from three periods acknowledges *The Crucible*'s status in *L.S.D.* as a reading, in the mid-eighties, of a 1950s
drama set in the seventeenth century" (Savran 1986, 174). The director

chose to reveal three different levels of historical time simultaneously, which thus became an element of its meanings.

For *Akropolis*, Grotowski rejected the use of costumes as providers of any historical or personal information; only mood and style resonate from the performers' costumes.

> The costumes are bags full of holes covering naked bodies. The holes are lined with material which suggests torn flesh; through the holes one looks directly into a torn body. Heavy wooden shoes for the feet; for the heads, anonymous berets. This is a poetic version of the camp uniform. Through their similarity the costumes rob men of their personality, erase the distinctive signs which indicate sex, age, and social class. The actors become completely identical beings. They are nothing but tortured bodies. (Barba and Flaszen 1965, 177)

Grotowski asks the costumes to vehemently project the agony and loss of self—nothing less.

Ariane Mnouchkine "has a special taste for costumes. She likes them to be lively, rich, exact, finished" (Féral 1989, 82). For her production of *The Terrible but Unfinished History of Norodom Sihanouk* the costumes were primary signifiers of locations, countries, professions, social contexts, ethnicity, time, and much more. The costumes were "more or less realistic—the changes from sarongs, to Western dress, to Mao suits, to Khmer Rouge pajamas help[ed] the audience to track events" (Blumenthal 1986, 9).

Robert Wilson uses costumes for every kind of signification possible—simultaneously. His epic productions, like *Death Destruction and Detroit II*, are assemblages of costumes from seemingly unrelated periods with different styles, textures, sizes, shapes, lines, and, to a lesser extent, colors. Spectators see a paratrooper in uniform, choir robes, Roman-style flowing robes, two large dinosaurs, an unnaturally large, almost perfectly round (obviously padded) man in a white suit, and a woman whose dress lights itself magically (fig. 14). A parade of costumes from Wilson's other productions would include a fifteen-foot-tall Abraham Lincoln in a period suit and hat, a giant cat that is so large that only her furry legs can be seen walking across the stage, animals of all kinds (realistic and not), nude men and women, eighteen ostrich dancers, an elegant yet simple long black dress, a woodsman dressed in punk-style green leather, a child in a diaper, a man in an oversized, padded-shouldered trench coat, soldiers in various uniforms, and monks in flowing robes. Many of these costumes are

Fig. 14. Production: *Death Destruction and Detroit II*. Director:
Robert Wilson. Photo by Ruth Walz.

realistic, many (like the woman in the lighted dress) are egregiously
theatrical, and most fall somewhere in between. The overriding impression one gets, however, is that Wilson has chosen each costume
carefully for its visual impact. The costumes are made to reveal movement and style and to signify every kind of information: period,
mood, style, emotional state of the character, occupation, pageantry,
time of year, weather conditions, and so forth. He chooses the sizes,
shapes, colors, and styles instinctively, at times even randomly, but

always with an eye toward unification at the intersecting level of the total production's signifiers. The costume signifiers are mixed, simultaneous, contradictory (black and white, loose and tight, giant and tiny, rough and smooth, expensive and cheap), yet when combined with the set, properties, and lighting they present global signifiers of epic and spiritual consequence for the spectators to assemble into meanings.

## Costume Designer's Responsibility

The design elements that are used by the costume designer are the same as those employed by the set designer: line, form, mass, color, unity, balance, and rhythm. The director and costume designer manipulate these elements in order to create costumes that will help tell a story, reflect the dramatic action of a playscript, or, in the case of some postmodern performances, depict disharmonious or abstract visual images. The costume designer does so in tandem with the other designers (unless one of them designs everything), because costumes are decoded within the context of the mise-en-scène as a whole. Some directors attempt to simplify the costume decoding process by keeping the setting and lighting simple in order to emphasize the communicative potential of the costumes. Such is the case with Peter Brook. For example, while the setting was kept quite simple for *The Cherry Orchard*, Chloe Obolensky (the designer) "pulled out all the stops with the costumes, designing a sumptuous array of lace work and beading on sculptured bodices." The critic's favorite touch was "the fur lining on Lopakhin's overcoat, visible for perhaps three seconds, but there just the same" (Gold 1988, 366). One of Brook's consistent strengths has been his insistence on simplicity and elegance. He believes that it is a sin to crowd the stage with too many competing signifiers. For his production of *King Lear*, Brook discovered a distinct method of achieving simplicity and focus through the use of costumes.

> When in a Shakespeare production you have thirty or forty equally elaborate costumes, the eye is blurred, and the plot becomes hard to follow. Here, we only gave important costumes to eight or nine central characters—the number one can normally focus on in a modern play. It was interesting to hear people saying, "How clear the play seems!" without realizing that the secret was related to the clothes. (Brook 1987, 90)

From Brook's perspective a costume not only vies with the setting, properties, and lighting for the audience's attention; each costume competes with the collective mass of costumes as well. Brook seeks clarity of communication; he reduces the possibility of competition though minimalist-inspired choices.

Many performances call for characters to change costumes to signify a change of place, time, or other circumstance. The director makes sure that all such costume changes happen at the appropriate moments. The rhythms and tempos required of the performance are reinforced by the way costumes appear and disappear from the stage. Under ideal circumstances costume, movement, gesture, and performer coalesce into a symbiotic multilevel sign system that can range from being highly unified to strangely discordant.

## Properties

Theater properties are physical objects that are seen by the audience and used by the performers. Set properties are furniture and stage decorations such as wall hangings, books, china, and the like. Hand properties are objects that are either carried onstage by performers or manipulated by them while onstage.

As a sign system, set and hand properties act in much the same way as do the set and costumes: they supply visual signifiers for the audience. A cane with a gold and diamond encrusted head signifies the status of its holder as does a cane made of a twisted tree limb. A room full of Louis XIV furniture signifies the socioeconomic status of the room's inhabitants, as does a room full of worn-out furniture.

Not surprisingly, contemporary directors use props with varying degrees of emphasis, although most directors use them as highlighting features of their mise-en-scènes. Jerzy Grotowski was the forerunner of many postmodern directors when he insisted on the minimal yet transformable use of properties for his laboratory theater. An example is his use of stovepipes in *Akropolis*.

> In the middle of the room stands a huge box. Metallic junk is heaped on top of it: stovepipes of various lengths and widths, a wheelbarrow, a bathtub, nails, hammers. Everything is old, rusty, and looks as if it had been picked up from a junkyard. The reality of the props is rust and metal. From them, as the action progresses, the actors will build an absurd civilization; a civilization of gas chambers, advertised by stovepipes which will decorate the whole room as the

actors hang them from strings or nail them to the floor. Thus one passes from fact to metaphor. (Barba and Flaszen 1965, 177)

Richard Foreman, on the other side of the continuum, is a fanatic about the use of properties as signifiers. His sets are literally strewn with an inexplicable assortment of props of all sizes, styles, and shapes: blackboards, clocks, lamps, miniature houses, chairs that sit at odd angles, picture frames, television monitors, and on and on. Properties take on such a strong focus for Foreman that he even uses them as a springboard for creating the written text for his productions. "With *Hotel China* I began to write plays by imagining intricate, strange objects that would suggest ways that desire, working through the performer, might cause them to be manipulated. I stopped working from outlines, and instead let the complicated physical objects that I imagined lead me in whatever direction they suggested" (1992, 80). Foreman uses props to lead him through the development of the dramatic action of the performance's text.

A world ruled by objects could also suggest, "I am a lamp, and over there is a bookcase. What are the possible relationships between a lamp and a bookcase? Well, let me, lamp that I am, go over and sit next to a book on a bookcase. Can you read me like you can read a book? Is a book as bright as a lamp?" I'd let my imagination run free: "I am a lamp. Usually, when you go to bed at night you take a book and read before you go to sleep. Tonight, try taking me, a lamp, to bed, and hold me in your arms, and look into the light, and tell yourself the story that you see looking into the light." (82)

To say the least, it is unusual to find properties as the driving signifier in a performance, but Foreman believes that there is profound meaning in the interaction between objects and human beings. How the objects are manipulated physically and the kinds of effects they have psychically on the characters is the seat of profound dramatic tension and visual signification. Props become the chief motivator of the dramatic action and the leading signifying system in many of his productions.

Properties also can play a seminal role in communicating vital information about the characters and given circumstances of a performance, especially when a director chooses not to use a set or chooses to use neutral, nonperiod costumes. Properties serve as signifiers that communicate the following information:

Historical period
Socioeconomic status
Style
Mood or atmosphere
Personality of a character
Location/place
Time of day
Ethnicity/nationality
Season
Weather conditions
Age
Profession or occupation
Shifting emotions
Femininity or masculinity

Most productions do not use properties to communicate all these elements. But for many productions—such as those that take place in arenas or environmental settings or that operate with a bare-bones budget—properties are a primary source of visual communication; they become strategically important to the production's mise-en-scène. As in all things, Peter Brook is highly selective in the use of props; those that appear on the stage are potent signifiers (their effectiveness is amplified by their scarcity). "And Brook knows well how to suggest large objects with a simple symbol or prop [as in *Mahabharata*]—a wheel representing a chariot, a red ribbon a gush of blood, a circle of fire the contours of a battlefield" (Brustein 1991, 139). Brook's use of properties is probably nowhere more ingenious than in "The Execution of the Aristocrats" scene from *Marat/Sade*.

At the beginning of the execution scene, the Herald cried, "The Execution of the Aristocrats!" Accompanied by loud raspings of broom handle and trapdoor against the central grate, a group of inmates came forward. As these "aristocrats" approached the down center trap, each in turn sharply jerked his head down and descended into the pit. Sade gave his speech about the perverse pleasure the aristocrats found in death. By the time he finished, the pit was full of severed heads with protruding tongues, goggling eyes, and twisted attitudes. In the stillness, the focus moved to Polpoch, one of the four singers, as he poured red paint (blood) from one bucket to another. A delicate run on the glockenspiel accompanied his symbolic action. (45 seconds had elapsed since the announcement.) During an elaborate fanfare (lasting 35 seconds), the aristocrats dispersed from the pit and introduced a dummy made from broom handles and bits of clothing, with a cabbage head and a carrot nose. The Herald then announced "The Execution of the King!" and the royal dummy was rudely pushed into the pit. Another bucket of blood was poured out, to the same accompaniment. But this blood was blue. (The scene was now 105 seconds old.) The inmates suddenly began to fight over the cabbage and carrot (Brecht to the rescue), until the guards subdued them and stuffed them down into the ring of traps.

The execution scene sounds simple enough, but it astonished the audiences. Everyone reviewing the play wrote about it, and everyone recalling the production mentions it. The pit of heads and the pouring of blood (the latter descended from the paint tropes of the Theatre of Cruelty workshop) were unforgettable pictures. (D. R. Jones 1986, 240)

Simple props creatively manipulated by the performers and imaginatively orchestrated by the director tell the wrenching story of mass execution in symbolic but emotionally affecting ways.


## The Semiotics of Properties

Set properties play a unique, multilevel role in the communication process. For example, a cane onstage may have a denotative, functional role; it may represent an object designed for walking. In a different scene, however, the cane could stand for a sword, in another scene for a large crucifix or a crowbar, and so on. Properties onstage are easily transformable. Directors use this knowledge when considering options for staging a playscript or performance piece. For example, a director may choose to think of all props as nontransformable or as fully transformable objects.

Realizing that properties have a denotative meaning and the potential for multiple connotative meanings, the director may or may not want to capitalize on the transformability of both stage and hand properties. Will the production use a single cane to represent a sword, a crucifix, and a crowbar, or will three different objects be used? In making this choice, the director is deciding the style of the production—on the one hand, fantasy or abstraction (in which properties are continually transformed), on the other, naturalism (in which each property is the actual object represented or a facsimile).

## Selecting Properties

The first decision a director makes is whether or not to use props, the second is whether they should be realistic or abstract, and the third is whether or not they should be transformable, as noted on the following continua:

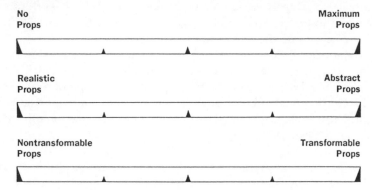

Once the director has located her production on these three continua additional questions need to be asked. How will set properties (especially furniture) contribute to the potential movement patterns of the performers? What size should the properties be relative to the size of the acting area? How many set properties should be used? Should the properties complement or contrast with the setting and costumes (in terms of style, color, and condition)? Do the properties need to be moved during the performance? If so, can they be shifted in the time allowed? What should be the properties' style, color, size, and shape?

In consort with his large-scale settings and use of massive space Robert Wilson meticulously selects or designs properties to fit his highly controlled yet eclectic style of visual communication. A bench flies into the air. Designer lounge chairs sit on the beach. A large black crow perches on a woman's arm. A giant, clear light bulb dominates a scene. Long thin ladders reach high into the fly tower. Real cabbages cover the forestage (fig. 15). Some of these properties are larger than life, some are smaller; some are realistic, some are abstract; most are black or white, a few are brightly colored; but all of them, when combined with all the other visual elements of Wilson's productions, present a unified grid of optic dynamism that is breathtaking to behold, if impossible to systematically codify.

Postmodern directors use properties in a variety of ways, but all

Fig. 15. Production: *the CIVIL warS* (Scene B, Rotterdam sec.). Director: Robert Wilson. Photo by Georges Meran.

appear to place special significance on their signifying verve and their transformability. In the postmodern theater, props are rarely treated as realistic objects unless they are used either as a foundation for juxtaposing the real and the unreal or unless they are mixed in a multistyled world created by intermingling the absurd with the real. There is no question, however, that postmodern directors see stage properties as having fathomless potential for meaning-producing signification.

## Lighting

The lighting designer is often charged with the greatest responsibility for achieving unity within the mise-en-scène. In part the lighting designer employs his art as a means of fusing the various designers' work into a unified mega–sign system. Why is this so? Partly because he is often the last designer to begin working on a production. Under normal circumstances a lighting designer does not begin to work until the sets, costumes, and props have been designed. In addition, many lighting designers wait until the movement patterns for a production have been determined, thereby gaining a full sense of the kinetic dimension of the production. Waiting can be an advantage: the lighting designer can see the shape, colors, form, and intensity of the other designers' work and the dynamics of the performers' movements, rather than having to visualize these elements based on discussions with the director.

The director first decides how pivotal lighting is to the performance and its mise-en-scène and second how realistic or abstract the lighting should be.

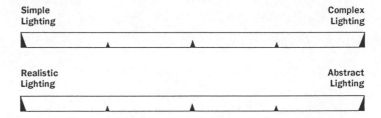

Does the director's vision include the extensive use of shifting and changing light as a central dynamic of the performance? Or does he want a fixed light pattern that remains unchanged during the entire performance? Or, in the case of environmental or outdoor theater, will natural light suffice?

The importance of lighting varies according to the director's style. Some directors believe strongly in using light as an active participant in the signification process, as do their designers.

> Lighting a scene consists not only in throwing light upon objects but in throwing light upon a subject. . . . We light the actors and the setting, it is true, but we illuminate the drama. We reveal the drama. We use light as we use words, to elucidate ideas and emotions. Light becomes a tool, an instrument of expression, like a paint-brush, or a sculptor's chisel, or a phrase of music. (R. E. Jones 1941, 118–19)

Robert Wilson and Josef Svoboda foreground lighting in their productions. Technological advances have allowed them to create walls of light, special isolation techniques, focused shafts of light coming from any direction, and blinding pulses of light, to name only a few special effects.

> In Wilson's theatre, light is as much a metaphysical force as a de-
> sign element, and its transforming powers are felt everywhere,
> from the starfilled nightscapes and glowing interiors to the lumi-
> nous sculptural forms which seem to grow out of his imaginary
> vistas. "For me light is the essential element in the theatre," Wilson
> often says. It is a primary component of composition, as integral
> to a piece as text, music or imagery. (Shyer 1989, 191)

In *Death Destruction and Detroit*, Wilson used light as a defining signifier of the mise-en-scène. Through a constantly shifting black/white,
shadow/bright, left/right motif emanating from the visionscape, lighting served as a dominant unifying and controlling agent (fig. 16).

Other directors, including Peter Brook, find a simple, one-level
lighting scheme sufficient for their productions.

> I now realize that I haven't touched a spotlight for at least ten
> years, whereas before I was forever climbing up and down lad-
> ders to adjust them, etc. These days I simply say to the lighting
> technician: "Very bright!" I want everything to be seen, every-
> thing to stand out clearly, without the slightest shadow. The
> same idea has often led us to use a simple carpet as our stage and
> set. I have not come to this conclusion through Puritanism, nor
> do I want to condemn elaborate costumes or ban colored lights.
> Only I've found that the true interest lies elsewhere, in the event
> itself as it happens at each moment, inseparable from the public's
> response. (Brook 1987, 14)

The relative complexity of theatrical lighting for a production is
dependent upon the lighting components available for possible use,
including:

Location, size, and type of performance space
Availability of natural lighting sources
Amount of electricity (number of outlets, wattage, etc.)
Number and kinds of lighting instruments
Number and lengths of connecting cable
Number and kinds of dimmer control systems
Number and location of places to hang lighting instruments
Range of color media

Fig. 16. Production: *Death Destruction and Detroit*. Director: Robert Wilson. Photo by Ruth Walz.

Contemporary lighting technology allows for an almost infinite array of lighting choices. Any imaginable lighting effect in terms of color, brilliance, size, angle, location, shape, and frequency or speed of manipulation is possible in today's computerized lighting environment. Coupled with advanced technology that fills the stage with what looks like "smoke," lighting can even become an architectural unit in space:

> During the past ten years Wilson has also become interested in what he calls "architectural light in the air"—the outlines of light traveling through space as held in mist or smoke. Such radiant light forms are usually triangular—"since light comes in triangles"—and often mirror other elements of the design. In *Einstein* these phantom triangles could be found nearly everywhere one looked; streaming from the lamp of a steam locomotive or the headlight of a bus, falling down upon the great bed in the courtroom scenes,

shooting out in long compressed shafts from the wings and beneath the stage in the final spaceship sequence. (Shyer 1989, 197)

Using light as an architectural shape brings the setting and lighting into symbiosis.

## Lighting as Communication

Several kinds of information can be sent to the spectator through the lighting:

Time of day
Season of the year
Weather conditions
Place
Mood or atmosphere
Emphasis (foregrounding or backgrounding)
Emotion
Theatricality
Style

The director and the lighting designer make several choices. Will lighting be used for general illumination only, leaving the scenery and/or costumes to serve as the primary visual signifiers? Or will lighting be employed as a primary means of communicating such elements as mood, time of day, and emotion? How much lighting variation is to be used is determined by the relative importance lighting is to play in the complex sign systems of a performance.

## Function of Theatrical Lighting

As a semiotic sign system in the theater, lighting has the following major functions.

### Visibility

In order for communication to take place there must be sufficient light for the audience to witness the production fully. Without light there can be no seeing, no signification through the eyes, no visual foregrounding.

*Composition*

Light is a medium for sculpting space. It can be used to accent or suppress details of the stage space. Through highlight, shadow, and color contrasts, lighting can be manipulated to aid in signification. The elements of visual composition—line, mass, form, balance, unity, color, and rhythm—are employed by the lighting designer (in collaboration with the set and costume designers) to create an aesthetic visual effect.

*Style*

The director and lighting designer can use light to depict a wide range of styles from naturalistic to highly abstract and theatrical. Naturalistic lighting is provided in outdoor performances by the sun and moon. For indoor performances naturalistic lighting can be achieved by using real lights onstage (lamps, candles, lanterns, flashlights) or by a natural-looking sun or moon (made by electrical lights) shining through the trees or a window. On the other hand, highly abstract theatrical lighting has no basis in reality; this lighting creates magical effects.

The style of lighting must relate to the style of the other visual elements. This does not mean that the lighting must always reflect the exact degree of naturalism or abstraction of the other elements of the production; indeed, the director may employ lighting as a contrasting or conflicting source of signification. Brecht insisted that the lighting instruments be in full view to remind the spectators that they were in the theater and thus prevent them from becoming too involved in the action. Robert Wilson wants lighting to be hidden from view so that he can create magical effects whose sources defy detection.

*Mood or Atmosphere*

Lighting is a dynamic tool for touching the spectator's emotions. In addition to providing visibility, lighting can be used to evoke a special mood. Its value in creating a specific atmosphere can be observed by comparing the lighting in nightclubs, art galleries, public streets, and people's homes.

Bright lights signify daytime, happiness, aggressiveness, celebration, comedy, energy, and a whole host of analogous emotions. Dark lights signify night, sorrow, submissiveness, fear, sleepiness, or dullness. A director can use lighting to elicit a single emotion, mood, or energy state or to reflect the ever-changing moods and emotions of a performance. A range of choices is available to directors and designers. Dim or bright? Monotone or multicolored? Cold or hot? Clear or shadowy? Stationary or moving? The director and lighting designer make these choices for the production as a whole and for each changing moment of the performance.

Richard Foreman vacillates between using no special lighting effects in his productions to using lighting to create mood, a personal style, a variety of levels of visibility, and, most important, an integrated visual composition.

> Finally, and perhaps most noticeably by virtue of quantity, is [Foreman's] lavish display of lights [in *Total Recall*]. In the ceiling there are three varieties of light, each with a different function. The hanging lights, with cone-shaped aluminum shades that direct the beam downwards, provide general illumination. They are bright, flat, and "spill" or overlap each other, eliminating shadows and, hence, the subtle effects of "mood lighting." One of these lights hangs only a few feet from the floor and marks the center point, from left to right, of the space framed by the two pillars. In this position the light cannot represent the "overhead light" of the room since it would not be over the heads of the performers except when in prone or sitting positions. The spectator must look "through" or past this light whenever it interferes with the line of vision to objects and activities occurring upstage of it. By interfering with the line of vision, it calls attention to itself and its position in the space. It not only functions to illuminate the space, but becomes as much a part of the setting as the major set pieces. The two brightest ceiling lights—upstage right and downstage left—are aimed directly at the spectators. These lights are glaring—uncomfortably bright and shining in the spectator's eyes—and as such, function primarily as a means of distancing the spectator from the work. Light aimed directly at the audience from the stage is characteristic of every Foreman production and one of the many ways of identifying a Foreman design. (Davy 1981, 42)

In his use of lighting Foreman creates compositions that signify and reinforce his hysterical, eclectic aesthetic: light provides both general illumination and architectural structure as well as contributing to the mood and emotional reality of the scene. As Foreman progressed in the development of his theatrical style, he learned that lighting (which he sometimes ignored in his early years) adds another track to his multitrack performances; indeed, lighting now serves as a unifier of his mise-en-scène.

Robert Wilson even found a way to use light as the central signifier, replacing the performer altogether.

> In what was perhaps the most remarkable scene in *Einstein*, light displaced the actor altogether and became the action: for nearly half an hour, spellbound audiences watched a bar of cold white light tilt upward from its horizontal position on an otherwise empty stage and rise into the sky. It would be no exaggeration to say that Wilson's works exist as much in the dimension of light as they do in time and space. (Shyer 1989, 192)

## Properties of Light

There are four major properties of light: intensity, distribution, color, and movement. By manipulating these properties, the director and lighting designer create signifiers for audiences to read.

### Intensity

Lighting for a performance can vary from dim to brilliant. The designer and director choose the intensity level of light for every moment of the performance and have options ranging from one setting for the entire performance to changes that take place every second.

Because spectators are seated at varying distances from the mise-en-scène, they may not all perceive the lighting as having the same degree of intensity. For instance, light that seems bright to someone sitting in the front row of a large theater may appear dull to a spectator sitting eighty feet away at the back. A spectator with sharp vision who is sitting at the back of the auditorium may experience more brilliance than a spectator sitting in the front row who has physically impaired vision. Also, one level of light may not appear brilliant in a dark, soft-textured setting, while the same level of light might be harsh in a white reflective setting. Again, when lights are brought up quickly from a dim level to a much brighter level, the sensibilities of the audience will be shocked: it takes time for the eye to adjust to sudden, severe changes in light levels. An extreme use of lighting intensity can be seen in Richard Foreman's production of *Woyzeck*. After Marie has been violently stabbed repeatedly and rhythmically, "a dozen blazing klieg lights all but blind the audience. The action itself convulses beyond visibility" (Kalb 1990, 71). Here, the pure intensity of the lighting is keenly (perhaps painfully) experienced by the spectators. They feel Marie's pain—but light, not a knife, delivers the message.

*Distribution*

Assuming that there are many lighting instruments available, a flexible means of controlling the light, and a variety of lighting positions that can be used to locate the different lighting instruments, there are numerous ways to distribute light in the theater. For example, the director and lighting designer may choose to light the whole theater (spectators' seating area and performers' playing space) or to keep the spectators' section dark and only light the playing space. For most productions the auditorium is lit before and after the performance and during intermission but is darkened during the performance. There is, however, a range of options that falls between these two extremes.

When the director and lighting designer choose to focus light on the stage space only, they face an additional spectrum of choices: pinpoint or flood, below or above, left or right, front or back. The direction of the light influences the signification process. For example, the facial features of the performers and the details of the setting and costumes are lost with pure back lighting; only the silhouettes of the three-dimensional objects onstage are seen. Such a severe lighting choice evokes a sense of mystery, suspense, or spookiness. At the same time, however, any use of facial expression, costume texture, set color, and makeup as a signifier is lost. Richard Foreman used shifting directional lighting to create a wonderful illusion.

In *The Book of Splendors*, as somewhat eerie music could be heard, the lights in the back of the space dimmed while those aimed at the audience became brighter. What appeared to be large, hulking, mysterious creatures could be discerned slowly lumbering down the rear ramp. Although a general shape and very peculiar movement could be perceived, it was not until the rear lights began to come up and the front lights dimmed that it was possible to see performers holding large, open umbrellas in front of their faces with square decorator pillows strapped to their ankles. (Davy 1981, 55)

By employing only direct, subtle front light, the audience is able to perceive facial expression, small gestures, and the color and details of the setting and costumes. Yet bright front lighting, which creates a two-dimensional effect, impedes the creation of mood as well as the indication of time and place. Fortunately, the direction and distribution of light can be altered hundreds of times during a performance so that the signifiers can be ever changing.

Robert Wilson's lighting designer, Beverly Emmons, has experimented with lighting style in order to meet Wilson's exacting demands.

> He wants the floor absolutely smooth—all one piece, completely separate from a sky or drop. No hot spots or cold spots. He likes light to come from below. He hates side lights hitting the scenery. Any set objects in the scene have to have a light completely separate from those lighting the floor, and any human figure has to have completely separate lighting as well. You can't light figures from above at an angle because you get a splotch of light. You have to light them from the side and light the rest of the floor with a German Flüter [a powerful lighting instrument]. Wilson is very particular about all that, but that's what makes his pieces seem so quiet and smooth. There are also requests, like lighting a hand so that it looks like a glistening diamond. He won't want the light to hit anywhere else but on the hand. (Emmons, quoted in Baker 1985, 96–97)

## Color

The theater can be literally painted with colored light. Any color the set and costume designers can produce can be reproduced with light. Colored light can change the mise-en-scène dynamically. More important, colored light has a psychological and emotional effect on the audience. Because the color of light ranges widely—from no color to multicolor, from cold to hot, from dull to brilliant—the director and the lighting designer have multiple color choices as signifiers. Traditionally, warm, bright colors are selected for farce and comedy and cool subtle colors for serious or tragic productions, but the span of possibilities is almost infinite. Modern technology has given directors and designers the opportunity to broaden their light pallet considerably. Some directors tend to prefer white and gray lights (Wilson, Foreman, Brook, and Svoboda), while others exploit the extremes of the color spectrum (Sellars, Mnouchkine, Akalaitis). Most of these directors have also found that fire onstage in its various manifestations—campfires, torches, candles, even a burning umbrella—adds a sense of naturalism, visual punctuation, or eerieness.

## Movement

Many types of movement take place during a performance. Performers move about the stage; sets, props, and costumes come and go; and lighting changes to project the ebb and flow of the dramatic action. Lights can be dimmed or brightened; they can be focused on one small part of the stage then moved to encompass the entire theater then moved again to focus on another, smaller part of the stage—all in a matter of seconds (quick movement) or minutes (slow movement). The movement of light is part of the mise-en-scène. For example, if the director decides to begin each act with the performers frozen in place or to shift the scenery in full view of the audience (outside the real time of the playscript), she triggers corresponding movements in lighting.

Movement of light results in changes in color, light, intensity, and areas lighted. These changes, together with their frequency and duration, contribute to a performance's tempo, rhythm, and style. For example, if the style of a production is exaggerated or farcical, the movement of light might be frequent, multidimensional, frantic, and staccatolike.

### Emphasis through Lighting

As a primary source of emphasis, lighting can direct the audience to look at a specific character or listen to a piece of dialogue. Variations in lighting can help guide the audience's concentration throughout a performance. Choosing to maintain a single level, color, and direction of light negates this possibility. Light can be manipulated in many dimensions to achieve emphasis.

Focus: Light can be limited to a small area of the stage or to only one performer, while the rest of the stage or remaining characters are dark.

Intensity: Even if the whole stage is lit, one area or character can receive a different level of light, thereby attracting attention.

Lighting direction and/or angle: If one performer or area of the stage is lit more clearly from the front and above, for instance, and the remaining performers or the rest of the stage is lit from

behind or below, the audience's attention will focus on the fron-
tally lit area or performer.

Color: A contrasting color will draw attention to a specific area of
the stage or to a specific performer. For example, if the stage is
lit with cool gray-blue color and one performer is bathed in hot
pink light, the distinct color attracts attention.

Movement: If the stage is lit with an even wash of light but
a moving follow spot is brought to focus on an object or
performer, the audience will track the movement of the
light.

Each of these lighting techniques can be used individually or simultaneously to help guide the focus of the audience. An example of the
use of all of these elements is Tadashi Suzuki's production of *The
Trojan Women*, which highlighted the use of rock music, intense
lighting, and images of Hiroshima and Nagasaki to portray the
horrors of modern life. "The rock [music] elliptically [brought] into
focus—as red lighting flashes in the background and the actors'
movements fractured by strobes intensif[ied] the impact of sound—
the nuclear holocaust" (Shevtsova 1989, 289). The audience was
assaulted visually by the violent color, rhythmic pulsing light, and
the fractured movement of the performers while thunderous, throb-
bing music drove the horror of the holocaust deeply into their
psyches.

The use of light as a medium for signification has been expanded
through modern technology and its creative manipulation by
postmodern directors and lighting designers. There is no unanimity
among directors, however, as each works with a designer to find the
best use of lighting for individual productions and for their evolving
theater aesthetic. Peter Brook rarely uses light as a signifier in his later
works: he went from many lighting changes, colors, and angles to
pure white light. Richard Foreman reversed this order: he went from
no formal theatrical lighting to a highly frenetic and often assaultive
deployment of lighting effects. Robert Wilson has consistently used
lighting as his central unifying element and a primary signifier in its
own right—but even he has moved toward a more precise and sophisticated use of lighting because of advances in technology and continual experimentation. Wilson has committed the time in rehearsal to
uncover a personal style of lighting. "During his lighting rehearsals,
which can last several weeks, he sits out in the darkened auditorium
like an artist before a canvas, detailing his composition moment by
moment" (Shyer 1989, 198).

# Color

Color is a vital dimension of sets, costumes, properties, performer's skin, makeup, and lighting. Spectators perceive the colors of the mise-en-scène and construct meaning from them. The director's primary choices include:

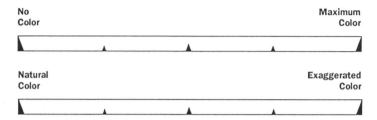

There are many possible perspectives from which to study color: that of the physicist (the physics of color), the chemist (the composition of color pigment), the psychologist (the emotional associations of color), and the artist (the aesthetics of color). The director's understanding of the aesthetics and psychology of color is of primary value, especially as it relates to semiotics and cultural codes.

## Elements of Color

The elements of color for the chemist and physicist are grounded in science: light waves, refraction, absorption, and reflection for the physicist and chemical composition for the chemist. This science of color, however, tells us little about why people choose certain colors or what impact such choices have on other people. When we ask people what their favorite colors are, we soon see that no two people experience color in exactly the same way.

> The sensation of color is usually caused by variations in the length of light waves radiated by self-luminous sources, reflected from objects, or transmitted through them. The rays enter the eye and through receptors in the eye their nature is communicated by the optic nerve to the brain. Because no two eyes and no two brains may operate in exactly the same way, no two persons are likely to sense color in exactly the same way. (Fischer 1974, 13)

The identification or development of a semiotic code for color becomes problematic, then, because not only does everyone react differently psychologically, emotionally, and spiritually to color, but people see colors differently; one person's blue is another person's purple.

## How Color Works

Color has two forms: chromatic color (red, blue, purple, etc.) and achromatic color (black and white). Most color schemes identify red, blue, and green as the three primary chromatic colors in light and red, blue, and yellow as the three primary chromatic colors in pigment. Secondary chromatic colors are yellow, orange, and purple in light and green, orange, and purple in pigment. There are many other chromatic colors, but they are derived out of a combination of the primary chromatic colors.

The primary chromatic colors, along with achromatic black and white, can be combined in various ways to produce the following qualities in an almost infinite variety of colors.

Hue: This term identifies the individual "colorness" of a color. A blue hue is different from a red hue.

Saturation: A color's saturation is its potency or vividness. A fully saturated red has no more potency; it is as red as it can be. Pink is a highly diluted version of red—it is capable of gaining more redness.

Brilliance: The relative lightness or darkness of a hue is responsible for its brilliance; light purple possesses more brilliance than dark purple.

Tint: A pure color can be combined with white to produce a variety of tints: the more white that is combined with a color, the further the color moves from its pure form. For example, if blue is mixed with a high volume of white it produces soft blue or light blue.

Shade: A pure color can be combined with black to produce a variety of shades. For example, a modest amount of red mixed with black will produce dark maroon.

Gray: Different tints and shades of gray are produced by combining black and white in various combinations.

The colors of a production's sets, costumes, and properties can produce a combinative aesthetic value that exceeds the sum of the individual colors. Also, colors can be chosen to reflect the changing dramatic action, contexts, emotional intensity, and story line. When used in this way color takes on a dynamic function: it is ever changing, adjusting to the different characters, scenes, movements, and tensions of the living performance. Many postmodern directors, however, choose to use monochrome or near monohue colors since they are more interested in communication through shape, mass, or other spatial aspects of a performance's mise-en-scène.

> Foreman works monochromatically in color as one means to achieve [a sense of the visual whole]. The dominant color of all the elements (stage floor, props, set pieces, curtains) in all Foreman's pieces was a deep but flat brown accented by white and a subdued gold. Foreman feels that a monochromatic color scheme promotes the meditative, unfocused kind of attention he is aiming for. (Davy 1981, 56)

Color is perhaps the only major sign system that Foreman does not allow to become hysterical. He senses that individual objects will become isolated by individual colors rather than be seen as aesthetically unified.

Robert Wilson works much the same way. "While Wilson has boldly explored most of light's properties, color is one element he applies with restraint. 'There's no color in Bob's lighting in the sense that he doesn't use red or green or yellow the way some designers do. He takes white light and treats it as different shades of white. It's extremely subtle'" (Emmons quoted in Shyer 1989, 198). There is also very little color in the majority of his scenic and costume elements. He is more interested in using shape and movement to signify meanings; bright colors disturb his sweeping, quiet, epic landscapes.

Color in light is of special significance, as its range includes all areas of the color spectrum from white to black (the absence of light). Moreover, light can change the color of any object, person, or piece of clothing on the stage. When a gray wall is flooded with intense blue light it turns blue. When a blue costume is illuminated by red light it turns purple.

Finding the right combinations of color for each element of the mise-en-scène and for every moment of a performance is a formidable task, but one that can bear much fruit in the signification process. Color has psychological and emotional (and perhaps even intellectual) reverberations for each spectator. Directors and designers have a sweeping array of color choices to make. Achromatic or chromatic color? Light tint or pure color? Dark shade or pure color? Monohue or multiple colors? No color change during a performance or constantly shifting colors? Cool or hot colors? Peter Brook employed subtle earthy colors throughout his production of *Carmen*, except for one costume that stood out to highlight an important dramatic moment. "When Escamillo makes his final entrance in full matador regalia, the evening's only bright costume is chillingly mocked by the premonitorily embalmed expression of the toreador's face" (Rich 1983, 125). The striking contrast of the single bright costume and the dead expression provided a heightened visual presence as well as a heightened dramatic moment.

Also, colors have unequal levels of "attention power." Some colors are more likely to dominate the attention of the spectators than are other colors. The following colors are listed in descending order of attention power:

red-orange
red
orange
yellow-orange
yellow
pink
yellow-green

(Birren 1961, 45)

By manipulating the attention power of colors on the stage, the director and designers orchestrate the spectators' focus.

Colors also possess "weight" (Birren 1961, 50). White and yellow are the lightest, blue-brown and black the heaviest. If spectators are greeted with a mise-en-scène that radiates heavy colors, they will most likely anticipate a serious, weighty, perhaps even onerous evening in the theater; light colors likely will evoke the opposite response.

### Traditional Color Codes

Cultural codes for colors vary with different peoples, times, cultures, and nations. Some of the most traditional are:

*Ancient Color Symbolism*
red—fire (heat, blood, sacrifice)
yellow—sun (light, wisdom)
blue—coldness (air, water, truth)
green—nature (life everlasting)
*Christian Mysticism*
blue—heaven

yellow—earth
red—hell
*Heraldry*
red—courage and zeal
gold/yellow—honor and loyalty
green—youth and hope
blue—truth and sincerity
purple—royalty and rank
silver/white—faith and purity
black—grief and penitence

(Birren 1961, 59–60)

It is possible (and perhaps useful) to suggest a cultural color code for contemporary Western audiences:

black—death, mourning, seriousness, evil
red—blood, hotness, sexiness, devil
blue—sky, baby boy, water, coolness
white—virginity, purity, cleanliness, goodness
pink—softness, femininity, baby girl
gray—dullness, business manner, somberness
yellow—springtime, happiness, brightness
green—nature, life, Irish, army
purple—mystery, offbeat quality, wealth, royalty

Directors and designers must make several choices about color as a sign system. How can color help underscore, reflect, and communicate the play's dramatic action? How can color be coordinated and changed to reflect the transforming moments of a performance? How can color be used to reflect harmony, contrast, or chaos? How can color affect the emotional, psychological, and spiritual experiences of the audience? How can color reflect the historical period and theatrical style of a production? For Peter Sellers' *Giulio Cesare* color helped to locate the production in the contemporary world of popular culture. "Sellers' Caesar, in an electric blue-green suit, is an oily, media-hyping politician, smirking and waving. His Cleopatra is a sleazy international bimbo; for one big number she wears a gold lamé playsuit, does bumps and grinds in time to her coloratura, and has a high old time tossing around a bag marked '$'" (Novick 1986, 17).

Color may draw the interest of the audience into the world of the performance, or it may repulse them. In one study, color preferences (in descending order of likability) were shown to be:

blue
red
green
yellow
purple
orange

(Birren 1961, 78)

Rarely, however, is a single color used in a performance; more often multiple colors coexist. The use of color becomes more complicated if the director and designers decide on a multicolor context. Yet even a single color may affect people differently depending on the visual context it finds itself in:

The deep blue of the sea and distant mountains enchant us; the same blue as an interior seems uncanny, lifeless, and terrifying. Blue reflections on the skin render it pale, as if moribund. In the dark of night, a blue neon light is attractive, like blue on black, and in conjunction with red and yellow lights it lends a cheerful, lively tone. A blue sun-filled sky has an active and enlivening effect, whereas the mood of the blue moonlit sky is passive and evokes subtle nostalgias. (Itten 1961, 130)

The design process requires a complex color plan (unless a monohue concept is used). How will a red dress look against a light blue set when illuminated by soft pink-and-blue lights? The best answer is to test the colors in the light lab—where a model set, a piece of red cloth, and colored lights can be observed and adjusted until the proper combination of colors is identified. Testing inspires creative solutions to a complex signification process.

Colors are dynamic signifiers; when chosen carefully they bring coded messages to the spectators for their individual interpretation. One vivid example comes from JoAnne Akalaitis's production of 'Tis Pity She's a Whore. In one scene Soranzo savagely brutalizes Annabella by slamming her against "a blood red wall" (Rich 1992, C14). This violent activity is made more vicious by providing the blood red wall as a backdrop. In her production of Cymbeline Akalaitis used counterpoints of visual images and color to tell her fractured tale. "Tsypin's setting spoke its own text: rock against water; the green world in contest with the hard, black-on-white world of corruption, threatened with the red of rape and war" (Fuchs 1989, 28). Akalaitis carefully chooses strong colors to signify the changing actions of her productions: the visual text is as punctuated with color as it is with highly stylized movement, makeup, and masks.

Postmodernists have profoundly eclectic tastes when it comes to the use of color in their works. Many use muted monotones, some use color as an infrequent visitor, and others employ color as a primary sign system.

## Summary

Visual sign systems are used by directors in a wide range of configurations to produce signification and meanings. Such choices as whether or not to use simple or elaborate scenery and costumes, vivid or dark colors, a large or small theater space, bright or dim lighting, and realistic or transformable properties affect the meanings that will be constructed by each spectator. Location, theater space, setting, costumes, properties, lighting, color, and the performer's body and its movement are independent sign systems that come together to form a symbiotic visual mega–sign system. A director's task is to orchestrate and overcode these visual sign systems so that they emit coordinated, simultaneous, and yet ever-changing stimuli that reflect and project a production's dramatic action. Luckily, modern technology gives enormous flexibility to what can be created, shifted, lit, and displayed onstage. Perhaps the most striking feature of postmodernist directing is the concentrated use of visual signification as a pivotal signifier. Audiences are asked to read the visual dimension of performance as a key language of the theatrical discourse. Many postmodern directors, designers, and technicians wed their knowledge of modern technology to produce optical magic and potent visual signification.

# Chapter 6

# Aural Systems

A spectator at a theater performance hears continuous sound. At times there is a virtual cacophony of overlapping sounds, and at other times for brief periods, there is absolute silence. "Sound evokes that part of our lives and that part of our experience which cannot be controlled by or reduced to verbal explanations. Sound evokes that part of our lives which is intuitive, that part of ourselves which can never be compromised, a world of pure feeling, being and unmediated experience" (Sellars, quoted in Kaye and LeBrecht 1992, vi).

The kinds of sounds a spectator is exposed to during a performance are spoken dialogue, paralinguistic vocal utterances (coughs, screams, sighs), sounds produced by physical movement (walking, sliding, jumping), sound effects (thunder, telephone ringing, door closing), music (instrumental, vocal), noise from mechanical systems (air conditioning, heating, stage rigging), and noise from the external environment (sirens, rain, airplanes).

Through live, electronic, or mechanical means the director and sound designer/technician can produce an infinite array of sounds to communicate meanings to spectators. Sound and music are capable of signifying the following:

Historical period: boogie-woogie music, antique automobile horn beeping
Geographic location: mariachi music, urban street noise
Socioeconomic circumstances: Beethoven quartet, rap music, belching, elegant manner of speech
Ethnicity/nationality: national anthem, Russian accent, "European" police siren
Specific location: traffic sounds, birds singing, *Grand Canyon Suite*
Weather conditions: wind, rain
Time of day: rooster crowing, lullaby

173

Character's personality: constant screaming, Gypsy violin music in the background as a character makes an entrance

Offstage activity: car arriving, doorbell ringing

Mood: blues music, wind, humming, whistling

Transition: circus music between scenes, wind at the conclusion of the performance

Emphasis: one character's voice louder than all others, thunder offstage to direct the spectator's attention to a major entrance

Examples abound to show how directors communicate information and affect emotions through sound and music. In his production of *The Fragments of a Trilogy* Andrei Serban asked Elizabeth Swados to create sound images for the time of day and weather: Serban asked "What is the sound of dawn? How can you make the light of the day and heat that it brings visible in sound?" (Serban interview, in Bartow 1988a, 291–92). Jerzy Grotowski employed a solo violin in *Akropolis* to signify a mood. He deliberately used "a hapless and tawdry little tune, redolent of vapid popular music." He did this knowing it would accentuate "the horror and pathos of his concentration camp setting" (Richie 1970, 208). As a transition into her production of Beckett's *Endgame*, JoAnne Akalaitis commissioned Philip Glass to introduce the performance with a brief overture. Music was not called for by the playwright; indeed, Beckett was upset by her distortion of his playscript (Brustein 1991, 200).

The director chooses whether or not to stress aural elements as a means of signification. The range of options is wide:

No Aural                                          Maximum Aural
Communication                                     Communication

In practical terms it is impossible to have no aural signification. Even if a director chooses to use no spoken words, music, or sound effects, there will be sound from the movement and breathing of the performers and noise in the theater from air conditioning or heating units, rustling programs, and coughing (or, if outdoors, from airplanes and birds). While some of these are incidental sounds, they contribute to the meanings of the experience if for no other reason than because they distract spectators from perceiving other signifiers. "Once a director becomes aware of what sound and music can add to his production, he'll be more likely to use it in the future. . . . Sound will be a new toy for him to play with, to manipulate more imaginatively and inventively each time around" (Kaye and LeBrecht 1992, 9).

After a director determines whether to emphasize or deemphasize the aural sign system for a production, she decides which style of sound and music to use, ranging from realistic to abstract sound and traditional to nontraditional music.

**Realistic**　　　　　　　　　　　　　　　　　　　　　　　　**Abstract**
**Sound**　　　　　　　　　　　　　　　　　　　　　　　　　　**Sound**

At the center of this continuum might be a production that mixes both realistic and abstract sound in order to present historic and future time simultaneously.

**Traditional**　　　　　　　　　　　　　　　　　　　　**Nontraditional**
**Music**　　　　　　　　　　　　　　　　　　　　　　　　　　**Music**

The director must choose music that is familiar and/or traditional or music that is highly abstract and/or artificial. Such choices help define the aural style of the production as a whole.

The director must also answer other questions. Should live or electronically reproduced music be used? Should the sound and music be amplified? Should dialects or bilingual dialogue be employed? Should all effects be natural and live? For his production of *Akropolis* Jerzy Grotowski chose not to use amplification; nevertheless, he was able to create an abstract soundscape through the phenomenal manipulation of the performers' voices. Grotowski created "a complex contrapuntal vocal score, composed of inarticulate shrieks, ragged whispers and patterned chants, underpinned by a percussive score of abrasive metallic clankings—words were treated as pre-rational incantation and physical sound. The result was an intricately constructed vision of the darkness of the human condition, an image of humanity destroyed" (Bradby and Williams 1988, 118). Richard Foreman creates a distinct kind of soundscape by using electronic sound, even for the spoken words, as a way of integrating the aural, visual, and linguistic sign systems: "The sound-layering I use—tapes of repeated words, noises, music—also serves to reflect the multiple pulls of the visual and ideational aspects of the manuscript" (Foreman, quoted in Davy 1981, 141).

## How Sound Works

Sound is made up of a series of pressure waves in the air. The major characteristics of sound waves are their intensity (loudness), frequency (pitch), and timbre (unique quality). Most sounds are complex: they are made up of several sound waves of various intensities and frequencies.

Like ocean waves, sound waves have greater intensity when larger and less when smaller. The level of intensity is measured in decibels (dB). The human ear can process dBs ranging from around 20 dB (a barely audible whisper or note) to around 130 dB, at which point the waves become so powerful that hearing is painful.

Frequency refers to the number of pressure waves per second. The higher the frequency, the higher the pitch; the lower the frequency, the lower the pitch. The human ear can hear frequencies of 16 to 16,000 Hz (Hertz).

Timbre is the unique quality of a sound; it makes one voice sound different from another or a saxophone sound different from a cello. Performers' voices sound different because of the size and thickness of their vocal cords and the configuration of their resonating chambers. Musical instruments sound different because of their shape, size, material, and method of producing sound (plucking or hammering strings, beating, blowing wind). Electronic music and sound equipment have the capability of digitizing the sound of every musical instrument and creating any abstract sound that can be heard by the human ear.

Using variations in intensity and frequency, performers produce a broad spectrum of vocal sounds, some of which are linguistic and others paralinguistic (moans, weeping, or screams). These utterances are created by the breath and vocal cords, which produce vocalized sound waves. Likewise, music is created with musical instruments or electronic synthesizers by producing variations in the intensity and frequency of sound waves. Music can either be recorded or performed live. Sound effects can be performed live and/or reproduced from recordings. It is also possible to combine music and sound to create special aural effects. For example, with a synthesizer, sampler, or other special recording equipment it is possible to produce the sound of a thousand wine glasses breaking simultaneously or the sound of a dozen horses screaming (*Equus*) or the distorted breaking of a musical string (*The Cherry Orchard*).

Sampling keyboards allow for digitized sound to be stored in a computer's memory so that any sound can be played back in any order with any frequency, and each sound can be manipulated to be played in higher or lower tones, in less or more time, or modulated in a number of other ways to produce wondrous sounds and music (Gorton 1991, 79). An example of how sound can be formulated to create unnatural effects comes from Robert Wilson's production of *The Forest*. "For the factory sequence in Act Two, Kuhn [Wilson's sound designer] has made an eight-track tape with eight different machine sounds, each of which emanate from different speakers on stage. Bird sounds will come from auditorium speakers to make the audience feel as if it is part of the forest environment" (Calhoun 1989, 50). In the same production "an actor sits in a metal tub dropping stones from his mouth. But instead of the sound of rocks hitting metal, the audience hears glass crashing" (48).

Postmodern directors are experimenting with and manipulating sound and music to enhance their performance's communication. For example, Richard Foreman sits in the front row during performances and manipulates recorded music and voices as well as his own voice (live and taped) as part of the event (see fig. 13, lower right corner). "For all my early plays I worked the tape recorder myself, because I liked to be able to regulate the rhythm of the performance by starting and stopping the tape, holding the pauses the way I felt they should be held for that particular audience" (1992, 34). Foreman uses sound as the commanding element of the performance; he manipulates sound and silence to dominate the entire performance.

The aural composition of a performance is limited only by the imaginative powers of the director, the vocal capabilities of the performers, the technical capabilities of the sound designer/technicians, the musical skill of the composer and musicians, and the sound reproduction and reinforcement equipment in the audio lab and performance space. Robert Wilson forges complex sound habitats.

> [Sound] ricochets off the walls and ceiling, moving instantaneously from stage to audience, dispersing bits of memory, data, noise and music into the darkness. To sit out in the auditorium is to be adrift on an ocean of sound, which like deep water can turn suddenly from calm to turbulent, lulling us one moment and buffeting us the next. Wilson may extol the values of distance and restraint in design and performance but audially his is a theatre of total immersion. (Shyer 1989, 233)

Wilson converses through sound and music that are chosen to reflect, reinforce, or serve as a counterpoint to the visual sign systems. He creates a theater in which the content and meaning of the performance are its visual and aural presence.

## Sound Conventions

The use of sound effects and music can be divided into four categories: framing effects, underscoring, transitions, and specific cues (Kaye and LeBrecht 1992, 20).

### Framing Effects

Sound and music can be used to set the context of a production. Music preceding the opening of the performance or between the scenes can prepare the audience for the 1950s, a frenetic farce, poetic language, or a funeral—depending upon the choice of music. For Ariane Mnouchkine's production of *The Orestia* "a slow, Kabuki-like crescendo of thunderous drumming compels the chattering to stop at the start of the play" (Ratcliffe 1991, H5). Mnouchkine uses drums to frame the impending event and to get the audience's adrenaline pumping.

### Underscoring

Sound and music can be used to create an atmosphere while the dramatic action is unfolding; it is not sound that is part of the dramatic action or sound that is specifically called for by the playwright. Sound or music used in this way is usually not heard by the characters, only by the audience. One type of underscoring that is part of the performance is the voice-over, where "the audience hears disembodied speech—sometimes embellished with effects—presenting information or thoughts" (Kaye and LeBrecht 1992, 23). Vocal amplification is a way of underscoring the speech act itself.

> With the aid of a harmonizer Kuhn [Wilson's sound designer] is also able to change the pitch of a performer's voice or transform its dimensions. In the first scene of the German *CIVIL warS*, for example, the voices of the two astronauts seen floating on ladders in

outer space occupied a vocal space unlike that of anyone else on stage, as though their words were reverberating within "an empty cathedral." On a few rare occasions an actor's voice may even be heard in its natural state—an often startling occurrence once the ear has become attuned to the prevailing sonic milieu. . . . (Shyer 1989, 237)

Wilson repeatedly underscores (overscores might be a more appropriate word) the natural voice with electronic reinforcement and manipulation in order to create a second language (a second discourse) that resonates beyond traditional linguistic discourse.

## Transitions

Sound effects and music can help connect scenes, actions, events, characters, and emotional shifts in a performance. "The connective can be music, which I sometimes use as the emotional climax of the previous scene or a comment on the next scene" (Douglas Turner Ward interview, in Bartow 1988a, 307). One form of transition (as well as framing device) is to use sound or music to introduce a character, as when the wind blows whenever Dracula enters the stage. One of the most fascinating uses of sound to underscore a character comes from Josef Svoboda's production of Goethe's *Faust*. Alfred Radok, the director, wanted Faust's servant and Mephistopheles to be played by the same actor. The problem was how to let the audience know when Mephistopheles inhabited the servant's body.

The stage floor provides the answer while at the same time creating a provocative theatrical sound effect—it echoes hollow footsteps when trod on by the servant, but under Mephistopheles' feet produces no sound at all. "The servant walks to the door," explains Svoboda, "and we hear the hollow sound of his steps in the vast room. He turns just as he reaches the door, and starts back—suddenly, silence! And we know, instantly, that it's the Devil." (Aronson 1987, 25)

This mystical sound effect underscores the change in character that would be cumbersome if not impossible to portray through costume or makeup changes.

## Specific Cues

There are three categories of specific cues: required music, spot effects, and ambiance (Kaye and LeBrecht 1992, 25). Required music is specific music that is called for by the playwright—a waltz for a required dance scene, Feste's singing in *Twelfth Night*, and so forth. Spot effects are specified sound effects such a doorbell or phone ringing. Gunshots that are required by the playwright as an integral part of the playscript's action and that require precise timing (as in *The Sea Gull*, *'night Mother*, and *Hedda Gabler*) are other examples of spot effects. Ambiance is generalized sound that usually covers a lengthy period of time and sets a required atmosphere. "The main difference between a spot effect and ambiance is that ambiance blends into the background, whereas a spot effect takes focus. Spot effects are often added to an existing ambient track" (Kaye and LeBrecht 1992, 26).

## Semiotics of Sound

In order for aural signifiers to be translated into meanings by an audience, spectators must have the ability to decode what they hear. For natural sound effects—a rooster crowing, rain falling, a car starting up and driving away—most spectators derive a shared literal meaning. For abstract sounds and for music without lyrics, however, there can be no absolute denotative meanings shared by the audience; there is no one-to-one semantic referent. Each individual spectator will be affected by the music or abstract sound in a personal way. "Pure music is an abstraction about emotion. . . . Music is a symbolic emotional experience" (Ostwald 1963, 199). Spectators with sophisticated musical knowledge, however, will receive more (or at least different) meanings from a portion of a well-known symphony used as preperformance music than will a classical music neophyte. "Our responses to music are the result of training and past experience in listening. Personal preferences for certain musical instruments, composers, and forms are involved, as well as cultural attitudes which determine whether music should be considered beautiful or ugly, popular or classical, desirable or undesirable" (Ostwald 1963, 192). Likewise, when an audience hears a screeching sound during a performance it may produce very different meanings for different spectators. It is likely that the meanings of music and sound will be visceral rather than intellectual for most audience members, although sound technicians, musicians, composers, and music lovers in an audience will be more aware of different dimensions of music than will non–musically oriented spectators.

Eero Tarasti (1979) contends that unique musical codes exist in specific cultures; encoding is done by the composer who understands acoustic codes, and decoding is done through an audience's culturally determined "patterns and symbols which permit a listener to interpret his responses to a musical work. . . . Consequently two different structures determine a musical communication: the first is manifested in the form which a composer sets upon the musical substance afforded by culture, while the latter is in the form which a culture gives to the individual listener's musical experience" (31). Directors who choose to incorporate music in a production seek music that reflects, underscores, or even dominates the dramatic action of the performance. By doing so, directors and composers reach beyond linguistic and visual signification to produce a deeper and richer sensory experience for the spectators.

There has been much debate about whether or not semiotics is a useful tool for the analysis of music because no musical semantic reference system exists. Orlov argues that "musical sound meets the definition neither of sign nor of the icon" (Orlov 1981, 135).

> If music is to be considered a sign system, then it is a very strange one: an icon which has nothing in common with the object it presents: an abstract language which does not allow for a prior definition of its alphabet and vocabulary, and operates with an indefinite, virtually infinite number of unique elements; a text which cannot be decomposed into standard interchangeable items. . . .
>
> Therefore, what appears as the icon on the surface acts, behind the surface, as an abstract sign—a symbol, but a special kind of symbol which is unique and otherwise undefinable. (Orlov 1981, 136)

Music has communicative power, but it operates quite differently from spoken language because it has no direct referent in the material or imaginational worlds. "Each single tone is contemplated and experienced by the listener as an inimitable multidimensional object, a piece of reality itself alive and rich with all sorts of meaning" (Orlov 1981, 134).

> If music (and sound) is viewed as a purely symbolic system, its value in performance increases enormously. The material quantification of sound or music may be technically helpful for the com-

poser, musicians and sound designer, but the meanings of those material manifestations contribute nothing to the audience's understanding. It is only through performance that meaning can be communicated to an audience, and when the aural sign-systems are viewed as purely symbolic, then sound takes its place as a theatrical element on the same level as setting, lighting, costuming, and movement. Even a highly realistic thunderstorm, such as that in Chekhov's *Uncle Vanya*, has enormous symbolic meaning to an audience, and the continual underscoring of scenes in American film and television has a tremendous effect in communicating the mood and symbolic relevance of the action to the viewers. (Westerman 1991, 13)

Many contemporary directors use aural sign systems in more dynamic and integrated ways than did directors of the past. Modern technology has made it easier to create abstract sounds and to amplify and distort the speaking voice. "I like to think that the microphone has come to occupy the place in contemporary theater that the mask occupied in the theater of ancient Greece. It is a device that creates both intimacy and distance, it conceals and it projects, it acts as a shield and as a medium of relentless exposure" (Sellars, quoted in Kaye and LeBrecht 1992, vii). Advanced technology is also used to produce music and to coordinate its use as an integral and constant presence in performances. Richard Foreman works meticulously to record, edit, and control the sound and music for his productions.

He gathers the performers and, in one or two sessions, records all of the dialog on tape, and then, he notes, "it takes me about a week to edit the tape, so that we can rehearse to it." During the week of editing, he adds music and noises until he has a complete sound score, explaining, "when I start rehearsing, it's really as if I had an orchestral score, it's really like choreographing—the piece is choreographed to the aural score." (Davy 1981, 164)

Foreman sees sound and music as the controlling and liberating elements of his productions.

## Sound Effects

Sound effects designers have at their disposal the following elements: rhythm, intensity, pitch, tone, speed, shape, and orderliness. Sound designers can imitate or record natural sounds through mechanical or electronic means, and by creating abstract sounds or distorting natural sounds they can achieve any sound imaginable. They can also combine music with nonmusical sound to achieve even more complex aural signification. "I mean, by playing special music with a special sound effect on top of it, suddenly you can change the whole mood by changing this one sound effect" (Kuhn, quoted in Calhoun 1989, 48).

In the not-too-distant past, sound effects were employed only to produce specific called-for information—a doorbell announcing an anticipated arrival, for example. Today sound effects are often scored to provide a continuous aural environment. A production set in the outdoors might have roosters crowing and other birds chirping in the morning, silence during the heat of the day, and night sounds (crickets, frogs, owls) after dark—all part of a continuous soundscape that could also incorporate ambient music, sounds, and carefully orchestrated performers' voices.

Normally, when a director chooses to use sound effects for a production, she layers her vision of an aural environment on top of her understanding of the dramatic action of the playscript or performance piece and the chosen production style. Only after developing a vision can a director work with a sound designer to create the individual sounds that, when blended into a sequence of sounds (including music), create a unified aural environment with a symbiotic relationship to the other sign systems of the production. Alternately, if a director chooses to use sound effects to shock or disorient his audience, then their selection must be guided by a desire for conflict or disunity. "The sound tracks for my plays became very loud, even assaultive, to echo the world as I experience it. I felt I needed something in my art that could match the degree of aggressiveness that washed over me as I walked the streets of New York" (Foreman 1992, 96).

At least two postmodern directors go about choosing music and sound effects before they do anything else. Elizabeth LeCompte first selects sound and music and then finds (through improvisation) dramatic action and related activities that reflect the mood and emotion that emanate from the music. "I find sound effects before I have the action for them" (LeCompte, quoted in Sommers 1991, 36). Richard Foreman's quest for music for *Livre des Splendeurs* led him to music stores where he picked up several records that looked interesting to him.

Then it's really amazing how sometimes when I get home . . . I put the records on and said, "Shit. I just wasted a hundred dollars buying all these records, they're useless." Then, next day, I'm bored and have nothing to do, so I put on the record again, and hearing it a second time, all of a sudden you hear a section that's . . . aha! It's great! The only time I really appreciated Cagian principles of chance is in getting music for the shows . . . it always works. (Davy 1981, 164)

This kind of chance or random selection of music and sound effects points to the importance of music and sound for these directors. They consider the aural sign systems important enough to let music and sound be a dominant force in the shaping of a production's dramatic action and physical and linguistic signifiers. First come the music and sound, then the other signifying systems.

Most directors, however, when piecing together a soundscape, choose each sound to reflect, project, or enhance a precise moment in the dramatic action. Each sound can vary in its intensity, rhythm, shape, duration, tone, pitch, and orderliness. Each series of sounds also can be adjusted to reflect the developing and varying progression of the performance's tensions and complications.

With modern sound technology the designer and technician can manipulate many different aspects of sound and music to signify shifting meanings.

The sound technician uses steady, sustained sounds to suggest continuous movement, directness, stability, and formality. Quiet sounds imply repose and tranquillity. Undulating sounds that vary in pitch or rhythm suggest purposeful movement and insistence. With intermittent sounds, the technician alludes to indecision, disorder, and lack of leadership. With sounds that suddenly increase in volume, he gives the feeling of climax, aggressiveness, and definite action. When sounds gradually get louder, they create suspense or relentless progress. Sounds that suddenly fade indicate cowardice, fear, and defeat: those that gradually fade evoke dejection or temporary defeat. Sounds that increase in volume and then suddenly stop or continue at a specific level create the illusion of opposition, conflict, and frustration. High-pitched sounds set a gay mood, whereas low-pitched ones suggest sadness. (Ostwald 1973, 27)

By manipulating volume, pitch, rhythm, intermittency, lengths of fades, speed of changes, and the order and structural relationships of sound and music, the designer and technician create aural signifiers that spectators cluster into ordered or disordered grids of meanings.

## Sound Reinforcement

Sound reinforcement can be used to amplify any sound in the theater. Live sound effects, music, and performers' voices are routinely amplified through electronic means. Reinforcement is particularly useful for large theaters or places where the acoustics are not good. Found spaces such as an old barn or an expansive hillside may need massive reinforcement, while a medium-size theater may call for modest amplification for those sitting in the back of the auditorium. The technology exists to bring the same loudness level and sound quality to every spectator in the theater. "Modern audiences demand that shows be easy to hear, and performers and producers expect the sound department to make this possible" (Ruling 1991, 39). The technology also exists to move the source and location of sound around the theater; sounds can come from in front, above, behind, left, or right, and they can be produced simultaneously, sequentially, or randomly. In *The Golden Windows* Wilson made extensive use of this technology.

> Actors onstage wear wireless body mics, with each mic feeding into a large mixing board with 24 input channels and eight output channels, which direct the sound to 26 speakers placed around the Opera House. Kuhn [Wilson's sound designer] and an assistant use a computer and the mixing board to direct the sound from the live feeds to the various speakers, according to an elaborate plan worked out with Wilson. "It's all done by stop watch," says Kuhn. "There's no improvising, not for one second." (Baker 1985, 22)

Wilson is pushing modern technology as far as it can go to create enormously expressive soundscapes that expand the horizon of expectation of his spectators. Choices about sound reinforcement—whether or not to use it and, if so, in what ways—have much to do with how effective the aural sign system will be as a vehicle for signification during a performance.

Not only may reinforcement be necessary to increase the volume enough to allow all spectators to hear what the director wants them to hear at each moment of the performance, but the volume, quality, direction, and naturalness of aural stimulation are signifiers in their own right. Amplified sound makes a clear statement about the style of a production and can be a device for reminding the members of the audience that they are in a theater witnessing a *theatrical* event (similar to Brecht's idea of using exposed lighting to remind audiences that they are in a theater). Directors may also use sound to wrench the audience physically.

> The effect of a loud sound, particularly a sudden, unexpected one, is to startle the listener. Startle reactions to sounds have characteristic physiological components. A reaction to the sound of a pistol shot, for example, includes elevation of the blood pressure; quickening of the heart beat; changes in breathing and sweating; and sharp muscular contractions over the entire body. (Ostwald 1973, 30)

Jolting sound can have one of two effects on spectators; it can snap them out of their concentration and involvement, or it can draw them more deeply into the event. Directors may, for example, deliberately distort the human voice, sound effects, and music to signify dehumanization, otherworldliness, or mechanization—all elements of the postmodern world.

### Options for Aural Communication

The questions a director, vocal coach, and sound designer face when designing the aural composition of a production are numerous and complex. Should they use no music or continuous music? No sound effects or maximal sound effects? Harmonic or discordant sound? Rhythmic or arrhythmic sound? Single-source or multiple-source sound? Unidirectional or multidirectional sound? Should a production use only live sounds? Should a production use only electronic sound? Or should a production juxtapose live and electronic sounds with music?

Directors are confronted with additional questions about the use of sound. If music, what kind? Jazz? Classical? Abstract? How loud or soft? How much time should each piece of music or sound effect take? From what direction should the sound come? As a director makes choices based on these questions (and others), she shapes the aggregate sound of the production and develops a rich texture of aural signification.

# Music

The musical elements that directors, composers, and musicians have at their disposal are "rhythmicity, intensity, pitch, tone, speed, shape, and orderliness" (Ostwald 1963, 25).

Of these seven attributes, some can be coded in a written form, such as the way written music codes rhythmicity and pitch (where anyone who understands the code of written music may decode the information), while other attributes may only be coded through the actual performance of the sound. Intensity can be described physically based on the logarithmic scale of decibels, yet in the coding of written music, intensity is given not precise but relative measurements. How loud is "forte"? How soft is "pianissimo"? "Crescendo" and "decrescendo" are simply a rise and a fall in intensity. The individual performance, not the material, determines how quickly and to what intensity that rise or fall is made. In written music, speed can be coded in a very precise way—such as a quarter note equals sixty beats per minute—or can be given only relative measures, as with the terms "lento" and "allegro," which the performers interpret according to their own experiences and biases. Similarly, tone and shape can be described very accurately, especially with the use of computer technology, but in written music, the codes that describe these attributes (such as the terms "pizzicato," "staccato," and "dolce," and the symbols of accents and/or dots above the notes) may be performed with a variety of sound qualities totaling the number of the different musicians and instruments that have ever performed music. Orderliness, however, is the attribute that depends mainly on the social adaptation and education of the individual audience members. . . . Of all the above attributes of sound, orderliness is the most difficult to predict how the coding will be interpreted and understood. The music of Bach has a very high degree of orderliness, yet few listeners have the education and capability to decode the complexity of where that orderliness lies. And many have so little understanding of the code that they feel only boredom and sometimes even resentment toward music of the genre. (Westerman 1991, 5–6)

Traditionally, music in the theater (for nonmusical productions) was relegated to preshow or intermission music, designed to put the audience in the right mood: somber for tragedy, upbeat for comedy.

Today, however, music is used in more imaginative ways. It is often used to project a character's individuality or a scene's emotional circumstance: scores of both sound and music are composed to reflect continuously changing emotional values, conflicts, and dramatic actions, and dialogue is turned into lyrics through musical composition and accompaniment. Music is also used as a counterpoint to other signifiers as a way of shifting a spectator's perceptions. Consequently, music is becoming a more dominant sign system in the theater.

> All my plays, including the classical plays and the contemporary plays that I haven't written, have music behind the text most of the time. If I'm working with a composer, I can't conceive of going into rehearsal without having the music completed, because that's going to be my play. . . . From the first day of rehearsal, I insist on having my soundman, who is busy shuffling these tracks, and it evolves organically as we're rehearsing. I spend just as much time altering my music as I do dealing with the performing and I think that all kinds of wonderful things happen that way. Again, I choose music that somehow takes a section of the text and makes a comment on it or lifts it into a slightly different plane. (Foreman interview, in Bartow 1988a, 135)

Directors are finding that the emotional and spiritual imprint of music can affect profoundly the impact of the dramatic action on the emotional experience of the audience. Thus, Peter Sellars has turned to opera because he believes that music is the primary signifier in the postmodern world.

> In an age when the interrelatedness of things is increasingly the issue, opera becomes the medium of choice. Multilingual, multicultural, multimedia, diachronic, dialogic, dialectical, and somehow strangely delectable, opera is the one form that seems to have a chance of reproducing and invoking the simultaneities, confusions, juxtapositions, bitter tragedy, and just plain malarkey that constitute the texture of recent history. (Sellars 1989, 23)

Sellars attempts to blend the music of traditional opera with the sights and sounds of contemporary society, not just to show that Mozart is contemporary but more importantly to show that the music can enlighten the meanings of contemporary life and art. "It is true that Mr. Sellars's productions . . . wrench the listener out of a complacent familiarity. Indeed their effect is not just to inspire a fresh response to

Mozart, but, for instance, to Spanish Harlem [the location of Sellars's production of *Don Giovanni*], which becomes not just the home of slum stereotypes but a place illuminated by the humanity of Mozart's music" ("Colas, Leather, Terrorism" 1991, 85).

The use of music as a counterpoint to other visual and aural elements of a mise-en-scène is commonplace in postmodern theater. Martha Clarke, for her production of *The Garden of Earthly Delights*, has a woman slowly and sensuously undulating to the "soothing sounds of a cello" only to be "pierced straight through with the pick-end of the instrument" (Copeland 1988, 14). Richard Foreman states, "I, on the other hand, was interested in introducing music that displaced the emotional quality of the scene; the music was *contra* to the dominant atmosphere. I wanted to make the scene other than it appeared to be through the text" (1992, 96).

Music has the power to soothe or enrage the emotions and psyche of spectators in ways that words, movement, costumes, and color cannot begin to achieve. Postmodern directors often assault the audience with aural signifiers that range from reinforcement and harmony with the other signifying elements of the mise-en-scène to negation and disharmony. In each case, however, spectators are expected to construct meanings from the performance through the carefully orchestrated or random choruses of sound and music.

## Summary

A director's vision often includes the use of sound and music to communicate a performance's meanings. The use of this sign system is effective only when it supports, enriches, amplifies, or serves as a counterpoint to a production's dramatic action, style, and mise-en-scène. The performers' speech, the music, and the sound effects must fit the overall style of the mise-en-scène or contrast with it for a discordant effect. For example, if a production is naturalistic, the music ought to be realistically motivated (emanate from a phonograph onstage) and historically accurate, and the sound effects and speech patterns should be authentic (appropriate dialects). For an abstract or absurd play the speech, music, and sound effects may need to be distorted, dreamlike, or ludicrously contradictory. By blending aural signifiers, the director enhances communication by reflecting or reinforcing the performance's structure, mise-en-scène, rhythms, conflicts, and harmonies or dissonances. Modern technology now allows for the radical reinforcement or distortion of natural sounds and the creation of otherworldly music, which enlivens the discourse between the mise-en-scène and the spectators. It also requires an aural stretching of the audience's horizon of expectations.

# Chapter 7

# Olfactoral and Tactile Systems

## Olfactoral Communication

Spectators encounter odors while attending a theatrical performance. They smell the polluted air of the freeway as they drive to the theater. They smell the fragrant odor of flowers as they walk to the theater from the parking lot. They become aware of a musty-moldy odor in the old theater lobby. They meet their friends in the lobby and become aware of two distinct body colognes (one masculine, one feminine). They smell the cigar of another spectator. They enter the theater and smell potent, sweet, cinnamony incense burning on the stage. They take their seats and notice they are sitting by someone who has not bathed recently. Each of these odors either frames or is an actual part of the performance.

Olfaction is considered a secondary communication system not because odors cannot have a profound impact on the audience but because olfaction is rarely used consciously by directors to affect the meaning of a performance. There are legitimate reasons for this: playwrights rarely concern themselves with smells as a meaningful force in their playscripts, there are few mechanical devices available in the theater to control and disperse fragrances, and the human sensory capability itself is limited in its ability to detect various odors. Nonetheless, directors can and do use specific odors to signify the following information:

Historical period: orange and cloves or sulfur burning
Geographic location: alfalfa or pine
Specific location: smell of fish or disinfectants
Socioeconomic circumstances: unpleasant body odor or expensive
    perfume

Ethnicity/nationality: the smell of Italian or Oriental food
Weather conditions: wood burning or flowers
Time of day: bacon frying
Mood: gunpowder or light perfume

The director decides first whether or not to use odors as a sign system.

No
Odors

Maximum
Odors

If she chooses to use odors, she must then decide how many odors, when to use them, and, more important, how to get them to the audience. The latter concern is great because, unlike the use of lights or properties (which can be changed quickly and often), an odor takes time to fill the theater and cannot be swept away instantly. If a director chooses to use the olfactoral sign system, it is likely she will use one fragrance to help locate the production in a certain place or socioeconomic level at the outset of the performance, and at most she may use one or two other odors later, perhaps after each intermission. If a performance is outdoors, the problem of distribution of the odors is exacerbated. (If there is a strong wind, the whole notion is moribund.) Outdoor productions are also susceptible to unwanted odors intruding on the performance—automobile pollution or skunk scent.

## How Olfaction Works

Olfaction is an interdisciplinary phenomenon involving chemistry, neurology, physiology, and psychology.

Smelling is a complex process. It starts with molecules in the outside world which possess certain special attributes. By virtue of these attributes, the molecules can interact with sensory receptors in the nose so as to send specific nerve impulse-patterns to the brain. The brain then compares the incoming signal with other signal-patterns held in a memory store and, depending upon whether or not it can find a matching pattern, it assigns a meaning to the signal and decides on the most appropriate response. (Wright 1982, 3)

The human nose is able to discern thousands of different odors if two thresholds are reached (Altner 1978, 233). The first threshold is detection. This means that there must be sufficient molecules in the air for a human to recognize that there is a special odor present, even though he may not be able to tell what the odor is. The second threshold is recognition. Normally it takes a high concentration of molecules to reach the recognition threshold—where the brain can match the odor with a distinct memory of that odor. Everyone has different threshold levels (of both varieties) as well as a different general ability to smell substances of all kinds. In other words, no two people are alike in their ability to detect and describe odors (Burton 1976, 108–9).

It is also significant that once an odor is perceived it is normal to lose comprehension of it. "Sensory fatigue is manifested by a reduced ability to perceive a certain sensation after a more or less prolonged exposure to a higher level of the stimulus in question" (Wright 1982, 166).

## The Semiotics of Olfaction

The semiotics of olfaction is complicated by the knowledge that individuals perceive odors differently in terms of their presence, strength, and meanings. Individual spectators are likely to detect odors at different times (and some not at all). It is also likely that individual spectators will have different recollections and meanings arising out of contact with individual smells. There is no one-to-one denotative referent between a single odor and each spectator's experience. For example, one spectator who grew up in the 1960s and frequently had incense burning in his commune will have a different recollection of what incense burning on stage means from another spectator who associates incense with the morning sickness she had every time she smelled it during her pregnancy. Likewise, the smell of cigarette smoke coming from the stage will have different meanings for one spectator who is trying to quit smoking and another who is allergic to the smoke. "A smell perceived is a message received. Chemical molecules are the medium, but the message is whatever interpretation is given to the signal by the recipient" (Wright 1982, 12).

Is there a cultural code for odors that can be employed by the director to help guide his choices as he determines which odors might be useful signifiers in a production? Furthermore, are there categories, labels, or words that can be used to communicate a director's choices to the technician who must find a way to provide the odor for the audience? There are some standard categories and words that describe odors:

Food: turkey roasting, steak frying, chili simmering, bread baking
Spices: garlic, onions, peppers, curries
Flowers: roses, lilacs, gardenias
Body odor: male, female, goat, elephant
Perfume: flowery, spicy, sweet, sensuous; or Old Spice, Tabu,
  Musk
Location: pulp mill, tire plant, bakery, outhouse
Air quality: car exhaust, ocean breeze, spring rain
Pungent odors: dead animal, skunk, excrement, fish
Candy: peppermint, chocolate, coffee, cherry

This brief list indicates that we do have a way of communicating about odors. Odors can also be described as being similar or dissimilar, friendly or unfriendly, pleasant or unpleasant, sweet or acrid, and the like. Scientists have attempted to classify odors, but no two scientists appear to agree. Their main purpose has been to establish a few general categories that are useful for grouping odors—for example, flowery, etheric, musky, camphorous, sweaty, rotten, and stinging (Altner 1978, 231). It is possible, then, to talk about odors and to develop a strategy for using them in a production.

There are, of course, certain odors that can be used safely to signify general meanings for an audience.

Smoke: fire or danger
Rose scent: love or romance
Baking bread: home or family
Heavy flowery scent: sex or decadence
Body odor: uncleanness, poverty, or barbarism
Pine: outdoors or bathroom
Turkey baking: Thanksgiving or family togetherness

This partial list suggests that there is at least a vague cultural code present in America that supports signification through olfaction.

## Options for Olfactoral Communication

Directors ask themselves several questions in regard to the use of odors in the theater. Should I use them? If so, how many? Where should they come from? Onstage? Offstage? In the lobby? Should they be realistically motivated or not? How strong should they be? When should they be introduced? How long should they last? How can one odor be cleared away so the next one can be admitted? In answering these questions, the director is able to shape the employment of odors as a contributing sign system for a production. Hospitals, barns, nurseries (both for babies and plants), basements, and pine forests have their own odor. Recognition will be given to these places if the appropriate odor invades the theater.

Peter Brook used incense to help set the location of his production of *Mahabharata* in India. Also, he habitually uses fire, torches, and candles onstage. In his production of *Carmen* the three bonfires in the mountain scene worked remarkably. "The fires' warmth, smell and above all the incantational properties of flame and smoke infiltrate[d] the audience, pulling us in" (Eder 1984, 9). At the opening of *Miss Julie* August Strindberg has the maid fry food as a way of reinforcing the extreme realism of the playscript. Tom, in *The Glass Menagerie*, smokes constantly to show both his uneasiness and his defiance of his mother. This smoke, however, also gets consumed by the audience (or at least the front rows in a large theater) and has a visceral effect on them. Productions that have pyrotechnics and gunfire, such as *Les Misérables*, produce a pungent, smoky odor, which adds significantly to the sense of struggle, death, and triumph that emerges. Robert Wilson uses fire and smoke in most of his productions: "open flames and banks of lighted candles were often seen in the early works" (Shyer 1989, 197). Human body odor also becomes a signifier in small environmental theaters in which audience and performers come in contact with one another. The Living Theatre and the Polish Laboratory Theatre placed spectators and performers within odor detection range. The object was to get all of the audience's sensors involved in the decoding process.

Even though olfaction may have limited uses in the theater, it can be a meaning-producing signifier. "It is well-known that odors may often tend to evoke a tremendous emotional response if they are associated in the memory with some event or situation which has been important in the experience of the individual" (Wright 1982, 162).

## Taste

A detailed analysis of the use of taste in the theater will not be provided here because it is so rarely used. Taste, however, is linked to olfaction and therefore deserves mention. The Bread and Puppet Theatre shares freshly baked bread after their performances, and it contributes to the communal meaning of their work. The Company of

Sirens' production of *Mother Tongues* began by assembling the audience for snacks before show time (S. Bennett 1990, 129). Sometimes candy is shared with children at a theater for youth performance, a parade, or a circus. Beer, wine, and soda are often served in the lobby before a performance and during intermissions, which provides a social frame. A production of *Bernie's Bar Mitzvah* re-created the Jewish ceremony for the audience, "complete with chopped liver, knishes, corned beef and pastrami—and then [came] the sit-down dinner" (Gussow 1992, C2). Ariane Mnouchkine had performers serve as waiters in the bar/snack area of her theater at Vincennes. The bar offered "rough red wine or beer for sale, together with sandwiches of coarse peasant bread" (Bradby and Williams 1988, 93). The choice of food and drinks and the way they were served (by performers) were signifying frames: champagne and caviar served on silver trays would have made an antithetical statement. It would be fascinating to provide such elite treats and service during an intermission for *The Grapes of Wrath* or Grotowski's *Akropolis;* the shock value from the contrast might jolt the audience into new perceptions.

Technically, taste works through a combination of information provided to the brain by olfaction and taste buds in the mouth. Scientists classify tastes in four general groupings: sweet, sour, bitter, and salt (T. L. Bennett 1978, 108). Each of these tastes elicits different reactions from each individual; no two people experience taste in exactly the same way. Most foods and drinks, however, offer a complex taste by blending the four general tastes.

The communal, religious, and family aspect of sharing food and drink before, during, or after a performance is a meaning-producing experience. A director may decide that such eating and tasting can aid in the signification process.

No Use
of Taste

Maximum Use
of Taste

After this decision is made a whole series of questions must be answered. What kind of food and/or drink should be served? Plain or elegant? Who will serve it? The performers? The staff? When should the food be served? Should it be part of the actual performance time-space? Or should it happen before or after the performance? By answering these questions, the director is on his way to providing spectators with an additional sensory experience—beyond those of traditional theater performances.

## Tactile Communication

Spectators engage their sense of touch when witnessing a theatrical event. Before the event begins a spectator may sit in a comfortable chair in the lobby, sense the heat in the theater, brush up against another spectator, and feel pain in his lower back as he stands up to enter the auditorium. In one theater a spectator may be asked purposefully to sit on a wooden bench, in another she may sit on a platform with no chair, and in yet another she may sit in a plush leather chair with built-in lumbar support. Or, as in Andrei Serban's production of *The Fragments of a Trilogy*, the audience may be required to stand and move about the playing space. Also, a spectator may be sat on, grabbed, kissed, or sprayed with water while witnessing a performance.

### How Touch Works

Skin has three different dimensions of sensation: pain, touch and pressure, and heat and cold (Schmidt 1978, 81). Human beings can sense these three dimensions simultaneously or individually. As with the other senses, every person has a different threshold for experiencing each of these sensations; one child may feel highly uncomfortable in freezing weather, while another loves to play in the snow. How well touch or temperature communicates to individuals is directly related to these threshold levels. The awareness of heat and cold tends to diminish over time, as does the awareness of touch and pressure. Pain, however, can be highly persistent. Since it is rare, however, for heat, cold, pain, or pressure to play a significant role as a signifier in the theater, this analysis will focus on touch, or tactile communication.

Skin is the sensory receptor for tactile sensations and is the largest sensory system in humans. It is not uniformly sensitive: some parts of the body (hands and feet, e.g.) are more sensitive than other parts (earlobes and elbows). Skin also reflects outward; that is, it serves as a signifier to others who view it.

Our skin, therefore, not only receives the signals that come to us from our environment and relays them to centers of the nervous system for deciphering, but also picks up signals from our inner world, all of which are then translated into quantifiable terms. The skin is the mirror of the organism's functioning; its color, texture, moistness, dryness, color, and every one of its other aspects, reflect our state of being, psychological as well as physiological. Our skin tingles with excitement and feels numb with shock; it is a mirror of our passions and emotions. (Montagu 1986, 12)

Performers use makeup to help communicate visual signs from their skin, but audience members also communicate with one another by observing people's skin—its color, condition, and health.

## The Semiotics of Touch

There is no comprehensive cultural code that matches clearly each tactile signifier with a standard signified or meaning. Different nations and their cultures have diverse tactile customs and codes.

National, cultural, and class differences in tactility run the full gamut from absolute nontouchability, as among upper- and middle-class Englishmen, to what amounts to almost full expression among peoples speaking Latin-derived languages, Russians, and many nonliterate peoples. (Montagu 1986, 353)

Directors adjust proxemic and gestural signifiers to communicate these cultural differences if they are part of what a production is attempting to mean.

Different kinds of touches have different meanings depending upon the given circumstances.

Touch, like all nonverbal behaviors, rarely has a unitary, unequivocal meaning. Whether it is a tap, a shove, or a caress, the meaning or message can vary profoundly depending upon a host of other factors. Because touching another's body generates an immediate demand for a response, as well as a special intimacy or threat unique among communicative behaviors, touch is probably the most carefully guarded and monitored of all social behaviors. (Thayer 1982, 266)

There are a few standard tactile sensations, however, that provide a general context for communication in American society, if not more universally:

Holding hands: friendship or kinship
Kissing the hand: respect

Kissing the forehead: kindness
Grabbing someone's shoulders: confrontation
Slapping someone's back: achievement or friendship
Slapping someone's face: hostility
Messing someone's hair: playfulness or teasing
Kissing someone's foot: servitude or humbleness
Pinching someone's ear: displeasure
Stroking someone's hair: tenderness
Stroking sexual areas: eroticism

## Touch in the Theater

While there are, then, a number of tactile events that communicate meanings, it is rare for spectators to actually engage in overt touching during a performance. Performers will touch, slap, stroke, and kiss one another, but it is not the norm for them to do any of these things to or with spectators. More often than not, a spectator can feel safe that he will not be touched directly by the performers. Touching among performers, on the other hand, is pervasive and can be a primary signifier of character relationships and personality. But this form of touching is not experienced by the spectator as a tactile sensation; it is experienced as a visual gestural-proxemic sign.

Most of the tactile sensations experienced by a spectator at a performance come during preperformance time or intermission, and the spectator herself can control how much tactile engagement she is willing to participate in. For instance, if the lobby is crowded, she might choose to stay outside to avoid making physical contact. Another spectator may fling himself into the middle of the lobby to socialize with acquaintances in the audience.

Even when performers physically touch spectators it usually happens to only a few of them (i.e., those sitting down front or near the aisle). Such touching can be highly meaningful, however. To have a performer hold hands with an audience member or reach out and touch her cheek is the ultimate personal signification. At this point the barrier is broken: the spectator and performer merge, even if for only an instant. "Touch is a language of its own with a very large vocabulary. Through touch we communicate what cannot be spoken, for touch is the true voice of feeling, for even the best words lack the honesty of touch" (Montagu 1986, 314). Moments of performer-spectator touching, if properly executed, embody a depth of sensory experience that can never happen through observation alone. Indeed, there is a whole science of healing associated with touch. For example, the laying on of hands is a time-honored religious rite that transcends cultures (Older 1982). This kind of intense spiritual touching seemingly transforms the touchee into a new realm of experience; he becomes healthy or a true believer or the like.

There is a risk, here, however: if the audience member who is touched has an aversion to such an invasion of personal space, the moment could turn into a disaster for the spectator and for the performer as well. There are many people in Western and especially American society who do not want to have their space invaded, let alone be touched intimately in public by a stranger. It is a calculated risk, one worth taking if fully planned for and if integrated into the total framework of the dramatic action. If personal confrontation is part of the meaning of a production, however, then invasion and touching might well be useful tactics for signification, even when unwelcome. Directors are offered a range of choices for the use of touching in the theater.

**No Touching**                                                           **Maximum Touching**

Most significant tactile communication in the theater take place in theaters that make an artistic commitment to developing a close, interactive relationship between the performer and the spectator—sometimes seeking bonding, sometimes confrontation. The Polish Laboratory Theatre, Performance Group, Open Theatre, and especially the Living Theatre developed their aesthetic roots from their desire to confront, contact, or involve the audience in an environmental theater experience. Close proximity, touching, smelling, and bonding with or assaulting the audience were part of the aesthetic of these groups and many like them.

There is only one element of which film and television cannot rob the theatre: the closeness of the living organism. Because of this, each challenge for the actor, each of his magical acts (which the audience is incapable of reproducing) becomes something great, something extraordinary, something close to ecstasy. It is therefore necessary to abolish the distance between actor and audience by eliminating the stage, removing all frontiers. Let the most drastic scenes happen face to face with the spectator so that he is within arm's reach of the actor, can feel his breathing and smell the perspiration. (Grotowski 1968, 42–43)

The Dionysian Theatre that leads the people into dance, wild hunting (we'll call it moving thru the world in search of what we deserve), and fucking, hints at what we are aiming at. But now we have not only to refer back to this suggestion out of human history, but to go thru it and find its double: other faces of body theatre, holy touch and use. (Beck 1972, 32)

These theater groups (as well as their contemporary counterparts) were committed ideologically to direct audience participation, which necessitated their exploitation of the tactile senses as a primary mode of signification.

If a director chooses to use tactile contact for a performance, she will need to consider several questions. How will the audience-performer relationship be defined spatially? Which performers will touch which spectators? At which moments during the performance will contact be made? In what manner? Touch hands? Kiss? Hug? Dance? Sit in a spectator's lap? Will the spectators be invited onto the stage? Will the performers go into the audience area? What happens if other audience members get into the swing of things and want to participate as well? What if a spectator does not respond to a gesture or verbal enticement for contact? Armed with answers to these questions, the director and performers are prepared to heighten the experience of the spectators through tactile communication. Even for those spectators who are never touched directly by the performers, the witnessing of physical contact and the breaking down of the distance barrier will allow associated meanings to be communicated.

## Summary

The engagement of the audience's senses of smell, touch, and taste play a secondary (or nonexistent) role in most traditional theater productions. This is an interesting phenomenon, because these three senses are the only three that cannot be employed in any meaningful way by the movies or television. Only during live performance can direct personal contact be made between performers and their audience. Touching, smelling bodies or other fragrances, and tasting food offered as part of the content of a performance can only happen in a live theater situation. Only a few directors and theater companies have explored these sign systems as a way of reaching deeper layers of meanings in the theater. This is theater at its most sensual and exposed—and most risky and nontraditional.

# Chapter 8

# Simultaneity in Performance

What next? We have reviewed twenty sign systems that operate during theater performances. We have seen how each acts as a signifier of meanings. We have seen that each is a complex system with its own cultural codes through which signification takes place and that the reading of signifiers produces meanings that are constructed by each spectator based on her education, socioeconomic background, theatergoing experience, and so forth. We have seen how each system can be manipulated by a director and coartists to produce a boundless array of signs as individual units of signification. We have also seen that signifiers rarely appear one at a time, or even five or ten at a time. Productions contain thousands of signifiers, which in turn produce an even larger number of signifieds. We have learned, then, that signification in a theater performance is an immeasurably complex form of communication that is troubling to quantify, codify, or qualify piece by piece. The sum is both greater and less than all the aggregate signs. The final and accumulated meanings of a theater performance are often perceived to be quite simple. The complexity of the interaction of the multiple sign systems is so pervasive, however, that it defies complete description or notation.

"A language is a system in which all the elements fit together, and in which the value of any one element depends on the simultaneous coexistence of all the others" (Saussure 1983, 113). The same might be said of a theater performance; that is, each of the elements of a production—its various sign systems, clusters of signs, and individual signifiers—can produce meaning only because they exist simultaneously with one another at each moment and throughout the total time frame of a performance. Patrice Pavis, Umberto Eco, and others have concluded that the isolation of a single sign as a unit of interpretation is not a useful way to discover how spectators construct meanings from a performance. Looking at clusters of signs and examining how they overlap and interact is a more rewarding method of exploration.

> Currently attention is moving away from this theoretical search for the minimal unit (too fragmenting), toward the grouping of signs according to a shared semiotic objective (or signifying function). In this way, in order to isolate the signified "explorer," it is enough here to add up the signifier "rifle," "helmet," "shorts," "whiteness," etc. Every performance reading proceeds by a back-and-forth motion between translation of the signifiers and the signifieds and attempts to find signifiers with which to corroborate the signifieds already identified. (Pavis 1982, 169)

Spectators are able to cluster signifiers and their multiple signifieds in complex interrelated ways that defy scientific explanation but which allow each spectator to read a performance interactively. Each spectator draws from a performance clusters of signifieds that they personally structure into some form of coherent grid, which ultimately leads to personalized meanings. In the case of a traditional production of a playscript that tells a sequentially developed story with a mise-en-scène that nourishes the text, most spectators easily find meanings and pleasure in the experience. It is effortless for the spectator to decode most traditional productions.

It is problematic, however, for many American spectators to construct meanings from Asian or postmodern productions that resist linear and logocentric readings.

> The spectator tends not to attribute a meaning value to the interweaving of simultaneous actions and behaves—as opposed to what happens in daily life—as if there was a favoured element in the performance particularly suited to establishing the meaning of the play (the words, the protagonist's adventures, etc.). This explains why a "normal" spectator, in the Occident, often believes he doesn't fully understand performances based on the simultaneous weaving together of actions, and why he finds himself in difficulty when faced with the logic of many Oriental theatres [or postmodern productions], which seem to him to be complicated or suggestive because of their "exotic-ness."
>
> If one impoverishes the simultaneity pole, one limits the possibility of making complex meanings arise out of the performance. These meanings do not derive from a complex concatenation of actions but from the interweaving of many dramatic actions, each

one endowed with its own simple meaning, and from the assembling of these actions by means of a single unit of time. Thus the meaning of a fragment of performance is not determined by what precedes and follows it, but also by a multiplicity of facets whose three-dimensional presence, so to speak, makes it live in the present tense of a life of its own.

In many cases, this means that for a spectator, the more difficult it becomes for him to interpret or to judge immediately the meaning of what is happening in front of his eyes and in his head, the stronger is his sensation of living through an experience. Or, said in a way which is more obscure but perhaps closer to the reality: the stronger is the experience of an experience.

The simultaneous interweaving of several actions in the performance causes something similar to what Eisenstein describes in reference to El Greco's *View of Toledo*: that the painter does not reconstruct a real view but rather constructs a synthesis of several views, making a montage of the different sides of a building, including even those sides which are not visible, showing various elements—drawn from reality independently of each other—in a new and artificial relationship. (Barba and Savarese 1991, 69–70)

Although Barba and Savarese are concerned with Asian theater, their evaluation also captures precisely the problem many American spectators have in experiencing enjoyment and constructing meanings from postmodern theater performances that often confront spectators with a new horizon of expectations. Postmodern theater offers simultaneous, overlapping, interwoven, disjointed, and nonsequential experiences that defy a simple narrative reading. The expansive, simultaneous bombardment of signifiers, signs, and sign systems in the postmodern theater has taken (and is continuing to take) spectators time to adjust to.

The distance between the actual first perception of a work and its virtual significance, or put another way, the resistance that the new work poses to the expectations of its first audience, can be so great that it requires a long process of reception to gather in that which is unexpected and unusable within the first horizon. It can thereby happen that a virtual significance of the work remains long unrecognized until the "literary [or theatrical] evolution," through actualization of a newer form, reaches the horizon that now for the first time allows one to find access to the understanding of the misunderstood older form. (Jauss 1982, 35)

Postmodern theater represents a paradigm shift from linear, story-oriented performance to something much more disjointed and layered. It has taken audiences some time to come to grips with this new paradigm, but there are growing numbers of people who are seeking the richness that this new theater brings. Directors who work in the postmodern theater world (even if they are not purely postmodern directors) must wrestle with this relatively new phenomenon and must understand how, even in more traditional productions, the employment of pluridimensional signifiers and sign systems is part of the consciousness of the contemporary audience. As people who were raised with MTV images and Walkman-generated music in their realm of experience come into the theater, the simultaneous and disjointed visual and aural phenomena become readily accepted.

There is no question that the study of signs in the theater is an entangled problem. This is why no system of notation (writing or drawing) has been advanced that can manage all of the dimensions of this complex issue. It is one thing to examine artificially each sign system as an independent system; it is another thing entirely to bring them all together and study them as one vast simultaneous system of signs that constitutes a live theater performance.

## The Director's Role

This is where the director steps forward. The best directors have complex minds and highly tuned sensory systems; they have the ability to process all of the simultaneous information and signification that accumulates during the planning, preparation, rehearsal, and performance of a playscript or theater piece. It is their special intellectual *and* intuitive knowledge of the communication process heretofore analyzed, coupled with their unique aesthetic sensibilities and knowledge of the theater and its artists, that allows them to orchestrate and fashion infinitely complex and multifaceted performance experiences. So few people are able to direct at the highest levels of artistic brilliance because only a handful of people are uniquely prepared and aesthetically dexterous and sensitive enough to perceive how signifiers and sign systems are manipulated, layered, juxtaposed, and unified to produce a stunning work of art. At the same time, it is clear that no director can govern every aspect of a production. "The role of the director is to decide which aspects of the performance he's going to control and which aspects he isn't. The final production is a dialectical interaction between the options of control and noncontrol. . . . No director can control every molecule of a production" (Foreman 1992, 266–67).

No megacomputer can do the work of a top-flight director. Artificial intelligence has not advanced far enough to allow computers to juggle all the communication variables of a theater performance. While it is possible to imagine a computer program that could notate and track the unfolding of a production through time for all twenty sign systems simultaneously, it is impossible to imagine a computer that could hypothesize about and observe all the sign systems in action during the incubation, preparation, design, and rehearsal process and then actually make the voluminous choices that need to be made to bring coherence, shape, and symbiosis to the final artistic product. Only a sensitive, smart, experienced, trained, yet highly intuitive human being can comprehend and produce a unified theater performance. Directors create a living work of art through the breathtakingly intricate coordination of the work of multiple artists who generate thousands of signifiers.

Only people with highly developed multiple intelligences—linguistic, musical, spatial, bodily-kinesthetic, and interpersonal (Gardner 1983)—possess the capability of observing and synthesizing all of the sign systems at work in a complex performance and of making the thousands of choices required to produce a coherent aesthetic event.

> One might go so far as to define a human intelligence as a neural mechanism or computational system which is genetically programmed to be activated or "triggered" by certain kinds of internally or externally presented information. Examples would include sensitivity to pitch relations as one core of musical intelligence, or the ability to imitate movement by others as one core of bodily intelligence. (Gardner 1983, 64)

Gardner's model for complex intelligences fits neatly the reality of multiple simultaneous signification systems for theater performances; that is, the director possesses problem-solving skills and information that can guide the creation of signifiers for each of the sign systems simultaneously at work in a performance.

> To my mind, a human intellectual competence must entail a set of skills of problem solving—enabling the individual *to resolve genuine problems or difficulties* that he or she encounters and, when appropriate, to create an effective product—and must also entail the potential for *finding or creating problems*—thereby laying the groundwork for the acquisition of new knowledge. (60–61)

This describes the director's work precisely: directors create art through visualization, interpretation, manipulation of signs, and problem solving.

There are certain guidelines and signposts that can aid directors in the selection and coordination of the various sign systems and signifiers as they are manipulated at each emerging moment of a performance. This final chapter examines them.

## Notation

At the end of *The Semiotics of Theatre and Drama* Keir Elam (1980) presents a complex eighteen-column table in which he attempts to notate the semiotic functioning of the first seventy-nine lines of *Hamlet*. Each segment of the dialogue is scored to indicate how eighteen different sign systems and theatrical elements work and change at different moments in the scene. It is a marvelous attempt to provide a comprehensive score of an imagined performance. Elam's system of notation fails, however, to provide a useful tool for practicing directors. The scheme is too cumbersome and limited in its descriptions; it does not begin to capture the true complexity of the performance experience. It is useful, however, in providing insights into just how labyrinthine making and perceiving theater is and how futile it is to attempt to notate and quantify live theater given the state of current notational systems (even those that are computerized).

Whatever the system of notation used, it is readily acknowledged that the notation of the performance simplifies it to the point of impoverishment. . . . Notation is inadequate, not because the necessary technology to make a record of the mise en scène is lacking, but because no description can do other than radically modify the objects it describes. To "notate" the performance inevitably means to interpret, to make a more or less conscious choice among the multitude of signs of performance deemed *noteworthy*. (Pavis 1982, 111)

During the preparation and rehearsal process, it is not unusual for directors to employ various notational methods to keep track of different elements of signification. Some directors record suggested or actual movements in their promptbook. Some directors write detailed notes on individual characterizations and how they ought to be represented through special gestures, makeup, vocal characteristics, motivational objectives, and the like. Some directors collaborate with composers to write and produce music and sound scores to undergird the entire production. Some directors develop elaborate storyboards that represent changing aspects of the mise-en-scène—its lighting, setting, and properties. Some directors require elaborate costume sketches that outline the dynamic flow and change of costumes through time. Some directors even prepare an outline of anticipated audience responses, especially for productions that require direct interaction between performers and spectators. Of course, some directors do none of these things, while others employ all these notational techniques and more.

Bertolt Brecht is famous for his *Reigiebuchs* (detailed promptbooks) which were prepared by multiple assistants who recorded every aspect of his productions—preparation, rehearsal, and performance. Brecht's goal was to preserve as much information as possible about a performance so that it might be re-created or be more closely understood by performance historians. "The production book of the *mise en scène* is one of the most valuable instruments available to us for obtaining an idea of the way the text has been staged. . . . At its best, it tends to become a second text, a stage text, which is superimposed over the dramatic text [the actual performance]" (Pavis 1982, 116).

## Directing Process

Since the process of signification is so complex, and the sign systems so plentiful and diverse, how can a director begin to get her arms around a performance's signs in order to produce great theater? As one of my students once said, "If everything is a sign and there are thousands of them and they are ever-changing, where do I begin?" I passed on Patrice Pavis's advice: "No isolated stage element acquires its meaning unless its role in the stage enunciation is understood" (1982, 118). I further advised the student to begin at the aggregate level by choosing a prioritized order of sign systems that she could use for a specific production and to work to insure that the highlighted sign systems are emphasized or deemphasized at different moments of the performance. At the end of chapter 1 I proposed two hypothetical productions of *King Lear*. What makes the productions significantly different from each other is the idiosyncratic use of sign systems. I cannot overemphasize how critical the choice, mix, and contrapuntal emphasis and deemphasis of sign systems are when it comes to shaping the style and meanings of a performance. How a director uses the twenty sign systems is the way he leaves his personal imprint on a production.

Esslin posits that there are several primary sign systems that serve as "key," or "clef," signs: level of language, color scheme, style of the set, costume period, acting style, and mood of the music. He contends that these are the sign systems that operate over a long period of time and therefore have special force or power in the overall signification scheme (1987, 111).

Esslin's list of key signs works, however, only for a traditional production. For instance, it is possible to have a performance with little or no linguistic communication, little or no color, neutral costumes, and no music. In such a case the key signs are very different. Esslin is correct, however, in saying that each production is likely to have some key sign systems that serve as touchstones for spectators as they interpret a performance's signification. In fact, a director who does not make clear choices about which sign systems function most predominantly and which ones communicate best the vision and meanings of her imagination will find she has not established a personal style or identity beyond the mundane and mediocre.

As we have seen, notable contemporary directors such as Richard Foreman, JoAnne Akalaitis, Peter Sellars, and Robert Wilson create productions with an idiosyncratic stamp; their works reflect a pattern of choices that produce vivid signification, a density of signifiers, and an authoritative orchestration of sign systems. These directors, and others like them, have each found a way of using the multivarious sign systems to tell their story in a personal, singular, and yet publicly consumable way. They have each created a directorial style of their own, presenting theater that is universally accessible but fundamentally unique.

## Synchronical Analysis

I use an exercise for my graduate directing class that may help demonstrate how directors analyze sign systems synchronically in order to understand how signs can be manipulated at any and every given moment of a performance. I ask three different groups of students to enact one moment from a hypothetical playscript, *Dracula*. The line of dialogue I give them is of a character, Lucy, saying: "I am afraid Dracula lurks nearby." Each of the three groups has the same line, but each is given a different mode of production (realism, farce, or melodrama), depth of character portrayal (naturalistic, exaggerated, or black and white), and period (late nineteenth century, the present, or early twentieth century).

I ask each group to work as a team of directors, designers, technicians, and performers who must decide how to use all of the twenty sign systems. Most important, they must choose which of the sign systems to highlight in their miniproduction. I give the groups two weeks and ask them to perform the moment and to explain how they would prioritize and manipulate the sign systems in order to communicate this one line from *Dracula*. The instructions given to three groups of students and their composite responses follow.

### Dracula Project 1

**Text:** Lucy says, "I am afraid Dracula lurks nearby!"

**Meaning:** This moment is intended to communicate Lucy's intense fear of Dracula.

**Given Circumstances:**
Lucy is in her bedroom.
Lucy is speaking to her father and Dr. Wilmer.
The men have just entered the room after hearing Lucy's earlier scream.
The location is a castle outside London.
The time is the late nineteenth century, very late at night.
These people believe in vampires.
Lucy is already under Dracula's spell.
Dr. Wilmer is an expert on the occult.

**Interpretation:**
The play is realistic and serious.
The theme is the fear of the unknown.
The characters are realistic and psychologically complex.

**Question:** How would you use the twenty semiotic sign systems to communicate this isolated moment to an audience in order to signify as fully as possible Lucy's *intense fear* of Dracula?

| Sign system | Group's Response |
| --- | --- |
| Spectator | Expected to watch, no physical involvement. |
| Audience | Sits close to performers in thrust stage. |
| Physical environment | Old theater on a small ivy league college campus. Theater is in a nine- |

| | |
|---|---|
| | teenth-century brick building surrounded by grand oak trees. Slightly spooky at night with lots of shadows and spotty, dim street lighting. |
| Publicity | Poster and programs with a realistic image of Dracula seducing a woman. Black, gray, and a touch of red for the color scheme. |
| Personality | Lucy is a tall, frail yet sensuously charismatic woman. |
| Voice | Lucy's line is delivered slowly, softly, hauntingly. |
| Facial expression | Trancelike, as in a drugged stupor. |
| Gesture | Frozen, Lucy directly faces the audience. |
| Movement | Still. |
| Makeup/hair | Long flowing brown hair (to the waist). |
| Space | Massive volume, tall and wide. |
| Setting | Realistic castle bedroom with stone and wooden beams, large window archway at center back (which Lucy is standing directly in front of). Color scheme is dark gray for stone and brown for beams and heavy woodwork. |
| Costume | Lucy wears a flowing, white, lace nightgown; it is sensuous and revealing. The doctor and father wear dark bathrobes, as if they had dressed quickly and just rushed into the room. |
| Properties | Ornate, heavy bedroom furniture plus one knocked-over chair. |
| Lighting | One candle near Lucy's bed. The massive arched window at the back is aglow with blue and silver moonlight. Lucy is thus silhouetted. The doctor and father stand near the door downstage right and are barely visible in the candlelight. |
| Color | Dark set. Blue and silver light dominate. Lucy stands out in a white nightgown. |
| Music | None (would not be realistic). |

| Sounds | Haunting, pervasive wind. |
| Touch | No contact with spectators. |
| Smell | Not used. |

**Summary:** Here the visual and aural stimuli evoke a realistic and frightening moment. Lucy is highlighted in her white gown, center stage, silhouetted against a blue and silver moonlit grand archway. She speaks in a possessed, whispering tone as the wind haunts the audience with its subtle, mysterious presence. The doctor and father play a minor role; they reflect a sense of urgency and horror through their frozen positions near the room's entrance.

### Dracula Project 2

**Text:** Lucy says, "I am afraid Dracula lurks nearby!"

**Meaning:** This moment is intended to communicate Lucy's intense fear of Dracula.

**Given Circumstances:**
Lucy is in her bedroom.
Lucy is speaking to her father and Dr. Wilmer.
The men have just entered the room after hearing Lucy's earlier
    scream.
The location is a castle outside London.
The time is the present, very late at night.
These people believe in vampires.
Lucy is already under Dracula's spell.
Dr. Wilmer is an expert on the occult.

**Interpretation:**
The play is a farce.
The theme is the fear of the unknown.
The characters tend toward being black or white (good versus evil).

**Question:** How would you use the twenty semiotic sign systems to communicate this isolated moment to an audience in order to communicate as fully as possible Lucy's *intense fear* of Dracula?

| Sign system | Group's Response |
| --- | --- |
| Spectator | No participation, except to laugh a lot. |
| Audience | Large proscenium theater. They are sitting out front and watching. |
| Physical environment | An early-twentieth-century vaudeville |

|  | theater with a balcony and ornate decoration in golds and reds. Audience members will be served red punch from a bowl that emits fog (because of dry ice). Camp, contemporary Dracula iconography will festoon the theater entrance and lobby. |
|---|---|
| Publicity | Cartoonlike images in black, pink, and red are used for the poster and program. |
| Personality | Star comedians. John Candy as Dracula and Goldie Hawn as Lucy. |
| Voice | Line is delivered with great vocal tension, haltingly and loudly. |
| Facial expression | Exaggerated fear. |
| Gesture | Lucy is jumping on her bed with hands outstretched as if fighting off a ghost. |
| Movement | Dr. Wilmer and the father have just rushed in and are standing on either side of the bed attempting to grab Lucy. |
| Makeup/hair | Lucy has on white face cream, and her hair is in large curlers. The two men have their hair messed up as if arising from a fitful sleep. |
| Space | Large, vaulting. |
| Setting | Lucy's bedroom looks like a Walt Disney cartoon with painted stone and beams. Contemporary brightly painted furniture fills the room as do large overstuffed animals. |
| Costume | Lucy is in a pink bathrobe, which is slightly exaggerated (padded shoulders). Dr. Wilmer and the father are in their underwear (boxer shorts, etc.). |
| Properties | The father carries a baseball bat and Dr. Wilmer wields a large tennis racket as weapons. |
| Lighting | Light coming through the large French doors at the back is reddish-purple. The room is dark except for a very |

| | bright light flooding the bed on which Lucy stands. |
|---|---|
| Color | The basic set is a Disneyesque purple-gray. The furnishings are pinks and blues, as are the costumes. |
| Music | Someone (perhaps Dracula) is gently humming "My Funny Valentine." This sound is amplified and distorted to create a slight echo. |
| Sound | Loud thunder immediately after Lucy speaks. |
| Touch | Not used. |
| Smell | The smell of cotton candy floats through the air. |

**Summary:** This miniproduction is obviously quite different from the production that emphasized the serious and realistic aspects of the line/moment. For this farcical production, the movement, gestures, and vocal presentation are exaggerated. The colors are brighter and richer, and the actors perform in outlandish ways. The audience is presented with a completely different set of sights, sounds, and smells, which are designed to elicit laughter and enjoyment.

### Dracula Project 3

**Text:** Lucy says, "I am afraid Dracula lurks nearby!"

**Meaning:** This moment is intended to communicate Lucy's intense fear of Dracula.

**Given Circumstances:**
Lucy is in her bedroom.
Lucy is speaking to her father and Dr. Wilmer.
The men have just entered the room after hearing Lucy's earlier scream.
The location is a castle outside London.
The time is 1930, very late at night.
These people believe in vampires.
Lucy is already under Dracula's spell.
Dr. Wilmer is an expert on the occult.

**Interpretation:**
The play is a melodrama.

The theme is the fear of the unknown.
The characters are black and white (good versus evil).

**Question:** How would you use the twenty semiotic sign systems to communicate this isolated moment to an audience in order to communicate as fully as possible Lucy's *intense fear* of Dracula?

| Sign system | Group's Response |
| --- | --- |
| Spectator | Expected to take an active role. They are asked through a preshow announcement by a master of ceremonies to hiss and boo for the entrance of the villain and the like. |
| Audience | Collective involvement of a large group. |
| Physical environment | An old, big movie house with balcony and side boxes and with an organ or piano. Opening night is on Halloween. |
| Publicity | Posters and programs bold and in black and white, with a drop of red. |
| Personality | Capable of histrionic acting—physical, athletic, and intense. |
| Voice | Lucy's line is delivered with a rising-pitch screech. Hysteria has overtaken her. |
| Facial expression | A deep grimace with fear in the eyes. |
| Gesture | Lucy's hands are raised slightly at both sides. She is frozen with fear and tension. |
| Movement | Dr. Wilmer and the father have rushed to her sides but freeze when they see horror and fear in her face. They are shocked and immobilized by Lucy's total agony. |
| Makeup/hair | Lucy is unnaturally pale; her usually perfect hair is in disarray. |
| Space | Large and expansive. |
| Setting | Lucy's bedroom is romanticized yet castlelike, with its stone and concrete arches and heavy painted furniture. The set is expressionistic rather than re- |

| | |
|---|---|
| | alistic. The colors are shades of gray with a red bedspread and a red grand drape. |
| Costume | Lucy is in a white, sensuous, revealing nightgown. The men are in black robes. All three have red sashes around their waists. |
| Properties | Both men hold large candles. Lucy holds a long, slim, sharp dagger. |
| Lighting | Sharp shafts of white moonlight pierce the darkness, leaving the men in partial shadows and Lucy in full, haunting view. |
| Color | The set is gray with red curtains. The costumes are black and white with a touch of red. |
| Music | None at this moment, but a house organ is used to underscore much of this production. |
| Sound | A door slams in the distance (and reverberates electronically) immediately following Lucy's line and screech. |
| Touch | None. |
| Smell | None. |

**Summary:** This melodrama uses the stereotypical black and white motif not only in the color but also in the style of acting and in the characterizations. Everything is exaggerated visually and aurally in order to signify the melodramatic production style and to create an environment that will entice the audience to participate vocally in the performance.

As the students' responses to the three different versions indicate, there is no single way to present even one moment of a playscript. Each of the three groups chose to foreground different sign systems and then proceeded to select very different signifiers to communicate the unique given circumstances, styles, and modes. Each group chose a different way of reading the line of dialogue: softly whispered, haltingly loud, or as a high-pitched screech. Each group chose different colors: black/gray, red, or purple. Each group chose different lighting: blue/silver silhouette, bright frontal spot light, or white shadowy shafts of light. Each group chose different sounds: haunting wind, loud thunder, or electronically reverberating door slam. Each group chose different facial expressions: trancelike gaze, exaggerated fear, or deep grimace.

It is also possible to imagine a postmodern production of *Dracula* in which Lucy's line of dialogue—"I am afraid Dracula lurks nearby"—is not spoken but flashed pulsatingly on a screen while she mouths the words. Simultaneously, two deafening tape loops juxtapose a repeating shriek and repeating echoed laughter (of Dracula), while her father and Dr. Wilmer do slow-motion somersaults backward across a nearly bare stage. Immediately following Lucy's attempt to deliver her line, she grabs one of two "columns" that have just descended from the heavens; what Lucy cannot see (but the audience does see) is that the column that she is grasping for security is really the left leg of an eighteen-foot-tall naked Dracula puppet-woman. This Wilsonesque description could go on ad infinitum, but perhaps the point is made that a director must match his vision with the artistic capabilities of his coartists and must make thousands of choices in order to create a unique work of art. As all four *Dracula* examples make clear, any line, any scene, any theme, any piece of music, any complete playscript, can be interpreted in a variety of ways by a director and her coartists.

> Thus any single moment in a performance can be analyzed with a view to understanding the interplay of all the signifiers . . . operating within it; or to put it the other way round: the director must decide which signifiers, and what type of interaction between them, to deploy at any given moment in a performance. He will, for example, have to decide whether any, and if so which, signifying system should play the *dominant* role at any given moment; the visuals or the words, the musical or natural sounds, the movement or gestures. (Esslin 1987, 109)

The results for an audience are quite unpredictable. If I am given a ticket to see a real production of *Dracula* and I know nothing about the production, I must be prepared to witness almost anything— from extreme realism to disjointed postmodernism. I will have to wait until I get to the theater to find out whether the performance will make me laugh or cry, whether I will sit on the edge of my seat or fall asleep, and whether I will receive meaningful insights or learn nothing at all.

# Diachronical Analysis

Performances do not just happen for one moment. They consist of thousands of individual moments that appear one after another relentlessly through performance time. Each moment of the performance is unique, and yet the collective moments, when analyzed diachronically, reveal patterns of emphasis and deemphasis of sign systems and signifiers that constitute the collaborative unity of the aesthetic event.

If I were to ask the same groups of students to provide the beginning and ending moments of a production of *Dracula*, they would likely utilize signifiers quite differently from the moment analyzed earlier in this chapter. It is easy to imagine that the opening scene might take place in bright daylight in the cheery living room of the castle, that the characters would be happy and healthy, and so forth. It is also easy to imagine that at the end of the play we might witness the destruction of Dracula in a dark, dangerous, and mysterious cave somewhere and that all the characters would show signs of great fatigue, having been through hell. Yet these shifts in location, characters' fortunes, and so forth are so great that they might easily threaten the integrity of the production. It is the task of the director to establish cohesiveness even when there is a great diversity of scenes and sign systems, unless it is the director's intention to shock or disorient the audience through incongruous sign shifts or a bizarre juxtaposition of signifiers that are intended to create chaos and disorientation.

How, then, does a director use her knowledge of semiotics to orchestrate a unified yet ever-varying deployment of signifiers during a performance? How does she move semiotically from happiness to crisis to epiphany to resolution—allowing continual adjustments of signifiers and even occasional wild variations in sign deployment—and still maintain some semblance of unity? The ability to do so lies in the careful choice of primary sign systems—or, as Esslin calls them, key, or clef, sign systems. For example, one director chooses to present a production of *Macbeth* using the complete text and, in so doing, automatically sets up a performance in which plot and words are of primary importance. Because the words are expressed as heightened, poetic language, they build in an additional diachronical significance—nonrealism. Another director chooses to present a production of *Macbeth* in which most of the dialogue is cut, leaving only a patchwork of words. His plan is to emphasize gesture and sound. This director presents *Macbeth* as a deconstructed collage—a collection of impressions that emphasizes music, visual aesthetics, and chronologically displaced fragments of language as signifiers. Once both directors have decided on their priority for use of sign systems, they employ them consistently across the time span of the performance, even though there will be ever-changing variations in the use of sign systems for each unique moment. That is, in the first production the words must take precedence consistently over the use of visual and nonlinguistic sounds (the mise-en-scène is subservient to the playscript), whereas in the second production the visual and musical aspects of performance must be highlighted throughout the fabric of the performance (the mise-en-scène dominates or substitutes for a playscript).

## Collaboration and Selection

The collaboration between Philip Glass and Robert Wilson led to one of the most influential productions in the development of Western postmodern theater: *Einstein on the Beach*.

It never occurred to us that *Einstein on the Beach* would have a story or contain anything like an ordinary plot. Bob, by then, had done a series of large theater works which, by their titles at least, were based on the lives of famous persons (Freud, Stalin, etc.). But how that title character appeared in the work could, in the end, be *very* abstract. It seemed to me that in Bob's previous work, the title merely provided an occasion for which a theatrical/visual work could be constructed. It functioned as a kind of attention point around which his theater could revolve, without necessarily becoming its primary subject. This freedom gave his work an extension and richness which often overshadowed the work of his contemporaries.

To me, this process took on a somewhat different meaning in the Einstein work (as I believe it did for Bob as well). I saw *Einstein on the Beach* more as a portrait opera. In this case the portrait of Einstein that we would be constructing replaced the idea of plot, narrative, development, all the paraphernalia of conventional theater. Furthermore, we understood that this portrait of Einstein was a poetic vision. Facts and chronology could be included (and indeed were) in the sequence of movements, images, speaking and sing-ing. Conveying that kind of information, though, was certainly not the point of the work. (Glass 1987, 32)

What Glass and Wilson began with was a clear idea about which performance sign systems they were going to emphasize throughout their production of *Einstein on the Beach*. The text of the performance was to be primarily visual and musical, not linguistic, and this deci-sion consistently shaped the aesthetic of this watershed production.

The process of directing is a process of visualization, experimenta-tion, and selection. The director calls upon her own and her coartists' imaginations and technical skills to develop sketches, movements, sounds, objects, music, and the like that she thinks best signify the meanings of the production. The director writes the performance by selecting and adjusting the signifiers that constitute the various sign systems she has chosen to emphasize.

The transition from written text to performance does not happen in a single uninterrupted process, and the various stages between the initial decision to stage a playtext and the opening night involve patterns of *selection* and *rejection* of alternatives in order to arrive at what seems to be a unified whole. And in that process of shaping, the words of the original written text (assuming that there is one at all) are only one language among many. (Bassnett-McGuire 1980, 48)

This mysterious process of selection is done differently by different directors, whose styles range from dictatorial to collaborative, with many variations between.

Single
Vision

Collaborative
Vision

Even with an open and collaborative style of direction, however, the director usually, in the end, steps forward and selects those precise signifiers and systems that will be actualized before the audience through performance.

Richard Foreman stands triumphantly at the single-vision end of the continuum. He creates performances that conform precisely to his theater aesthetic.

A fundamental impulse behind Richard Foreman's approach to theatre is Wagner's concept of a "total artwork," or a *Gesamtkunstwerk*.
Foreman is not only concerned with an effective, unified interplay
among the elements of theatre in performance, he is also adamant
about theatre art as a "total creative process" that does not necessarily involve a group of specialists. He believes that playwrights
should be their own directors, explaining, "I am interested in a
work of art that . . . is a total creation of a personality." Writing in
1969 about his reasons for founding the Ontological-Hysteric Theatre in 1967, Foreman stated: "At that point, [I] realized I had my
own total vision of the kind of theatre I wanted, and . . . [that] I'd
have to do it all myself." Several years later, during an interview
with Michael Feingold, Foreman mentioned that he had "always
been obsessively interested in all the arts." "Doesn't that make
specializing difficult?" asked Feingold. "But I don't specialize, really, because in my Ontological-Hysteric Theatre I function as composer, designer, writer, director, dance director . . . everything,"
Foreman replied. There is no collaboration in Foreman's work—
every Ontological-Hysteric Theatre piece is the product of a single
creator. (Davy 1981, 159)

Robert Wilson directs with a singular vision. He selects all the final
images and sounds, but he relies on many collaborators to actualize
his imagistic conceptions.

"When [Wilson] first goes over a piece with me, he draws the
pictures that he usually publishes in the program, and as he draws,
he describes the scene, and as he describes the scene, he describes
an effect. He will describe each one as he goes along. This is never
in technical terms. Just the way it is supposed to happen, what it
is, where it is. How it looks and how it happens." Then, it is up to
the various designers and technicians to come up with a way to do
the things Wilson wants. These methods are then presented to
Wilson for approval. (Julia Gillett, quoted in Baker 1985, 25)

Bob began thinking about trains and courtrooms [for *Einstein on the
Beach*]. We looked at quite a number of ideas before we settled on
three. The way we worked was that Bob proposed images to me
and I would say, "I like that" or "No, nothing." What we were
trying to do was arrive at a group of images we both felt we could
work with. We had agreed to work on things we both felt strongly

about. To me the biggest problem in the theatre is always what the piece is about. (Philip Glass, quoted in Shyer 1989, 216–17)

From the beginning, [Wilson's] art has rested on an understanding of the complex relationship between order and chaos. He has usually explored this by choosing the elements of his theatre pieces almost at random—assembling a cheerfully chaotic assortment of images, words, lights, objects—and then arranging them into patterns of striking gracefulness and precision. (Sterritt 1991, 11)

Clearly, Wilson is in charge of his productions. His dominant original ideas and his careful selection of the suggested images, music, movement patterns, gestures, and so forth lead to the final vision and soundscapes that are the signatures of his work.

Martha Clarke works much more collaboratively at the outset of her directorial work. She sees the rehearsal process as a kind of sifting ground for testing and selecting.

If you watched a rehearsal of mine, you would see that nine-tenths of it is in such disarray. I flounder. If you walked in you would see absolutely nothing except me being uncertain. You would say, "These people are never going to get anything together." I'm not temperamental or a screamer or anything like that, but I'm foggy a lot of the time. And the actors and dancers have to search as much as I do. We're all children dropped on another planet at the beginning of this process and, tentatively, hand-in-hand, we find our way through this mire to whatever. The day-by-day process couldn't be more collaborative. It's really a workshop. Sometimes I just sit back and watch them and don't say anything all day except, "I like this." Sometimes they'll be doing something facing in one direction and I'll stand behind them and say, "It's great from the back, just turn it around." The dancers make up physical material. The actors have suggestions about what they want to do with the text. Happy accidents happen all the time. Things we love get thrown out and things we don't like get better. It's just like other directors' processes in that respect. During the last tenth of the process I get very decisive. Then I want precision. All those finishing elements—lights, costumes and sets—are very important to me. I'm in pain unless there's a chance to work over every cue, every button on a high-button boot. (Bartow 1988b, 16)

Clarke's work as a director is highly collaborative and yet infused with a personal aesthetic that materializes in the later stages of the rehearsal when she selects the simultaneous and disordered sights and sounds. "That's the essence of the work, that it's collaborative. It will ultimately be my weaving that makes the whole, but the input of everyone who's involved with it is of paramount importance" ("Martha Clarke" 1988, 39).

Elizabeth LeCompte's directing process is also highly collaborative. Her work with the Wooster Group, which is dedicated to collective artistry, is based on the selection of images and sounds that arise out of the prerehearsal and rehearsal process.

> [LeCompte's] technique as a director is to develop strong, emotionally charged images through the juxtaposition of words, images, and movements suggested by the actors, and to combine them in a mixed-media collage. The working process begins by assembling a pool of "source" texts that can be pictorial, literary, choreographic, or structural. These are then explored, reworked, and rearranged with images from cultural history, images of public events, and with other ideas that emerge from the collective experiences of Group members. LeCompte also adds the television techniques of cutting, editing, distancing, storytelling, the combination of live characters and animation in commercials and quick pacing. (Durham 1989, 523–24)

In choosing to work in a theater collective, LeCompte has defined her directorial approach as collaborative. She even goes one step further, however, and also makes choices based on chance occurrences in rehearsal. "I call it chance work, like throwing a handful of beans up in the air. And when they come down on the floor, I must use that pattern as one pole against which I work my dialectic" (quoted in Savran 1986, 51). For LeCompte's productions the collective will, experience, and abilities of the entire company of performers and designers are tapped as primary source material for signification.

Andrei Serban's rehearsals are exploratory. He champions the work of the performers yet centers their focus on the written text.

> Serban rehearses a production by exploring all the possibilities of a text. He may start with the absolute opposite of what one might expect of a scene; if it is between two characters who traditionally are softly cooing, he may have them shouting at one another across the stage, and then he will try fifteen or twenty other ways of

approaching the scene until he finds the right one. (Bartow 1988a, 288)

[Serban] draws more from his actors, collaborates more, is willing to deal with improvisation. He loves the give and take of working with a company. Friends claim he often goes into rehearsals giving the impression that he isn't sure what to do with the play, so that actors will feel encouraged to contribute more and ultimately get the feeling that the production is their own invention. "It very much suits the American actors," said one Romanian who has worked with Serban. "But I don't believe for a minute that he doesn't know exactly what he wants, even from the beginning." (Steele 1985, 10)

Here we see a slight twist on the idea of collaborative selection. Serban asks the performers to improvise, to try many different ways of performing a text. Serban is the final arbiter, however: he selects from the myriad possibilities explored in rehearsal.

The selection, layering, and orchestration of signifiers can be accomplished through a variety of working processes. Each director develops a method of working that suits his personal style. Each director produces a unique production through the conscious and intuitive selection and arrangement of the signifiers of the mise-en-scène. All the planning in the world can only result in a generalized concept of what a production might end up looking and sounding like. Only through the process of design, rehearsal, trial and error, experimentation, and confrontation and cooperation between multiple artists can a fully staged production be actualized for the audience. Depending on her personal working methods, a director can tightly control the conception and selection of signifiers or she can rely heavily on the creative imaginations and activities of her coartists to develop the performance. The postmodern directors that we have examined generally fall into one end of the collaborative continuum or the other; rarely do they work at a midpoint. They either dominate every aspect of the mise-en-scène or they allow their coartists significant authority to contribute.

## Prioritizing Signifiers

There is no formula for setting priorities for the use of signifiers in the theater. I wish there were, and at one time I thought one might be developed, but the more I research and observe the work of other directors, and the more I use semiotics as a tool for my own directing and teaching, the clearer it becomes that each director must make his choices and set his own priorities. One director's choice is another director's anathema.

> Every director and every performer can and does decide to some extent the order of the signals and hence pre-empts to some degree the possible relationships between them. To this extent, any performance generates a bewildering, rapid succession or sequence of puzzles: why that colour with that shape, why that movement with that sound, why that gesture after that word . . . ? The new signs normally resolve the puzzle (closure is, however, never definitive: even as a performance selects one option, the others remain open as shadowy alternatives and potential critiques: there are other ways to speak any sentence, other gestures to accompany it. . . . (George 1989, 73)

What makes every production truly special is that directors always choose to emphasize different sign systems and choose distinct colors, performers, spaces, and so forth, because each director is fundamentally unique.

There are no formulas for creating a theatrical performance or for choosing and arranging individual and collective signs. Many directing textbooks and how-to books by directors offer prescriptions for emphasizing one sign system or individual signifiers over another (such as the often-stated rule that movement will always overpower the speaking of words, so you had better not have people move during important linguistic moments; or the advice that performers' faces must always be lit brightly so they can be seen at all times). Today's postmodern theater, however, has rejected or twisted these rules and indeed has fashioned a new aesthetic that eschews all formulas for theatrical communication. Simultaneous complex signifiers constitute the theater's new agenda.

> What I love is that theatre is not like television, which features one thing at a time. You move in on a close-up of her face or whatever. But theatre has three or four things happening at once and you have to decide what to look at. I try and leave it open to the audience what to look at. Obviously I guide the eye in certain situations. I also leave it open so that two people sitting next to each other saw different shows because they were each looking at a different place

at a given moment. Two people watching a TV show see the same thing. (Peter Sellars interview, in Bartow 1988a, 284)

It is not uncommon for directors to juxtapose movement, words, music, and scenic changes to create an animated collage of signifiers—whose meanings derive from the juxtaposition rather than from the individuation of signifiers. The senses do not even take these multiple signifiers in one at a time; rather, they are processed coinstantaneously. In the same production, of course, a single signifier can be presented—an amplified sigh in the dark at the end of the performance—but it has meaning only because of the context in which it is offered.

The director's role is to envision a hypothetical production, work with the designers, performers, and technicians to create thousands of signifiers, and then monitor and arrange the deployment of these signifiers at each moment and throughout the performance time. Keeping track of every signifier and how each one is dominant or subordinate to each of the other multiple signifiers is an impossible task, especially if a director thinks of this tracking and orchestration as a totally rational, sequential, and technical process. But it is not. A special aesthetic sense is present in the artists of the theater and especially the director. Distinctive directors employ their multiple intelligences in near-mystical ways to create the myriad signifiers that ebb and flow in number, complexity, and simultaneity over the course of a performance. Personal artistic choices are what make each production and each performance truly unique. There is no way to write a prescription for the creation of profound theater. Semiotic analysis and a knowledge of reader-response theories, however, can help animate a director's thinking, seeing, hearing, smelling, feeling, and decision making in order to guide her judgments and shape theatrical communication.

It must be remembered, however, that it is the work of the spectator who reads the performance that gives meanings to a performance. The audience acts as coproducer of the performance as it witnesses the dialectical interchange between the playscript (if there is one), the director's metatext, and the living mise-en-scène.

## Summary

While synchronic analysis of a moment in a performance is easily achievable and highly useful, diachronic analysis of the use of signs and sign systems in a performance is often perplexing. An attempt to trace and notate the employment of twenty sign systems and thousands of signifiers over the course of a three-hour performance inevitably leads to the use of vast amounts of computer disk space or paper (Brecht's *Reigiebuchs* were huge, and they recorded only a few sign systems) and produces a technological analysis of only one performance. It also often produces as much frustration as paperwork. Directors do not need technical data about their production to help them create an aesthetically engaging work of art. They blend their artistic sensibilities and detailed knowledge of how performances communicate through signification with the capabilities and knowledge of their coartists to create a potent and enlightening theater event.

Semiotics gives the director a framework for making choices about which sign systems should dominate a production as a whole, which signifiers should take precedence at any given moment of a performance, and how signifiers can be orchestrated through time to create a meaningful, coherent, and symbiotic artistic statement. Each spectator in turn perceives selectively different signifiers and absorbs the impact of the accumulated signifieds, which produce a singular set of meanings tailored from the spectator's psychic and physical uniqueness. Such is the stuff that produces renowned directors and superlative theater.

# Works Cited

Albright, Harry D. 1959. *Working Up a Part*. 2d ed. Boston: Houghton Mifflin.

Alter, Jean. 1990. *A Sociosemiotic Theory of Theatre*. Philadelphia: University of Pennsylvania Press.

Altner, H. 1978. "Physiology of Olfaction." In *Fundamentals of Sensory Physiology*, ed. Robert F. Schmidt. New York: Springer-Verlag.

Arnink, Donna J. 1984. *Creative Theatrical Makeup*. Englewood Cliffs, N.J.: Prentice-Hall.

Aronson, Arnold. 1987. "The Svoboda Dimension." *American Theatre* 4 (Oct.): 24.

Baker, Rob. 1985. "The Mystery Is in the Surface." *Theatre Crafts* 19 (Oct.): 22.

Barba, Eugenio, and Ludwik Flaszen. 1965. "A Theater of Magic and Sacrilege." *Tulane Drama Review* 9 (Spring): 173–89.

Barba, Eugenio, and Nicola Savarese. 1991. *A Dictionary of Theatre Anthropology*. Trans. Richard Fowler. London: Routledge.

Barnes, Clive. 1988. "Orchard Grows in Brooklyn" (*New York Post*, 25 Jan. 1988). *New York Theatre Critics' Reviews* 5 (11 Jan.): 364.

Barthes, Roland. 1967. *Elements of Semiology*. Trans. Annette Lavers and Colin Smith. New York: Hill and Wang.

———. 1974. *S/Z*. Trans. Richard Miller. New York: Hill and Wang.

Bartow, Arthur. 1988a. *The Director's Voice*. New York: Theatre Communications Group.

———. 1988b. "Images from the Id." *American Theatre* 5 (June): 10.

Bassnett-McGuire, Susan. 1980. "An Introduction to Theatre Semiotics." *Theatre Quarterly* 10 (Summer): 47–53.

Beck, Julian. 1972. *The Life of the Theatre*. San Francisco: City Lights Books.

Bennett, Susan. 1990. *Theatre Audiences*. New York: Routledge.

Bennett, Thomas L. 1978. *The Sensory World*. Monterey, Calif.: Brooks/Cole.

Birren, Faber. 1961. *Color, Form, and Space*. New York: Reinhold.

Blumenthal, Eileen. 1986. "The Unfinished Histories of Ariane Mnouchkine." *American Theatre* 3 (Apr.): 4–11.

Bradby, David, and David Williams. 1988. *Directors' Theatre*. New York: St. Martin's Press.

Braun, Edward. 1982. *The Director and the Stage*. New York: Holmes and Meir.

Brecht, Stefan. 1970. "On Grotowski." *Drama Review* 14 (Winter): 178–92.

Brook, Peter. 1987. *The Shifting Point*. New York: Harper and Row.

———. 1992. "Any Event Stems from Combustion (An Interview by Jean Kalman)." *New Theatre Quarterly* 8 (May): 107–12.

Brušák, Karel. 1976. "Signs in the Chinese Theater." In *Semiotics of Art,* ed. Ladislav Matejka and Irwin R. Titunik. Cambridge, Mass.: MIT Press.

Brustein, Robert. 1991. *Reimagining American Theatre.* New York: Hill and Wang.

Burton, Robert. 1976. *The Language of Smell.* London and Boston: Routledge and Kegan Paul.

Burzynski, Tadeusz, and Zbigniew Osinski. 1979. *Grotowski's Laboratory.* Trans. Boleslaw Taborski. Warsaw: Interpress.

Calhoun, John. 1989. "Creating an Audio Environment." *Theatre Crafts* 23 (Jan.): 46–51.

Carlson, Marvin. 1989. *Places of Performance.* Ithaca: Cornell University Press.

———. 1990. *Theatre Semiotics.* Bloomington: Indiana University Press.

Clay, James H., and Daniel Krempel. 1967. *The Theatrical Image.* New York: McGraw-Hill.

Coe, Robert. 1985. "The Extravagant Mysteries of Robert Wilson." *American Theatre* 2 (Oct.): 4.

———. 1987. "What Makes Sellars Run?" *American Theatre* 4 (Dec.): 12.

"Colas, Leather, and Terrorism." 1991. *Economist* 319 (Apr.): 85–86.

Copeland, Roger. 1988. "Master of the Body." *American Theatre* 1 (May): 14–15.

Corson, Richard. 1975. *Stage Makeup.* 5th ed. Englewood Cliffs, N.J.: Prentice-Hall.

Davy, Kate. 1981. *Richard Foreman and the Ontological-Hysteric Theatre.* Ann Arbor: UMI Research Press.

Durham, Weldon B. 1989. *American Theatre Companies, 1931–1986.* New York: Greenwood Press.

Eco, Umberto. 1976. *A Theory of Semiotics.* Bloomington: Indiana University Press.

Eder, Richard. 1984. "The World according to Brook." *American Theatre* 1 (May): 4.

Elam, Keir. 1980. *The Semiotics of Theatre and Drama.* London: Methuen.

Esslin, Martin. 1987. *The Field of Drama.* London: Methuen.

Féral, Josette. 1989. "Mnouchkine's Workshop at the Soleil." *Drama Review* 33 (Winter): 77–87.

Fischer, Howard T. 1974. "An Introduction to Color." In *Color in Art,* ed. James M. Carpenter. Cambridge, Mass.: Fogg Art Museum.

Foreman, Richard. 1992. *Unbalancing Acts.* Ed. Ken Jordan. New York: Pantheon.

Fotheringham, Richard. 1984. "The Last Translation." In *Page to Stage,* ed. Ortrun Zuber-Skerritt. Amsterdam: Rodopi.

Fuchs, Elinor. 1989. " 'Cymbeline' and Its Critics." *American Theatre* 6 (Dec.): 24–31.

Gaggi, Silvio. 1989. *Modern/Postmodern.* Philadelphia: University of Pennsylvania Press.

Gardner, Howard. 1983. *Frames of Mind.* New York: Basic Books.

George, David. 1989. "On Ambiguity." *Theatre Research International* 14 (Spring): 71–85.

Glass, Philip. 1987. *Music by Philip Glass.* New York: Harper and Row.

Gold, Sylviane. 1988. "Theater: Peter Brook's 'Cherry Orchard'" (*Wall Street Journal,* 26 Jan. 1988). *New York Theatre Critics' Reviews* 49 (11 Jan.): 365–66.

Gorton, Rob. 1991. "Samplers." *Theatre Crafts* 25 (Aug./Sept.): 42.

Grotowski, Jerzy. 1968. *Towards a Poor Theatre.* New York: Simon and Schuster.

Gussow, Mel. 1992. "Who's Acting? Who's Watching?" *New York Times,* 28 Feb.

Hafrey, Leigh. 1991. "He's Back Home But Is He the Real Robert Wilson?" *New York Times,* 3 Feb.

Hall, Edward T. 1966. *The Hidden Dimension.* Garden City, N.Y.: Doubleday.

Hanna, Judith Lynne. 1983. *The Performer-Audience Connection.* Austin: University of Texas Press.

Harrop, John, and Sabin R. Epstein. 1982. *Acting with Style.* Englewood Cliffs, N.J.: Prentice-Hall.

Hassan, Ihab. 1980. "The Question of Postmodernism." In *Romanticism, Modernism, Postmodernism,* ed. Harry R. Garvin. Cranbury, N.J.: Associated University Presses.

Holland, Bernard. 1989. "A Glass Adaptation of Poe Tale." *New York Times,* 16 July.

Holland, Norman N. 1975. *5 Readers Reading.* New Haven: Yale University Press.

Holmberg, Arthur. 1990. "'Lear' Girds for a Remarkable Episode." *New York Times,* 20 May.

Hornby, Richard. 1987. *Script into Performance.* New York: Paragon House.

Huston, Hollis. 1992. *The Actor's Instrument.* Ann Arbor: University of Michigan Press.

Itten, Johannes. 1961. *The Art of Color.* New York: Reinhold.

Jauss, Hans Robert. 1982. *Toward an Aesthetic of Reception.* Trans. Timothy Bahti. Minneapolis: University of Minnesota Press.

Jellicoe, Ann. 1967. *Some Unconscious Influences in the Theatre.* Cambridge: Cambridge University Press.

Jones, David Richard. 1986. *Great Directors at Work.* Berkeley: University of California Press.

Jones, Robert Edmond. 1941. *The Theatrical Imagination.* New York: Duell, Sloan, and Pearce.

Kalb, Jonathan. 1990. "The Iconoclast and the Underdog." *American Theatre* 7 (May): 22.

Kaye, Deena, and James LeBrecht. 1992. *Sound and Music for the Theatre.* New York: Backstage Books.

Kettle, Martin. 1990. "High on Mozart." *New Statesman and Society* 3 (18 May): 44.

Kirkpatrick, D. L., ed. 1988. *Contemporary Dramatists*. 4th ed. Chicago: St. James Press.

Kissel, Howard. 1977. "'The Cherry Orchard'" (*Woman's Wear Daily*, 22 Feb. 1977). *New York Theatre Critics' Reviews* 5 (21 Mar.): 339–40.

———. 1988. "Half of the 'Orchard'" (*Daily News*, 25 Jan. 1988). *New York Theatre Critics' Reviews* 49 (11 Jan.): 363.

Kott, Jan. 1980. "After Grotowski." *Theatre Quarterly* 10 (Summer): 27–32.

Kowzan, Tadeusz. 1968. "The Sign in the Theatre." *Diogenes* 61: 52–80.

Kueppers, Harald. 1982. *The Basic Law of Color Theory*. Trans. Roger Marcinik. Woodbury, N.Y.: Barron's.

Laban, Rudolf. 1960. *The Mastery of Movement*. 2d ed., ed. Lisa Ullmann. Estover, Eng.: MacDonald and Evans.

LeNoir, Nina. 1993. Research notes. University of Texas. Typescript.

MacDonald, Heather. 1991. "On Peter Sellars." *Partisan Review* 58 (Fall): 707–12.

McMullan, Frank. 1962. *The Directorial Image*. Hamden, Conn.: Shoe String Press.

Marowitz, Charles. 1986. *Prospero's Staff*. Bloomington: Indiana University Press.

"Martha Clarke." 1988. *Horizon* 31 (May): 37–40.

Merriam-Webster, A. 1989. *Webster's Ninth New Collegiate Dictionary*. Springfield, Mass.: Merriam-Webster.

Mielziner, Jo. 1965. *Designing for the Theatre*. New York: Atheneum.

———. 1970. *The Shapes of Our Theatre*. Ed. C. Ray Smith. New York: Charles N. Potter.

Miles-Brown, John. 1980. *Directing Drama*. London: Peter Owen.

Miller, Jonathan. 1986. *Subsequent Performances*. New York: Viking.

Montagu, Ashley. 1986. *Touching*. New York: Perennial Library.

Nadin, Mihai. 1979. "Sign Functioning in Performance: Ingmar Bergman's Production." *Drama Review* 23 (Dec.): 105–20.

Nadotti, Maria. 1988. "What Becomes of the Brokenhearted?" *Artforum* 27 (Sept.): 117–21.

Novick, Julius. 1986. "Interlopers in the Opera House." *American Theatre* 3 (May): 10–17.

Older, Jules. 1982. *Touching Is Healing*. New York: Stein and Day.

Orlov, Henry. 1981. "Toward a Semiotics of Music." *In The Sign in Music and Literature*. Ed. Wendy Steiner. Austin: University of Texas Press, 131–37.

Ostwald, Peter F. 1963. *Soundmaking*. Springfield, Ill.: Charles C. Thomas.

———. 1973. *The Semiotics of Human Sound*. The Hague: Mouton.

Pavis, Patrice. 1982. *Languages of the Stage*. New York: Performing Arts Journal Publications.

Penrod, James. 1974. *Movement for the Performing Artist*. Palo Alto, Calif.: National Press Books.

Quinn, Michael L. 1990. "Celebrity and the Semiotics of Acting." *New Theatre Quarterly* 6 (May): 154–61.

Ratcliffe, Michael. 1991. "The Greeks, with an Accent on the French." *New York Times*, 28 July.

Rich, Frank. 1983. "Theater: Peter Brook's 'Tragedie de Carmen'" (*New York Times*, 18 Nov. 1983). *New York Theatre Critics' Reviews* 44 (7 Nov.): 124–25.

———. 1992. "Jacobean Tale of Lust and Revenge Updated to the Facist 1930s." *New York Times*, 6 Apr.

Richie, Donald. 1970. "On Grotowski." *Drama Review* 14 (Winter): 205–11.

Rojo, Jerry N. 1974. "Environmental Design." In *Contemporary Stage Design USA*, ed. Elizabeth B. Burdick, Peggy C. Hansen, and Brenda Zanger. Middletown, Conn: International Theatre Institute of the United States.

Ruling, Karl G. "Wireless Microphones." *Theatre Crafts* 25 (Aug./Sept.): 39.

Russell, Douglas A. 1980. *Period Style for the Theatre*. Boston: Allyn and Bacon.

Saussure, Ferdinand de. 1983. *Course in General Linguistics*. Ed. Charles Bally and Albert Sechehaye. Trans. Roy Harris. Oxford: Duckworth.

Savran, David. 1986. *The Wooster Group, 1975–1985*. Ann Arbor: UMI Research Press.

Schechner, Richard. 1973. *Environmental Theater*. New York: Hawthorn Books.

Schmidt, Robert F. 1978. *Fundamentals of Sensory Physiology*. New York: Springer-Verlag.

Selden, Raman. 1989. *Practicing Theory and Reading Literature*. Lexington: University Press of Kentucky.

Selden, Samuel. 1969. *Theatre Double Game*. Chapel Hill: University of North Carolina Press.

Sellars, Peter. 1989. "Exits and Entrances: Peter Sellars on Opera." *Artforum* 28 (Dec.): 22–24.

Seymour, Allen. 1963. "Revelations in Poland." *Plays and Players* 11 (Oct.): 33–34.

Shevtsova, Maria. 1989. "The Sociology of the Theatre, Part Three." *New Theatre Quarterly* 5 (Aug.): 282–300.

Shyer, Laurence. 1989. *Robert Wilson and His Collaborators*. New York: Theatre Communications Group.

Sommers, Michael. 1991. "Why Do You Need Sound, Anyway?" *Theatre Crafts* 25 (Aug./Sept.): 36.

Steele, Mike. 1985. "The Romanian Directors." *American Theatre* 2 (July/Aug.): 4–11.

Sterritt, David. 1989. "Making Mozart Postmodern." *Christian Science Monitor*, 14 Aug.

———. 1991. "With Ibsen Play, Wilson Opens New Chapter in His 'Theatre of Images.'" *Christian Science Monitor*, 21 Feb.

Styan, J. L. 1975. *Drama, Stage and Audience*. London: Cambridge University Press.

Tarasti, Eero. 1979. *Myth and Music.* The Hague: Mouton.

Thayer, S. 1982. "Social Touching." In *Tactual Perception*, ed. William Schiff and Emerson Foulke. Cambridge: Cambridge University Press.

Westerman, Ken. 1991. "The Semiotics of Music." University of Texas at Austin. Typescript.

Wright, R. H. 1982. *The Sense of Smell.* Boca Raton, Fla.: CRC Press.

Zorn, John W., ed. 1968. *The Essential Delsarte.* Metuchen, N.J.: Scarecrow Press.

# Index

*Agamemnon,* 118
Akalaitis, JoAnne, 3, 45, 89, 94, 110, 132, 142, 162, 170, 174, 210
*Akropolis,* 21, 81, 89, 142, 145, 148, 174, 175, 196
Albright, Harry D., 91, 229
Alter, Jean, 11, 229
Altner, H., 192, 194, 229
*Angelface,* 102
Arnink, Donna J., 109, 229
Aronson, Arnold, 114, 134, 139, 179, 229
Artaud, Antonin, 82, 90
Articulation, 72, 74, 82–83, 93
Asian theater, 9, 21, 80, 89, 90, 93, 112, 203, 204
*Atrides, Les,* 136
Audience: and aural systems, 177, 178, 179, 180, 181, 182, 185, 186, 187, 188, 189; and communication, 1, 6, 7, 9, 10, 11, 15, 26, 61–63, 68, 79, 83; and framing systems, 33–36, 38, 39–49, 53, 113; and horizons of expectations, 33–36, 42–46, 48–49, 78, 107–8, 190, 205–6; influences on, 51–56, 65, 69; and olfactoral systems, 191, 192, 201; and perfor-mance, 5, 10, 11, 16, 19, 23, 26, 27, 30, 51–63, 71, 73, 76, 77, 78, 81, 83, 85, 88, 90, 97, 100, 101, 105, 106, 107, 108, 111, 112, 211, 213, 215, 216, 217, 218, 219, 221; as signifier, 16, 26–27; as sign system, 11–12, 56–58, 100; and tactile systems, 197, 198, 200, 201; and taste, 196, 201; and visual systems, 113–18, 119,

124, 127, 131, 139, 140, 143, 148, 151, 159, 160, 161, 162, 163, 164, 169, 171
Aural systems, 2, 4, 5, 10, 14, 26, 27, 30, 31, 38, 39, 51, 56, 57, 58, 61–62, 71–85, 91, 103, 113, 119, 139, 140, 173–90, 206, 209, 210, 212, 213, 215, 217, 220, 221, 222, 223, 226, 227

*Baal,* 139
Backgrounding, 23, 27
Baker, Rob, 162, 185, 222, 229
*Bald Soprano, The,* 34
*Balm and Gilead,* 39
Barba, Eugenio, 22, 82, 93, 145, 149, 205, 229
Barnes, Clive, 123, 229
Baroque-style theater, 41, 42
Barthes, Roland, 6, 18, 229
Bartow, Arthur, 2, 3, 65, 127, 174, 179, 188, 223, 225, 227, 229
Bassnett-McGuire, Susan, 54, 90, 221, 229
Beck, Julian, 201, 229
Beckett, Samuel, 43, 83, 174
Bennett, Susan, 16, 33, 36, 44, 47, 52, 53, 69, 196, 229
Bennett, Thomas L., 196, 229
Bergman, Ingmar, 27
*Bernie's Bar Mitzvah,* 196
Birren, Faber, 145, 168, 169, 170, 229
Blocking, 122–29
Blumenthal, Eileen, 145, 229
*Book of Splendors, The,* 161
Bradby, David, 59, 89, 96, 102, 109, 118, 120, 142, 175, 196, 229

Braun, Edward, 114, 229
Bread and Puppet Theatre, The, 195
Brecht, Bertolt, 11, 139, 158, 186, 228
Brecht, Stefan, 96, 229
Brook, Peter, 3, 34, 35, 52, 85, 91, 114,
    122, 123, 135, 142, 147, 148, 150,
    155, 162, 164, 167, 195, 229–30
Brušák, Karel, 21, 230
Brustein, Robert, 39, 60, 70, 132, 136,
    139, 150, 174, 230
Bunraku theater, 90
Burlesque, 44
Burton, Robert, 193, 230
Burzynski, Tadeusz, 81, 116, 230

Calhoun, John, 177, 183, 230
Carlson, Marvin, 33, 37, 44, 230
Carmen, 136, 167, 195
Charisma, 67, 68–69
Chekhov, Anton, 122, 182
Cherry Orchard, The, 122–23, 135, 147,
    176
Chicano theater, 38
Chinese theater. See Asian theater
CIVIL warS, 79, 81, 129, 153, 178
Clarke, Martha, 3, 43, 82, 91–92, 94,
    126, 127, 132, 189, 223, 224
Clay, James H., 55, 230
Codes, definition of, 8–11
Coe, Robert, 129, 230
"Colas, Leather, Terrorism," 189
Color, 10, 12, 15, 27, 30, 31, 38, 48,
    68, 80, 111, 113, 114, 130, 137, 138,
    140, 141, 142, 143, 145, 146, 147,
    152, 154, 155, 156, 158, 160, 161,
    162–63, 164, 165–71, 210, 212, 215,
    217, 226
Comedy, 9, 96, 187
Company of Sirens, The, 195–96
Constant Prince, The, 61
Copeland, Roger, 92, 189, 230
Corson, Richard, 108, 230
Costumes, 47, 53, 58, 65, 66, 100, 111,
    113, 127, 131, 140–48, 152, 154, 155,
    157, 161, 162, 163, 165, 166

Crucible, The, 144
Cymbeline, 45, 110, 170

Davy, Kate, 120, 136, 140, 159, 161,
    167, 175, 182, 184, 222, 230
Deafman's Glance, 34
Death Destruction and Detroit, 79, 97,
    155, 156
Death Destruction and Detroit II, 61,
    145, 146
Delsarte, François, 87, 88, 92, 93
Diachronical analysis, 219–20, 227
Dionysian Theatre, 201
Distance, 123–27
Don Giovanni, 98, 189
Dracula, 210, 211, 218, 219
Dracula project, 211–17
Durham, Weldon B., 224, 230

Eco, Umberto, 6, 8, 11, 203, 230
Eder, Richard, 195, 230
Einstein on the Beach, 51, 56, 102, 156,
    160, 220, 221, 222
Elam, Keir, 5, 6, 9, 11, 21, 24, 72, 73,
    91, 93, 208, 230
El Greco, 205
Elizabethan theater, 30, 34, 121, 122
Emmons, Beverly, 162, 167
Emperor Jones, 84
Endgame, 43, 174
Epstein, Sabin R., 97, 230
Equus, 176
Esslin, Martin, 4, 6, 7, 11, 48, 66, 210,
    218, 219, 230
Ewell, Tom, 44
Expression. See Facial expression

Facial expression, 15, 30, 65, 66, 85–
    89, 92, 161, 168, 212, 214, 216
Fall of the House of Usher, 96
Farce, 97, 210, 213, 215
Faust, 179
Faust, Wolfgang Max, 79
Faustus, Dr., 120
Féral, Josette, 145, 230

Film. *See* Video
Fischer, Howard T., 165, 230
Flaszen, Ludwik, 22, 82, 145, 149, 229
Foregrounding, 23, 27, 85, 129, 144, 154, 157, 217
Foreman, Richard, 3, 22, 32, 43, 51, 65, 70, 73, 75–76, 78–79, 96, 97, 98, 101, 102, 110, 113, 114, 120, 131, 132, 136, 138, 139–40, 142, 143, 144, 149, 159, 160, 161, 162, 164, 167, 175, 177, 182, 183, 188, 189, 207, 210, 221, 222, 230
*Forest, The*, 136, 177
Formalist school, 34
Fotheringham, Richard, 55–56, 230
Fourth wall, 60
*Fragments of a Trilogy, The*, 81, 174, 197
Frames: control of, 32, 35–36, 44, 47, 48, 49; definition of, 31–35; theatrical, 32–35. *See also* Framing systems
Framing systems: and audiences, 33–36, 38, 39–49, 53, 113; historical, 33, 42–43; horizons of expectations, 31–34, 36, 42, 44, 46, 48, 49, 52, 69, 70, 78, 85, 97, 107; intellectual, 42–43; physical, 32–33, 36–42, 52, 63; postperformance, 48, 49, 161; preperformance, 39–40, 45, 46–47, 49, 57, 59, 161; publicity, 32–33, 43, 44–48, 49, 52, 212, 214, 216; social, 33, 42–43; and spectators, 31–34, 38, 39–49. *See also* Frames
François, Guy-Claude, 136
Fuchs, Elinor, 45, 170, 230

Gaggi, Silvio, 3, 230
*Garden of Earthly Delights, The*, 189
Gardner, Howard, 207, 231
George, David, 226, 231
*Gesamtkunstwerk*, 2, 222
Gesture, 4, 9, 15, 57, 62, 65, 66, 89–98, 99, 100, 105, 112, 123, 148, 161, 198, 199, 208, 212, 214, 216, 220, 223, 226
Gillett, Julia, 222
*Giulio Cesare*, 169

Glass, Philip, 43, 56, 174, 220, 221, 223, 231
*Glass Menagerie, The*, 195
Goethe, Johann Wolfgang von, 179
Gold, Sylviane, 147, 231
*Golden Windows, The*, 84, 185
Goldoni, Carlo, 60
Gorton, Rob, 177, 231
*Grapes of Wrath, The*, 196
*Grease*, 40
Greek theater, 39, 58, 182
Grotowski, Jerzy, 3, 21, 61, 80, 81, 82, 85, 89, 94, 96, 114, 115, 117, 120, 142, 145, 148, 174, 175, 196, 200, 231
Guerilla theater, 117
Gueroult, A., 87
Gussow, Mel, 60, 196, 231

Hafrey, Leigh, 96, 231
Hairstyle, 65, 108–12, 212, 214, 216
Hall, Edward T., 121, 123, 124, 126, 231
*Hamlet*, 208
*Hamletmachine*, 123
Hanna, Judith Lynne, 90, 231
Harrop, John, 97, 231
*Harvey*, 44
Hassan, Ihab, 3, 4, 231
*Hedda Gabler*, 180
Hoffman, Dustin, 69
Holland, Bernard, 96, 231
Holland, Norman N., 17–18, 231
Holmberg, Arthur, 95, 107, 231
Horizons of expectations: and audiences, 33–36, 42–46, 48–49, 69, 70, 78, 107, 190; and spectators, 31–34, 42–46, 48–49, 52, 67, 69–70, 85, 97, 185, 205
Hornby, Richard, 131, 231
*Hotel China*, 22, 149
Huston, Hollis, 26, 126, 231

Ibsen, Henrik, 65
Icons, definition of, 7

*Imaginary Invalid, The,* 111
Indexes: definition of, 7
Inflection, 72, 74, 78–80
Ionesco, Eugène, 34, 43
Israel, Robert, 132
Itten, Johannes, 170, 231

*J. B.,* 46
Japanese theater. *See* Asian theater
Jarry, Alfred, 43
Jauss, Hans Robert, 31, 34, 35, 205, 231
Jellicoe, Ann, 57, 231
Jones, David Richard, 151, 231
Jones, Robert Edmond, 134, 154, 231

Kabuki theater, 65, 90, 96, 106, 110, 178
Kalb, Jonathan, 110, 161, 231
Kalfin, Robert, 60
Kamm, Tom, 120
Kathakali, 9, 80, 90
Kaye, Deena, 173, 175, 178, 180, 182, 231
Kettle, Martin, 106, 231
*King Lear,* 27–30, 66, 107, 147, 209
Kirkpatrick, D. L., 78, 232
Kissel, Howard, 118, 135, 232
*Kitchen, The,* 96, 102
*Kordian,* 61
Kott, Jan, 46, 232
Kowzan, Tadeusz, 11, 232
Krempel, Daniel, 55
Kuhn, Hans-Peter, 81, 84, 177, 178, 183, 185

*L'Age d'Or,* 117–18
*L.S.D.,* 144
Laban, Rudolph, 99, 232
Lahr, Bert, 44
Language. *See* Linguistic systems
Laterna Magika Theatre, 139
*Lava,* 75–76

LeBrecht, James, 173, 175, 178, 180, 182, 231
LeCompte, Elizabeth, 3, 19, 183, 224
LeNoir, Nina, 11, 232
Lighting, 2, 9, 39, 47, 61, 84, 100, 113, 114, 127, 130, 131, 140, 141, 143, 146–47, 148, 153–64, 165, 167, 170, 171, 209, 212, 214, 217, 223
Linguistic systems, 4, 5, 10, 12, 203, 210, 221
*Little Foxes, The,* 70
*Little Mary Sunshine,* 59
Living Theatre, 45, 46, 195, 200
*Livre des Splendeurs,* 183
Lobel, Adrianne, 132
Loudness, 72, 74–76
*Love's Labor's Lost,* 51

*Macbeth,* 219, 220
MacDonald, Heather, 104, 232
MacLeish, Archibald, 46
McMullan, Frank, 54, 232
*Madame De Sade,* 27
*Mahabharata,* 136, 150, 195
Makeup, 4, 12, 65–66, 69, 88, 89, 108–12, 161, 171, 179, 198, 206, 208, 212, 214, 216
Malayan theater, See Asian theater
Malina, Judith, 46
*Marat/Sade,* 150
Marowitz, Charles, 133, 232
*Marriage of Figaro, The,* 103, 104
Masks, 66, 86, 89, 110, 171, 182
Melodrama, 96, 210, 215, 217
Metatext, 16, 71
*Midsummer Night's Dream, A,* 34, 35, 117, 135–36
Mielziner, Jo, 39, 137, 232
Miles-Brown, John, 52, 232
Miller, Arthur, 144
Miller, Jonathan, 14, 15, 77, 232
Mime, 21, 73, 90, 91
*Minotarus, The,* 65, 139
*Miracolo d' Amore,* 82
Mise-en-scène, 14–16, 21, 30, 60, 62,

89, 103, 106, 114, 121, 126, 127, 129, 131, 132, 133, 137, 138, 140, 141, 143, 147, 148, 150, 153, 154, 155, 160, 162, 163, 165, 167, 168, 189, 190, 204, 209, 220, 225, 227
*Misérables, Les,* 195
*Miss Julie,* 195
*Mistress of the Inn, The,* 60
Mnouchkine, Ariane, 3, 59, 65, 96, 102, 106, 109, 117, 136, 142, 145, 162, 178, 196
Modernism. *See* Postmodernism
Montagu, Ashley, 198, 199, 232
*Mother Courage,* 59
*Mother Tongues,* 196
Movement, 9, 10, 12, 15, 57, 58, 61–62, 65, 66, 70, 84, 90, 92, 93, 94, 97, 100, 102, 103, 104–8, 111, 112, 123, 126–30, 148, 152, 154, 163, 164, 166, 171, 173, 174, 212, 214, 216, 221, 223, 224, 226, 227
Mozart, Wolfgang Amadeus, 98, 106, 188, 189
Müller, Heiner, 79
Müller, Richy, 95
Music. *See* Aural systems
*Music Man,* 40

Nadin, Mihai, 11, 232
Nadotti, Maria, 82, 83, 232
New Criticism, 17
*'night Mother,* 180
Noh theater. *See* Asian theater
*Normal Heart, The,* 111
Notation, 206, 208–9
Novick, Julius, 81, 169, 232

O'Neill, Eugene, 84
Obolensky, Chloe, 147
Occidental theater. *See* Asian theater
Odors. *See* Olfactoral systems
*Oedipus,* 142
Older, Jules, 200, 232
Olfactoral systems, 4, 5, 10, 14, 26, 30, 31, 51, 191–95, 201, 213, 215, 217

Olivier, Lawrence, 69
Ontological-Hysteric Theatre, 22, 32, 222
Open Theatre, 200
Opera, 98, 106, 188, 220
*Orestia, The,* 178
Oriental theater. *See* Asian theater
Orlov, Henry, 181, 232
Osinski, Zbigniew, 81, 116
Ostension, 23–24
Ostwald, Peter F., 180, 184, 186, 187, 232

*Paradise Now!,* 45
Paralinguistic elements. *See* Vocal elements
*Parisian May,* 45
Pavis, Patrice, 6, 7, 8, 14, 15, 26, 30, 203, 204, 208, 209, 232
Penrod, James, 86, 107, 232
Performance Group, 200
Performers: and aural systems, 174, 176, 185, 189; as celebrities, 32, 67, 68, 69–71; and communication, 27, 52, 60–61, 62, 209, 224, 225; personal qualities of, 67–71, 89, 214, 216, 226; as signs, 58, 65–66, 89–98; and tactile systems, 199, 200; and visual systems, 115–18, 121, 122, 124, 126–31, 139, 143, 145, 148, 151, 160, 164, 165, 171. *See also* Performer systems
Performer systems: charisma, 67, 68–69; facial expression, 15, 30, 65, 66, 85–89, 92, 161, 168, 212, 214, 216; gesture, 4, 9, 15, 57, 62, 65, 66, 89–98, 99, 100, 105, 112, 123, 148, 161, 198, 199, 208, 212, 214, 216, 220, 223, 226; hairstyle, 65, 108–12, 212, 214, 216; makeup, 4, 12, 65–66, 69, 88, 89, 108–12, 161, 171, 179, 198, 208, 212, 214, 216; movement, 9, 10, 12, 15, 65, 84, 90, 91, 92, 93, 94, 97, 98–108, 111, 112, 126–30, 148, 152, 154, 163, 171, 212, 214, 216, 221,

Performer Systems: movement (*continued*) 223, 224, 226, 227; voice, 56, 65–67, 69–70, 71–85, 91, 93, 98, 109, 111, 112, 174, 175, 176, 177, 178, 181, 182, 185, 186, 208. *See also* Performers

Picturization, 122–29

Pierce, C. S., 7

Pinter, Harold, 83

Pitch, 72, 76–77, 78, 79, 176, 182, 184, 187

*Plague, The*, 111

Playscript. *See* Text: written

Polish Laboratory Theatre, 81, 89, 195, 200

Postmodernism: definition of, 3–4

Postperformance, 48, 49, 161

Preperformance, 39–40, 45, 46–47, 49, 57, 59, 161

Properties, 12, 22, 30, 39, 113, 122, 127, 130, 131, 147, 148–54, 165, 167, 170, 171, 209, 212, 214, 217

Proxemics, 121–22, 126, 198, 199

Proximity, 57, 140, 200

Publicity, 32–33, 43, 44–48, 49, 52, 212, 214, 216

Quinn, Michael L., 67, 68, 69, 233

Rabe, David, 25

Radok, Alfred, 179

Ratcliffe, Michael, 136, 178, 233

Reader-response theories, 17–20, 30, 227

*Real Inspector Hound, The*, 47

Realism: definition of, 210

Reception theories. *See* Reader-response theories

*Reigiebuchs*, 209, 228

Resonance, 72, 80–82

Restoration theater, 39, 58

*Rhoda in Potatoland*, 143, 144

Rhythm: and design, 137, 140, 147, 148, 158; and movement, 84, 100, 103–4; of performance, 15, 177; and sound, 182, 184, 186, 187; and voice, 72, 75, 77, 84

Rich, Frank, 89, 136, 168, 170, 233

*Richard II*, 106

Richie, Donald, 89, 174, 233

Rojo, Jerry N., 118, 233

*Romeo and Juliet*, 43

Roth, Stephanie, 96

Ruling, Karl G., 185, 233

*Rumstick Road*, 19

Russell, Douglas A., 95, 106, 233

Saussure, Ferdinand de, 6, 203, 233

Savarese, Nicola, 93, 205, 229

Savran, David, 19, 144, 224, 233

Scene design. *See* Setting

Schechner, Richard, 115, 233

Schmidt, Robert F., 197, 233

Schneider, Alan, 44

Script. *See* Text: written

*Sea Gull, The*, 180

Selden, Raman, 6, 18, 20, 22, 34, 43, 233

Selden, Samuel, 51, 233

Sellars, Peter, 2, 3, 27, 43, 68, 98, 104, 106, 126, 132, 142, 143, 162, 169, 173, 182, 188, 189, 210, 227, 233

Semiotics: definition of, 5–6 ; of olfaction, 193–94; of properties, 151; of sound, 180–82; of touch, 198–99

Seneca, 142

Serban, Andrei, 3, 73, 81, 85, 94, 103, 118, 132, 174, 197, 224, 225

Setting, 2, 4, 12, 22, 27, 30, 39, 45, 47, 53, 58, 100, 103, 113, 114–22, 127, 131–40, 141, 143, 147, 148, 152, 154, 155, 157, 161, 162, 163, 165, 166, 171, 209, 210, 212, 214, 216, 223, 227

*Seven Year Itch, The*, 44

Seymour, Allen, 81, 233

Shaffer, Peter, 9

Shakespeare, 51, 84, 96, 106

Shakespearean theatre, 21, 30, 39, 40, 65, 147

*Shakuntala*, 81
Shevtsova, Maria, 91, 164, 233
Shyer, Laurence, 70, 79, 81, 84, 102, 115, 120, 123, 155, 157, 160, 164, 167, 177, 179, 195, 223, 233
Signs: definition of, 6–8
Simon, Neil, 33
Smell. *See* Olfactoral systems
Sommers, Michael, 183, 233
Sophocles, 68
Sound. *See* Aural systems
Space, 15, 113, 114–131, 140, 171, 212, 214, 216, 226
Spectators: and aural systems, 173, 180, 181, 185, 186, 188, 189; and communication, 6–7, 10, 61–63, 85, 209; and framing systems, 31–34, 38, 39–49; and horizons of expectations, 31–34, 42–46, 48–49, 52, 67, 69–70, 185, 205; influences on, 6–7, 8–9, 51–56, 171; and olfactoral systems, 191, 193; and performance, 1, 4, 8–9, 10, 12, 14, 15–17, 18, 19–20, 23, 30, 51–63, 66, 67, 69, 72, 74, 77, 78, 85, 86, 88, 89, 90, 94–95, 97, 101, 103, 106, 112, 203–5, 210, 211, 213, 216, 228; as sign systems, 4–5, 11, 25–27, 56–58; and tactile systems, 197, 199, 200, 201; and visual systems, 113, 114, 115–20, 122, 124, 126–28, 129–31, 137, 139, 140, 143, 145, 147, 158, 159, 160–61, 165
Speech. *See* Voice
Stanislavsky, Constantin, 11
Steele, Mike, 103, 225, 233
Stein, Douglas, 132, 139
Sterritt, David, 98, 223, 233
Stoppard, Tom, 47
*Streamers*, 25
Strinberg, August, 195
Styan, J. L., 63, 233
*Suddenly Last Summer*, 84
Sutton, Sheryl, 102
Suzuki, Tadashi, 164
Svoboda, Josef, 3, 27, 65, 114, 123,

134, 136, 139, 154, 162, 179
Swados, Elizabeth, 174
Symbols, definition of, 7
Synchronical analysis, 210–18, 227

Tactile systems, 4, 5, 12, 14, 30, 51, 60, 197–201, 213, 215, 217
Tarasati, Eero, 181, 234
Taste, 195–96, 201
Taylor, Elizabeth, 70
*Teatro Campesino*, 38
Tempo, 15, 72, 74, 76, 83–84, 102, 103, 148, 163
*Terrible but Unfinished History of Norodom Sihanouk, The*, 109, 145
Text: performance, 3, 17, 18–20, 22, 209; spoken, 1, 2, 12, 27, 30, 65–67, 71–75, 90, 103, 140, 173, 174, 178, 189, 211, 213, 215, 221, 224, 227; written, 1–3, 9, 12, 14, 15, 17–18, 20, 22, 26, 27, 30, 32, 33, 34, 36, 39, 42, 63, 66, 71–72, 75–76, 79, 84, 85, 91–93, 95, 107, 114, 119, 122, 126, 127, 128, 131, 139–40, 143, 147, 151, 163, 188, 189, 191, 204, 206, 217, 218, 219, 220, 225
Thayer, S., 198, 234
Theater for the deaf, 93
Theatre of Cruelty, 151
Theatre of Dionysus, 34
*Thérèse Raquin*, 41, 42
*'Tis Pity She's a Whore*, 89, 170
*Total Recall*, 159
Touch. *See* Tactile systems
Tragedy, 96, 187, 188
Transformability, 21–23
*Trojan Women, The*, 164
*Twelfth Night*, 180

*Ubu*, 91
*Uncle Vanya*, 182
Underscoring, 178–79

Video, 2, 65, 71, 123, 139, 140, 200
*Vienna: Lufthaus*, 92

*View of Toledo*, 205
Visual systems: and audience, 26,
    113–18, 119, 124, 127, 131, 139, 140,
    143, 148, 151, 159, 160, 161, 162,
    163, 164, 169, 171; color, 10, 12, 15,
    27, 30, 31, 38, 48, 113, 114, 130, 137,
    138, 140, 141, 142, 143, 145, 146,
    147, 152, 154, 155, 156, 158, 160,
    161, 162–63, 165–71, 210, 212, 215,
    217, 226; costumes, 4, 12, 15, 27, 30,
    47, 53, 58, 65, 66, 100, 111, 113, 127,
    131, 140–48, 152, 154, 155, 157, 161,
    162, 163, 165, 166, 168, 170, 171,
    179, 209, 210, 212, 214, 217, 223;
    lighting, 2, 9, 39, 47, 61, 84, 100,
    113, 114, 127, 130, 131, 140, 141,
    143, 146–47, 148, 153–64, 165, 167,
    170, 171, 209, 212, 214, 217, 223;
    and performers, 115–18, 121, 122,
    124, 126–31, 139, 143, 145, 148, 151,
    160, 164, 165, 171; properties, 12,
    22, 30, 39, 113, 122, 127, 130, 131,
    147, 148–54, 165, 167, 170, 171, 209,
    212, 214, 217; setting, 2, 4, 12, 22,
    27, 30, 39, 45, 47, 53, 58, 100, 113,
    114–22, 127, 131–40, 141, 143, 147,
    148, 152, 154, 155, 157, 161, 162,
    163, 165, 166, 171, 209, 210, 212,
    214, 216, 223, 227; space, 15, 113,
    114–131, 140, 171, 212, 214, 216,
    226; and spectators, 51, 113, 114,
    115–20, 122, 124, 126–28, 129–31,
    137, 139, 140, 143, 145, 147, 158,
    159, 160–61, 165
Vocal elements: articulation, 72, 74,
    82–83, 93; inflection, 4, 72, 74, 78–
    80; loudness, 72, 74–76, 78, 79, 85,
    111; pitch, 72, 76–77, 78, 79, 81;
    resonance, 72, 80–82; rhythm, 15,
    72, 75, 77, 84; tempo, 15, 72, 74, 76,
    83–84
Voice, 9, 56, 65–67, 69–70, 71–85,
    91, 93, 98, 109, 111, 112, 174, 175,
    176, 177, 178, 181, 182, 185, 186,
    208, 212, 214, 216. *See also* Text: spo-
    ken

Wagner, Richard, 222
*Waiting for Godot*, 44
Ward, Douglas Turner, 179
Wesker, Arnold, 102
Westerman, Ken, 182, 187, 234
*When We Dead Awaken*, 34, 65
Williams, David, 59, 89, 96, 102, 109,
    118, 120, 142, 175, 196, 229
Williams, Tennessee, 19, 84
Wilson, Robert, 3, 27, 33, 34, 43, 51,
    56, 61, 65, 70, 73, 79, 81, 83, 84, 94,
    96, 97, 102, 104, 107, 115, 117, 120,
    123, 129, 132, 136, 142, 145, 146,
    152, 153, 154, 155, 156, 158, 160,
    162, 164, 167, 177, 178, 179, 185,
    195, 210, 218, 220, 221, 222, 223
Woodruff, Robert, 3, 139
*Woyzeck*, 110, 136, 160
Wright, R. H., 192, 193, 195,
    234

Yeargan, Michael, 132

Zola, Emile, 41
Zorn, John W., 87, 93, 234